THREE VERSIONS OF JUDAS

BibleWorld

Series Editor: Philip R. Davies, University of Sheffield

BibleWorld shares the fruits of modern (and postmodern) biblical scholarship not only among practitioners and students, but also with anyone interested in what academic study of the Bible means in the twenty-first century. It explores our ever-increasing knowledge and understanding of the social world that produced the biblical texts, but also analyses aspects of the Bible's role in the history of our civilization and the many perspectives – not just religious and theological, but also cultural, political and aesthetic – which drive modern biblical scholarship.

Published:*

History, Literature and Theology in the Book of Chronicles
Ehud Ben Zvi

Women Healing/Healing Women
The Genderization of Healing in Early Christianity
Elaine M. Wainwright

Jonah's World:
Social Science and the Reading of Prophetic Story
Lowell K. Handy

Symposia: Dialogues Concerning the History of Biblical Interpretation
Roland Boer

The Ontology of Space in Biblical Hebrew Narrative
Luke Gärtner-Brereton

Mark and its Subalterns:
A Hermeneutical Paradigm for a Postcolonial Context
David Joy

Linguistic Dating of Biblical Texts:
Ian Young, Robert Rezetko and Martin Ehrensvärd

O Mother, Where Art Thou? An Irigarayan Reading of the Book of Chronicles
Julie Kelso

Sex Working and the Bible
Avaren Ipsen

Redrawing the Boundaries:
The Date of Early Christian Literature
J. V. M. Sturdy
Edited by Jonathan Knight

The Archaeology of Myth:
Papers on Old Testament Tradition
N. Wyatt

Jesus in an Age of Terror:
Scholarly Projects for a New American Century
James G. Crossley

On the Origins of Judaism
Philip R. Davies

The Bible Says So!:
From Simple Answers to Insightful Understanding
Edwin D. Freed and Jane F. Roberts

From Babylon to Eternity:
The Exile Remembered and Constructed in Text and Tradition
Bob Becking, Alex Cannegieter, Wilfred van der Poll and Anne-Mareike Wetter

The Production of Prophecy:
Constructing Prophecy and Prophets in Yehud
Edited by Diana V. Edelman and Ehud Ben Zvi

Judaism, Jewish Identities and the Gospel Tradition:
Essays in Honour of Maurice Casey
Edited by James G. Crossley

A Compendium of Musical Instruments and Instrumental Terminology in the Bible
Yelena Kolyada

Jesus beyond Nationalism:
Constructing the Historical Jesus in a Period of Cultural Complexity
Edited by Halvor Moxnes, Ward Blanton and James G. Crossley

The Social History of Achaemenid Phoenicia:
Being a Phoenician, Negotiating Empires
Vadim S. Jigoulov

Biblical Resistance Hermeneutics within a Caribbean Context
Oral A. W. Thomas

Edward Said, Contrapuntal Hermeneutics and the Book of Job
Alissa Jones Nelson

Secularism and Biblical Studies
Edited by Roland Boer

* Space precludes a full listing of published BibleWorld titles – for this, please go to http://www.equinoxpub.com/books/browse.asp?serid=11

THREE VERSIONS OF JUDAS

RICHARD G. WALSH

equinox

LONDON   OAKVILLE

Published by

UK: Equinox Publishing Ltd
Chelsea Manor Studios
Flood Street
London SW3 5SR

US: DBBC,
28 Main Street,
Oakville, CT 06779

www.equinoxpub.com

First published 2010

© Richard G. Walsh 2010

All rights reserved. No part of this publication may be reproduced or transmitted in any form or by any means, electronic or mechanical, including photocopying, recording or any information storage or retrieval system, without prior permission in writing from the publishers.

British Library Cataloguing-in-Publication Data
A catalogue record for this book is available from the British Library.

Library of Congress Cataloging-in-Publication Data
Walsh, Richard G.
  Three versions of Judas / Richard G. Walsh.
    p. cm. -- (Bibleworld)
  Includes bibliographical references and index.
  ISBN 978-1-84553-701-2 (hb) -- ISBN 978-1-84553-702-9 (pb) 1. Gospel of Judas--Criticism, interpretation, etc. 2. Judas Iscariot. I. Title.
  BS2860.J832W35 2010
  229'.8--dc22
                          2009054293

ISBN-13 978 1 84553 701 2   (hardback)
         978 1 84553 702 9   (paperback)

Typeset by ISB Typesetting Ltd, www.sheffieldtypesetting.com
Printed and bound in Great Britain by Lightning Source UK Ltd., Milton Keynes and Lightning Source Inc., La Vergne, TN

Contents

Preface	vii
Chapter 1 From the Gospel to Borges and Back Again	1
Chapter 2 The Canonical Judas: Oracular Betrayal	22
Chapter 3 The Cooperative Judas: True Believer, Phantom of the Infinite	51
Chapter 4 The Ascetic Judas: Judas the Scapegoat and Judas the Jew	85
Chapter 5 Judas the God	120
Chapter 6 Adding Evil to the Son	151
Bibliography	163
Index of Borges' Writings	172
Index of Authors	173
Index of Scriptures	176
Index of Films	179

Preface

Judas has long puzzled and intrigued me. I suppose this is because I, like most in my profession, am doubly alienated. I share the alienation inherent to modern individualism and also have a modern academic's sense of alienation from the Christian tradition in which I was raised. Growing up in the 60s also increased this cynicism. Such a background prepared me to think that Judas "got a raw deal."

Accordingly, I read William Klassen's *Judas: Betrayer or Friend of Jesus?* (1996) with great interest when it splashed onto the SBL scene. While I was unable to bring myself to agree with his historical approach or results, I still appreciated his charity. Subsequently, Kim Paffenroth's *Judas: Images of the Lost Disciple* (2001b) gave me a sense of the incredible variety of the Judas stories that belied apparent canonical fixity and finality. More recently, the media and academic furor associated with the publication of the Gospel of Judas has only served to remind me of the enigma and intrigue of Judas.

Other scholarly interests also contribute to the specific musings on Judas that follow, which are best summed up as readings of the work of Jorge Luis Borges. I explore these interests in the first chapter below, with particular attention to Borges' "Three Versions of Judas" (1962: 151-57), which is, in my opinion, still the most insightful interpretation of Judas yet offered. From Borges' fiction, I return to the gospels and the canonical Judas that first perplexed me, but now read as Borges' precursors. The result replaces apparent canonical finality (and the search for a "real" Judas) with multiple fictions.

Essentially, then, this work moves from the canonical and popular Judas to modern struggles with that image. The struggle creates more sympathetic and, on rare occasions, heroic versions of Judas. This work also moves from the notion of the infinite book, with its corollary of the secret plot (read myth), to modern horror in the face of such an absorbing and degrading determinism.

Consequently, this work also moves from myth to fiction. Readers might also expect to find the move from myth to character, but Frank Kermode (1979) has nicely shown that the modern notion of character is itself the product of a myth. If humans cannot escape myth, they can learn to tell better fictions more self-consciously. From myth to fictions, then, is a better description of the trajectory of this work. After all, Borges offers, in essence, repeated lessons in the near revelations and near beliefs of fictions. In these days of true believers, such fictional lessons seem more important daily. Fictions may suspend our true belief unto death and challenge us to live more graciously. Consequently, this work does not provide the one, true, or final interpretation of Judas superseding and correcting the mistakes of everyone else. Instead, it asserts the beneficial effects of multiple versions of Judas.

Chapter 1 sets out an interpretation of the aesthetic worldview of Borges' fictions with special attention to his "Three Versions of Judas." That analysis provides this work's interpretative lens on Judas. Chapter 2 discusses the canonical Judas—the oracular betrayer—that so dominates interpretations of Judas, including Borges'. Chapters 3 through 5 read the gospels and selected, subsequent interpretations of Judas in scholarship and in the arts in light of Borges' three Judases. Chapter 3 examines Judases that cooperate with the gospels' secret plots to their own demise. Chapter 4 discusses both the Judases who scapegoat themselves and those whom various mythic systems make their scapegoats. Chapter 5 discusses supernatural Judases, both demonic and divine. As the readings in the chapters move freely back and forth between the gospels and their interpretation, the canonical and other Judases appear throughout these chapters. The last chapter reflects on the mythic work undertaken with these various Judases, the evil that inevitably haunts such mythic work, and the possibility of finding more helpful fictions.

I owe a debt to many people, which the footnotes and bibliography only intimate. For anyone wishing to undertake work in the history of the interpretation of Judas, Kim Paffenroth's work (2001b) is a mine of information. The staff of the Methodist University library, including Ms Helen Graham, procured many of the works I have used here. For my notion of fantastic fiction, I acknowledge a debt to my friend George Aichele that I can never repay. Finally and most importantly, I gratefully acknowledge the support that my wife Jennifer provides me through her constant friendship, humor, and intellectual curiosity and through her own work on telling the best possible fictions.

Chapter 1

From the Gospel to Borges and Back Again

The Beginning is Not the End[1]

For the Christian canon, the story of Judas is over before it begins. Judas is the "bad guy" in the gospels. He is the one who "handed" Jesus "over"[2] (Mk 3:19; Mt. 10:4), the one who became a traitor (Lk. 6:16), or the demonic unbeliever (Jn 6:64-71). Nothing good—at least, for Judas—can come of such an introduction.[3] From the beginning, the canonical Judas is the hero's disloyal friend, the one opposed to the things and to the people of God. Inside the canon, he is the outsider. Not surprisingly, he comes to his "just desserts" (Acts 1:16-26).

This story is so dominant that the name "Judas" still stands for perfidy

---

1. As the best-known collections of Borges' fiction in English are *Ficciones* (1962) and *Labyrinths* (1964), this study cites them wherever possible. When materials are not available in them, this study employs the three-volume Penguin collection of Borges' work (1999a, 1999b, 2000a). Biblical quotations are from the NRSV unless noted.

2. English versions normally translate the forms of παραδίδωμι in Mk 3:19 and Mt. 10:4 as "betrayed." Klassen argues that "handed over" would be a better translation (1996: 41–61). See Chapter 3 below. If Klassen is correct, the introductions in Mark and Matthew may not condemn Judas. While Saari agrees with Klassen's analysis of παραδίδωμι, he argues that Mark's "one of the twelve" depicts Judas negatively (2006: 18–55). If he is correct, only Matthew possibly begins Judas' story non-pejoratively. As a matter of fact, positive interpretations of Judas rely most often upon Matthew (or some non-canonical source). Such interpretations, however, require a non-canonical reading of Matthew, reading Matthew, i.e., as a historical or literary text separate from the canon. Despite heroic scholarly efforts, it is hard to get the canon on one's side in the endeavor to find a positive interpretation of Judas. See, e.g., Anderson, 1991: 31; and Robinson, 2006: 49–51.

3. The technique of damning Judas from his introduction is also present in films, like Cecil B. DeMille's *The King of Kings* (1927), which introduces Judas as the one disciple with political ambitions. DeMille's Judas misunderstands the nature of Jesus' ministry. As DeMille joins Judas' introduction with the story of the "conversions" of a young Mark and Mary Magdalene the courtesan, Judas' damnation is clear. Intriguingly, Jesus films typically offer a very canonical Judas. See Walsh, 2006a: 37–53.

and betrayal in cultures influenced by the Christian Bible (see Hand, 1942). Nonetheless, the canonical Judas has puzzled many and, therefore, theological, artistic, historical, literary, and political readings of Judas have multiplied.[4] Despite the canonical finality, stories of Judas proliferate.

Jorge Luis Borges' "Three Versions of Judas"—and Borges' aesthetic worldview generally—provides this work's perspective on that multiplicity. Borges' short story is a posthumous review of the work of a fictional, modern-day gnostic, Nils Runeberg, who spends his life obsessing over the canonical story of Judas (1962: 151–57).[5] Runeberg's first work on Judas, *Kristus och Judas* (*Christ and Judas*), begins with Thomas De Quincey's famous claim that everything supposedly known about Judas is false. Following certain German theologians, De Quincey contends that Judas betrayed Jesus in order to force Jesus to act to free Israel from Roman occupation (De Quincey, 1897: 8:177–82).[6] Borges' Runeberg offers a more metaphysical solution.

Assuming the Christian Bible's perfection, Runeberg reasons that all acts therein are predetermined parts of the divine drama of redemption. The mystery, then, is Judas' precise role in that redemption.[7] Making another assumption with a more gnostic flavor—that the earthly mirrors the heavenly—Runeberg further contends that Judas' role as betrayer is to provide a mirror of the incarnate Word's sacrificial descent into flesh. To complement the divine sacrifice, Judas commits the most dishonorable transgression and, then, deliberately destroys himself.[8]

---

4. For an excellent review of the interpretation of Judas, see Paffenroth, 2001b. He arranges his review according to attitudes that various interpreters have adopted toward Judas: "object of curiosity," "object of horror," "object of hatred and derision," "object of admiration and sympathy," and "object of hope and emulation." Another excellent review, but available only in German, is Klauck, 1987: 17–32.

5. Runeberg's books are as fictional as he is. As the story proceeds, one begins to believe that Borges named this character *Rune*berg purposefully. Borges frequently mingles fiction and reality. Genette refers to such transgressions of narrative levels as "metalepses" (1980: 234–37). Barrenechea calls such transgressions the key to Borges' fiction (1965: 15–16). Sarlo prefers the phrase *structure en abîme* for this common feature of Borges' style (1993: 56–58). See below.

6. Klassen traces positive interpretations of Judas in Germany to Klopstock's *Messias* (1996: 20). The political understanding of Judas remains popular. It informs, e.g., the depiction of Judas in Nicholas Ray's film *King of Kings* (1961).

7. Judas' role in salvation is a major motif in Paffenroth's discussion (2001b: 1–15, 70–82, 135–42). For Christian interpretations of Judas, the ultimate question is almost always whether Judas is "saved" or not.

8. In "Biathanatos" (1999b: 335–36), Borges describes the death of Jesus as a divine suicide and that suicide as the reason for the world's creation. For a discussion

1 From the Gospel to Borges and Back Again 3

After orthodox critics impugn him, Runeberg turns from theology to ethics to explain Judas in a different way. Asserting that an interpreter should assume the best about one that Jesus chooses to participate in his preaching and healing ministry, Runeberg contends that a spiritual asceticism, rather than greed, motivates Judas. The resulting Judas still mirrors Jesus, but now the reflection is inverted. Knowing goodness and happiness to be divine prerogatives, Judas knows evil and sorrow to be his all too human lot. Accordingly, Runeberg's second Judas humbly eschews virtue and commits the worst offenses to depict the greater glory of God as in an inverse mirror (cf. 1 Cor. 1:31).

Pursuing these ideas further, Runeberg publishes *Dem hemlige Fralsaren* (*The Secret Savior*) to which he attaches Jn 1:10—"the world knew him not"—as an epigraph. For Runeberg, the "him" is Judas, who replaces Jesus as the incarnate one. To justify this assertion, Runeberg argues that Isa. 53:2–3—"despised of men and the least of them"—describes Judas far more precisely than it does Jesus. In Runeberg's logic, to become a man means to become able to sin and to suffer ultimate degradation—for example, the ignominy of betrayal—not merely to suffer for a mere afternoon. Judas, not Jesus, truly plumbs the depths of human suffering.

The story's denouement segues from Judas to Runeberg, as Runeberg becomes his Judas. At least, Runeberg's fate mirrors that of his Judas. Ignored by the world, Runeberg becomes convinced that God is punishing him for revealing the secret name of God (Judas). In a final reversal, Runeberg in his last pathetic days hopes to share hell with his Redeemer. Not surprisingly, Runeberg dies.[9]

Reading (Interpreting) the Gospel Judas with Borges

Borges' Runeberg struggles with the gospels in order to interpret the canonical Judas. His endeavors make "Three Versions of Judas" a micro-

---

of the deaths of Jesus and Judas as suicides, see Droge and Tabor, 1992. They claim that Christians developed a uniformly negative attitude toward suicide only after Augustine. For similar arguments, see Whelan, 1993: 505–22; Klassen, 1996: 160–76; and Saari, 2006: 15–18, 59–76.

9. This meshing of Runeberg and Judas is another metalepsis. The narrator adds, as a final comment, that Runeberg adds evil to the son. This parting observation is one of the most intriguing lines in the entire short story. Has the narrator adopted Runeberg's increasingly gnostic conceptions? Has he decided that the world is an evil place, a false creation? Mirror-like, the observation sends the reader back into the story yet again. As is so common in Borges, it leaves reality enigmatic and humans obsessed with ill-fated solutions. See Chapter 6 below.

cosm both of the act of interpretation generally and of interpretations of Judas specifically. In fact, one can understand many, if not most, of Borges' stories in this interpretative mode.[10] An overview of Borges' aesthetics, with particular attention to his interpretative play with previous stories and with "reality," may clarify this claim. At least, the overview of Borges' aesthetics will set the stage for this work's attempt to read the gospel Judas(es) as Borges' precursor.

Borges' first collection of prose, *A Universal History of Iniquity*, consists of stories derived from his reading of "true detective" stories (1999a: 1–64). In a preface to a later edition of the collection, Borges dismisses these early stories as "the irresponsible sport of a shy sort of man who could not bring himself to write short stories, and so amused himself by changing and distorting (sometimes without aesthetic justification) the stories of other men" (1999a: 4). Despite Borges' reductive tone, the description aptly summarizes Borges' lasting tendency to create new stories out of and about earlier literature. The process creates stories alongside one another. As a result, no one story reigns uncontested. In *A Universal History of Iniquity*, the style transforms "true stories" into fiction or, more accurately, into *Ficciones*. From a Borgesian perspective, all interpretation—even that of the gospels and of their Judas(es)—functions similarly.

In his literary autobiography, Borges claims he began to write his internationally famous short fictions only after he suffered a near-fatal injury. Uncertain that he could write as he had before as a journalist and in *A Universal History of Iniquity*, he opts for a new style and creates the famous "Pierre Menard, Author of *Don Quixote*" (1962: 45–55). Despite his assertions about his new aesthetic directions, however, Borges still creates stories out of story. Like Runeberg, Menard is a fictional creation and is obsessed with a classic. Unlike Runeberg, Menard does not wish to write a new, better story. He wishes to remain Menard and to rewrite— "to channel," not to copy—*Don Quixote* verbatim. He aspires to be an absurdly faithful tradent.

In a posthumous review of the understandably fragmentary results of Menard's lifework, Borges' narrator selects Menard's exact reproduction of a section of chapter nine of *Don Quixote* as an example of his work:

---

10. Rodríguez-Luis claims that Borges' stories provide allegories about artistic creation in the context of the demise of the West (1991: 34–46, 104). Sturrock asserts that to read Borges is to study fiction as a genre (1977: 3).

> [truth, whose mother is history, who is the rival of time, depository of deeds, witness of the past, example and lesson to the present, and warning to the future.] (1962: 53)

Borges' narrator, however, observes that Menard's exact reproduction fails to mean as the original did:

> History, *mother* of truth; the idea is astounding. Menard, a contemporary of William James, does not define history as an investigation of reality, but as its origin. Historical truth, for him, is not what took place; it is what we think took place. The final clauses – *example and lesson to the present, and warning to the future* – are shamelessly pragmatic. (1962: 53)

In short, the same words mean differently because the words occupy a new cultural location. Even verbatim repetition creates stories. It does not simply reprise "the original." It adds to it.

Matters turn more quixotic in Menard's reproduction of part of chapter thirty-eight of *Don Quixote*. There, Cervantes' Don Quixote prizes arms above letters. Borges' narrator cannot imagine Menard, the artist, arriving at a similar position, so he attributes Menard's thirty-eighth chapter to Menard's ironic disposition, to his habit of saying the opposite of what he meant. Now, the same words mean the opposite of what they once meant because of their new speaker. Once again, even "exact" repetition transforms the precursor. Finality vanishes. Stories proliferate.

In the preface to *Ficciones*, which includes the story about Menard and which was the first international collection of his famous short fictions, Borges describes his creative method:

> The composition of vast books is a laborious and impoverishing extravagance. To go on for five hundred pages developing an idea whose perfect oral exposition is possible in a few minutes! A better course of procedure is to pretend that these books already exist, and then to offer a résumé, a commentary....I have preferred to write notes upon imaginary books. (1962: 15 16)[11]

Anthony Kerrigan, the editor of *Ficciones*, accordingly describes Borges' "notes" as "a species of international literary metaphor" (1962: 9).[12] Borges

---

11. Other stories in *Ficciones* taking this approach include "The Approach to Al-Mu'tasim" (1962: 37–43), "An Examination of the Work of Herbert Quain" (1962: 73–78), and, of course, "Three Versions of Judas" (1962: 151–57).

12. For a comparison of Borges' fictions to (Jesus') parables, see Crossan, 1976. Sarlo claims that Borges' fiction is always on the edge, and she points to the importance of the *orillas*, the suburbs between the city and the mysterious plains of the gauchos of Argentine legend, in Borges' fiction (1993: 3–5). She claims that his fiction

6   *Three Versions of Judas*

deliberately places his stories alongside earlier—real or imagined—literature, and his stories take their meaning by commenting upon and, thereby, revising this earlier literature. In this process, Borges, the interpreter, creates and betrays his precursors. "Three Versions of Judas," for example, does this to the canonical gospels. In Borges' view, each author/interpreter—even if he repeats his precursors' words as exactly as Menard does—acts similarly.[13]

As a result, whether the canon/classic is read by the heretical Runeberg or by the absurdly orthodox Menard, the results are always multiple stories. Despite canonical fixity, Judas is always already in another story. Canon always becomes interpretation.[14] Unfortunately, scholarly readings often deny this necessity as they proffer the one, true interpretation (of Judas).[15] Reading the canon from the aesthetic perspective of Borges helps avoid such hubris. From the perspective of Borges, interpretation cannot uncover the one, true Judas. Interpretation necessarily multiplies Judases. The justification for such interpretative and artistic plurality lies in the death of Runeberg (see below) or, more broadly, in Borges' aesthetic worldview.

Borges' Aesthetic Worldview, Fantastic Fiction

A look at Borges' "Funes, the Memorious" introduces Borges' aesthetic worldview more fully. In that story, Borges depicts a young man crippled

exploits every possible meaning of the *orillas*: "edge," "shore," "margin," and "limit." In "The Argentine Writer and Tradition" (1964: 184), Borges asserts that the place of Argentines (like those of the Jews and of the Irish) on the margin of the Western tradition allows them an irreverent and innovative perspective on tradition.

13. Sturrock claims that Borges sees no distinction between quotation and misquotation because both transform the original (1977: 159).

14. One might also read "Three Versions of Judas" as an allegory of the general trajectory of biblical interpretation. See n10. Like Runeberg, modern biblical critics, whether early deists or recent postcolonialists, have moved from theology to ethics (or politics). Moreover, modern biblical interpretation pursues anthropology, not theology. The human replaces God, Jesus replaces Christ, and Judas' motivation replaces Judas' theological fate. Cf. Happel, 1993. Despite these changes, "Three Versions of Judas" also indicates that biblical interpretation invariably continues in the shadow of the canon. For example, the common scholarly idea that one can find the one, true interpretation of Judas—revealing the desire to end Judas' stories with a final, true interpretation—fastens interpretation to a perspective quite like that of the canon. See Walsh, 2001: 133–64.

15. Kermode claims that interpretation is so hard that one easily falls back into "truth" (1979: 123).

1 *From the Gospel to Borges and Back Again*   7

by an accident and, more horribly, afflicted by an infallible perception and memory (1962: 107–15). For Funes, the result is an insomniac life of details, a life incapable of thought, because "[t]o think is to forget a difference, to generalize, to abstract. In the overly replete world of Funes there were nothing but details, almost contiguous details" (1962: 115).[16] When Funes dies, the story's denouement attributes his death to a pulmonary congestion, but Funes seems to die from a surfeit of reality.

Borges sees "reality" as something akin to Kant's noumena or the mystic's ineffable infinite. For Borges, this reality is ultimately incomprehensible and is apathetic toward humans, if not vaguely destructive (see Barrenechea, 1965). What Borges says in an essay, the point of which is the refutation of time, concisely expresses his complex view about reality as a whole: "Time is the substance I am made of. Time is a river which sweeps me along, but I am the river; it is a tiger which destroys me, but I am the tiger; it is a fire which consumes me, but I am the fire. The world, unfortunately, is real; I, unfortunately, am Borges" (1964: 234).

Nonetheless, many of Borges' protagonists, like Runeberg, strive to grasp reality, the absolute truth (e.g., about Judas), or God. Most of them die without achieving their goal. Those who do reach the goal of their quest lapse into something other than normal human life; they fall, like Funes, into the silence of infinity. Thus, when the imprisoned priest in "The God's Script" finally finds the magical sentence that God wrote on the day of creation that might ward off the eschatological devastation of his people, he does not speak it because he has lost himself:

> Whoever has seen the universe, whoever has beheld the fiery designs of the universe, cannot think in terms of one man, of that man's trivial fortunes or misfortunes, though he be that very man. That man *has been he* and now matters no more to him. What is the life of that other to him, the nation of that other to him, if he, now, is no one. (1964: 173)[17]

While Borges sees this dissolution in infinity (a river of time and sensation) as human destiny,[18] he still strives to resist these effects of

---

16. For an essay on thought's distance from reality, see Borges, "The Postulation of Reality" (1999b: 59–64).

17. Similarly, the immortals in "The Immortal" know that ultimately all things happen to all men (1964: 105–18). Given infinite time, every human is all humans, so moral distinctions collapse. Accordingly, the immortals lapse into indifferent inactivity, into a subhuman troglodyte existence, until they discover the salutary prospect of a river that grants mortality. They set off in search of this river believing that death makes humans "precious and pathetic" (1964: 115).

18. Borges has little respect for modern individualism. See Borges, "A Note on

time/reality, so, in story after story, he lumps reality, infinity, and divinity together as inhuman, horrible territory. "Funes, the Memorious," for example, makes it clear that human life depends upon their opposites, upon abstracted thought, upon forgetfulness, and upon death. In an essay on language, Borges explicitly states that humans live in language, not in unmediated reality: "It will be our destiny to mold ourselves to syntax, to its treacherous chain of events, to the imprecision, the maybes, the too many emphases, the buts, the hemisphere of lies and of darkness in our speech" (Borges, 1999b: 39).[19] Reality, by contrast, lacks syntax. Consequently, reality is unspeakable and ultimately beyond human ken.[20]

According to Carter Wheelock (1969: 62), Borges' view of language resembles Nietzsche's. In "On Truth and Lies in a Nonmoral Sense" (1873: 114–23), Nietzsche argues that language is inevitably metaphorical and, therefore, not truthful. Language does not represent reality. Truth is "a moveable host of metaphors," "illusions which we have forgotten are illusions," "metaphors that have become worn out," and "the duty to lie according to a fixed convention" (1873: 117).[21]

For Borges, (literary) art also fails as a representation of reality. It adds something to reality,[22] an addition that Borges sometimes finds distasteful. In fact, one should probably add "art" to the list of the abominable in his famous line: "mirrors and copulation are abominable, since they

(toward) Bernard Shaw" (1964: 213–16), in which he castigates lyric poetry, the novel, and existentialism, which "foment that illusion of the ego which the Vedanta censures as a capital error" and "flatter our vanity" (1964: 216). In Borges, "Everything and Nothing" (1964: 248–49), Shakespeare (the author in Borges' estimation) and God are "many and no one."

19. Cf. his "John Wilkins' Analytic Language" (1999b: 231–32). His position resembles Hume's famous debunking of causality. Berkeley and Hume are among Borges' favorite philosophers.

20. In "Inferno, I, 32," Borges describes the world as "exceedingly complex for the simplicity of men" (1999a: 323).

21. Cf. Nietzsche: "Ultimate skepsis.—What are man's truths ultimately? Merely his irrefutable errors" (1974: 265). Nietzsche begins "On Truth and Lies in a Nonmoral Sense" with a fable about the unimportance of humans vis-à-vis reality: "Once upon a time, in some out of the way corner of that universe which is dispersed into numberless twinkling solar systems, there was a star upon which clever beasts invented knowing. That was the most arrogant and mendacious minute of 'world history,' but nevertheless, it was only a minute. After nature had drawn a few breaths, the star cooled and congealed, and the clever beasts had to die" (1873: 114).

22. See Borges (1999a: 310). Sturrock observes that in Borges there is no way out of literature into life and argues as well that Borges' realism mimics literary conventions, not reality (1977: 81–84, 204).

both multiply the numbers of man" (1962: 17).[23] Interpretation certainly belongs in this list. It, for example, can never arrive at the true Judas. It necessarily multiplies Judases. From Borges' perspective, despite his admitted distaste, such additions are the human condition. Borges describes this situation most succinctly with the symbol of a labyrinth. For Borges, the labyrinth represents both reality's mysterious nature and the invariably convoluted, fictitious constructs that humans create to map and depict that reality.[24]

Despite their realism, then, Borges' fictions do not mimic reality.[25] Instead, they intrude upon commonsense or cultural assumptions about reality, transgressing the comfortable lines between that (construct of) reality and acknowledged fictions.[26] Thus, "Three Versions of Judas" is a review of the work of a theologian who exists only in Borges' fiction, yet the fictional Runeberg exists in the story alongside the real Thomas De Quincey. Further, the story, like much of Borges' fiction, poses as a factual essay, citing sources and offering erudite footnotes. Moreover, these footnotes refer to both real and imaginatively created sources. Borges writes poetry and attributes it to Runeberg. Borges footnotes a theological position with a reference to a work by Jaromir Hladík, yet another character created by Borges in "The Secret Miracle" (1962: 143–50). This transgressive style challenges cultural commonsense about reality or human constructs posing as reality. It challenges human certainty about the nature of things and claims to certainty about characters or people like Judas.

23. Fittingly, the quote comes not from Borges directly but from a character in "Tlön, Uqbar, Orbis Tertius" who remembers that a heretic of Uqbar expressed this opinion. The narrator of "Hakim, the Masked Dyer of Merv" repeats a very similar judgment (1999a: 43). For more on Borges' aversion to mirrors, see his "Covered Mirrors" (1999a: 297–98); and his horror stories about meeting his younger or older self: "The Other" (1999a: 411–17); "August 25, 1983" (1999a: 489–93); and "Borges and I" (1964: 246–47).

24. The most famous collection of Borges' short stories, other than *Ficciones*, is *Labyrinths* (1964). The classic example of Borges' use of the labyrinth symbol is "The Library of Babel" (1962: 79–88). The labyrinth appears as horror in "The Immortal" (1964: 105–18); and in "The House of Asterion" (1964: 138–40). Its confusion is the prerogative of God in "The Two Kings and the Two Labyrinths" (1999a: 263–64).

25. They do sometimes have their own labyrinth quality.

26. See n5. These metalepses, combined with Borges' erudition and puzzle-like story structures, leave many readers of Borges with the sense that they have been or are about to be "had." Naomi Lindstrom asserts, "In learning to deal with Borges's stories, readers come to suspect all references either of being outright inventions or of making misleading use of an extant work" (1990: 13).

The classic example in Borges' fictions is "Tlön, Uqbar, Orbis Tertius," in which Borges, as narrator and character, searches for the version of an encyclopedia that contains an entry on the heresiarchs of Uqbar (1962: 17–35). When he finally finds a volume with the entry, Borges discovers therein a vague description of a territory whose literature refers to the imaginary territories of Mlejnas and Tlön. Two years later, the eleventh volume of *A First Encyclopaedia of Tlön*, belonging to his recently deceased friend, Herbert Ashe, comes into Borges' possession. The volume details the idealist world of Tlön, a world that sounds remarkably like one from the fantasies of the idealist philosopher George Berkeley.

The description of Tlön ends the story proper, but it leaves the identity of the inventor of Tlön unknown. A postscript, dated ten years later, clarifies this mystery. It claims that a seventeenth-century British secret society, later including Berkeley, invented a country. Later, a millionaire American ascetic expanded the society's country into the planet Tlön, decided that the plan would be kept secret, and authorized the production of an encyclopedia of the imaginary planet. Ashe was involved with this group in some way. In the interim between Borges' discovery of this plot and the writing of his postscript, objects from Tlön have begun to appear in Borges' world, including a copy of the full forty-volume encyclopedia of Tlön. Moreover, the story's world has steadily given ground to Tlön in place after place so that soon the "world will be Tlön" (1962: 34–35). Nonetheless, Borges ignores Tlön's intrusion and works on producing a tentative translation of Sir Thomas Browne's *Urn Burial*, which he does not intend to publish.

This character's aesthetic isolation is akin to that of the priest in "The God's Script" (1964: 169–73) and the ennui of "The Immortal[s]" (1964: 105–18). On one hand, one might castigate such passivity, as many critics have castigated Borges himself, for a lack of social activism.[27] On the other hand, one might see this aesthetic isolation as itself an ethical stance rejecting human constructs that masquerade as reality and, thereby, opposing all dogmatism and all totalitarianism. Tlön testifies to the ability of constructs, metaphysics, and interpretations (of Judas, e.g.) to become what their adherents (wrongly) believe to be reality.

---

27. Should one read the end of "Tlön, Uqbar, Orbis Tertius" as an ironic riposte to Borges' many activist critics? For a review of the criticisms of Borges' elitism, conservatism, and non-activism, see Stabb, 1991: 101–20. For a nuanced defense of Borges, see Sarlo, 1993. For Borges, fiction's uselessness is its inherent value. It distracts from life and from the inevitability of death. See Sturrock, 1977: 204–12.

Tlön exemplifies the transgressions of reality and fiction that fascinate Borges. His favorite examples include Don Quixote reading the novel of which he is a part, Hamlet staging and watching a play quite like that in which he is the protagonist, Scheherazade embarking on the tale of *1001 Nights* on one of the nights within that story, and Royce's description of a map of England so detailed that it includes the map that includes the map, and so on to infinity (1964: 193–96). For Borges, such metalepses threaten readers' realities. As fictional characters transgress fictional boundaries and near the place of readers, they suggest that readers and their commonsense reality may also be fictional. Reflecting upon these examples, Borges concludes, "In 1833, Carlyle observed that the history of the universe is an infinite sacred book that all men write and read and try to understand, and in which they are also written (1964: 196)."[28] Here, "history" stands both for mysterious reality and for the human constructs that purport to depict it. Borges' transgressive play illustrates the uncertainties of both.

The device of the dream can be as corrosive. In "The South," the librarian protagonist has an accident similar to the one that Borges claims led to his literary transformation (1962: 167–74). Thereafter, the protagonist travels to the South, becomes involved improbably in a duel, and is killed. The story intrigues because it is impossible to determine whether the protagonist actually travels to the South or whether he dreams the story while dying in a hospital. The narrator pointedly remarks that the people that the protagonist meets on his journey southward look suspiciously like people in the hospital. All that one is really sure of in the end is that the protagonist dies. Such corrosive uncertainties leave one in the position of Chuang Tzu who dreams he is a butterfly and, then, awakes uncertain whether he is a man dreaming he is a butterfly or vice versa.[29]

Dreams consume fixed reality even more completely in "The Circular Ruins" (1962: 57–63). In this story, an unfeeling, gray man from the South comes to a ruined, circular temple. Somehow, he knows his obligation is to dream, and he desires to dream a man and foist him on reality. After a great struggle, the gray man brings forth his dream Adam and sends him to another ruined temple. Before he does so, however, he wipes out his son's memory so he will think himself a man (1962: 61–62).

---

28. Playing with similar ideas in "On Exactitude in Science," Borges imagines cartographers that make a map so exact that it grows to the size of the empire it maps, proves useless, and ruins geography in the empire (1999a: 325).

29. Borges makes specific reference to this dream in "A New Refutation of Time" (1964: 230–31).

Years later, messengers tell the gray man of a man in another temple who walks through fire unharmed. Knowing they speak of his son, the gray man worries that his son will meditate upon his peculiar abilities and recognize, to his humiliation, that he is another man's dream. His anxieties end when the sanctuary in which he serves is destroyed by fire because he does not feel the flames: "With relief, with humiliation, with terror, he understood that he also was an illusion, that someone else was dreaming him" (1962: 63).

Borges uses such metalepses to corrupt reality or, more exactly, to corrupt the human hold on constructs, which pose as reality:

> Let us admit what all idealists admit: the hallucinatory nature of the world. Let us do what no idealist has done: seek unrealities which confirm that nature. We shall find them, I believe, in the antinomies of Kant and in the dialectic of Zeno.
>
> "The greatest magician (Novalis has memorably written) would be the one who would cast over himself a spell so complete that he would take his own phantasmagorias as autonomous appearances. Would this not be our case?" I conjecture that this is so. We (the undivided divinity operating within us) have dreamt the world. We have dreamt it as firm, mysterious, visible, ubiquitous in space and durable in time; but in its architecture we have allowed tenuous and eternal crevices of unreason which tell us it is false. (1964: 208)[30]

Thus, metaphysic, the human understanding of reality, becomes a branch of fantasy:

> The fact that any philosophical system is bound in advance to be a dialectical game, a *Philosophie des Als Ob*, means that systems abound, unbelievable systems, beautifully constructed or else sensational in effect. The metaphysicians of Tlön are not looking for truth, nor even for an approximation of it; they are after a kind of amazement. They consider metaphysics a branch of fantastic literature. They know that a system is nothing more than the subordination of all the aspects of the universe to some one of them. (Borges, 1962: 25)

---

30. Cf. Borges: "The title of this book [*The Book of Imaginary Beings*] would justify the inclusion of Prince Hamlet, the point, the line, the plane, the hypercube, all generic nouns, and, perhaps, each one of us and the divinity as well. In sum, virtually the entire universe" (2005: xv). Barrenechea discusses, at length, the deconstructive effects of Borges' play with infinity, pantheism, time, and idealism on ordinary notions of the reality of the universe, the self, and time (1965: 16, 144–45). David Hume, one of Borges' favorite philosophers, comes immediately to mind as does the Buddha.

1 *From the Gospel to Borges and Back Again* 13

While this quote specifically describes the view of some of Borges' fictional creatures, it also speaks of Borges' own fascination with philosophy, with religion, and with ideas as aesthetic fodder, potential "as if" or "perhaps" starting points, for his tales.[31]

As they unsettle one's certainties, Borges' fictions have the potential to liberate. Joseph Campbell claims myth acts similarly:

> Such a highly played game of "as if" frees our mind and spirit, on the one hand, from the presumption of theology, which pretends to know the laws of God, and, on the other, from the bondage of reason, whose laws do not apply beyond the horizon of human experience...
>
> The opaque weight of the world—both of life on earth and death, heaven, and hell—is dissolved, and the spirit freed, not *from* anything, for there was nothing from which to be freed except a myth too solidly believed, but *for* something, something fresh and new, a spontaneous act.
>
> ...for the sheer delight of play, transubstantiates the world—in which actually, after all, things are not quite as real or permanent, terrible, important, or logical as they seem. (1969: 28–29)[32]

Defiantly unreal, Borges' fictions imagine other possible realities (and Judases in "Three Versions of Judas").[33] Like Nietzsche, Borges believes that art can smash conventional constructions of reality in order to put them "back together in an ironic fashion" (Nietzsche, 1873: 122).[34]

Borges, then, does not believe in any of the metaphysics, which he takes as his starting points, nor does he want his readers to believe his fictions.[35] His metalepses aggressively call attention to his fictions as fic-

---

31. Barrenechea refers to Borges' fiction as "the territory of perhaps" (1965: 137). The original Spanish title of her work, *La expression de la irrealidad en la obra de Jorge Luis Borges*, more aptly captures this aspect of Borges. Crossan calls "perhaps" Borges' favorite word (1976: 91).

32. One does not need to wax romantic on this point. The scientific method also eschews dogmatism and certainty. Wheelock compares Borges' fiction to myth, claiming, in particular, that Borges writes fiction to deal with the mythic conflict between the contingent perspective—best set out in Borges' "The Zahir" (1964: 156–65)—and the absolute—best set out in Borges' "The Aleph" (1999a: 274–86)—through adopting a skeptical, fluid point of view that imagines multiple, possible realities (1969: 12–26).

33. Borges claims that art "requires visible unrealities" (1964: 207).

34. Wheelock claims that Borges' stories "suggest other ways of interrelating the parts of the universe, ontologies which we have forgotten or not yet made" (1969: 5).

35. Embarking on his "New Refutation of Time," Borges remarks that he does not believe his argument even though it is present in all his works (1964: 218). After completing this argument—which extends the ideas of Berkeley and Hume—Borges

tions, as do stories that are swallowed up by the dreams of their protagonists, the failures of heroes or narrators to find the absolute truth or revelation that they seek, and the narrators that simply fall into silence. When revelations do occur, they remain untold as in "The God's Script" (1964: 169–73) or they disappoint as in "The Immortal" (1964: 105–18). Borges' fictions invariably end with and evoke uncertainty. In fact, in a preface to one of his last collections of fiction, he describes the creation of uncertainty as one of his enduring aesthetic tricks (1999a: 331). Such uncertainties make it impossible to accept any one story, even the canonical story of Judas, as the unimpeachable truth. Such uncertainties bathe all metaphysics and all stories in an "as if" quality.

While Campbell argues that myth has this "as if" capacity, most critics think of myth as a community's charter story or its cultural commonsense in narrative form. Most critics think myth supportive of a culture's ordinary conception of reality. If one thinks of myths so, one might better think of Borges' fictions as parabolic or fantastic.[36] His fictions abut the cultural tradition and its ordinary conception of reality in order to challenge it.[37] John Dominic Crossan thinks that Jesus' parables function similarly, and, in a comparison of Borges' fictions and Jesus' parables, he claims they both induce playfulness and laughter: "Laughter purifies from dogmatism, from the intolerant and the petrified; it liberates from fanaticism and pedantry, from fear and intimidation, from didacticism, naïveté and illusion, *from the single meaning, the single level*, from sentimentality."[38]

Julio Rodríguez-Luis has provided the most thorough examination of Borges' work in light of critical conceptions of the fantastic (1991: 3–27).[39] His work relies upon Tzvetan Todorov's analysis of the fantastic

---

dissents from himself yet again and grudgingly acknowledges time's existence (1964: 234).

36. Irwin defines fantasy as "the persuasive establishment and development of an impossibility, an arbitrary construct of the mind with all under the control of logic and rhetoric" (1976: 9). This definition also makes a very nice, brief depiction of the "as if" starting points and the tightly structured plots of Borges' short fiction. Borges, in his preface to *Artifices*, printed as part two of *Ficciones*, refers to "Three Versions of Judas" as a "Christological fantasy" (1962: 106).

37. For a discussion of myth and parable's different relationships to cultural reality, see Crossan, 1975: 9, 47–62.

38. Bakhtin, *Rabelais and His World*, 123, cited in Crossan, 1976: 126 (italics added by Crossan).

39. For a postmodern discussion of fantasy, see Aichele, 1985; and Aichele, 2006: 1–81. In the first work, Aichele places Borges on the side of self-referential fiction and semiotic play, i.e., fantasy, rather than on the side of the certainties of genre, ideology,

as a reader's hesitation when confronted with a supernatural event in a seemingly realistic narrative. This fantastic hesitation ends if the reader does not accept the narrative as realistic, taking it instead as poetry or as allegory. The fantastic also ends if, at the end of the reading, the reader decides that normal laws of nature can explain the event or if the reader decides that altogether new laws are called for to account for the event. In the former case, the fantastic slides into the genre of the uncanny and, in the latter, into the marvelous. Notably, Todorov also locates fantastic narratives in a particular historical era—after the development of the realist novel and before the development of psychoanalysis, which reduces the supernatural to unconscious drives (Todorov, 1973: 25–64, 160–73).

While not quite the same as Todorov's theory of the fantastic, Sigmund Freud's notion of the uncanny also involves an interpretative glitch. For Freud, the uncanny is the experience of frightening events that bring modern, scientific individuals to an impasse threatening the return of repressed, primitive ideas. In less anxious times, moderns typically dismiss such ideas as superstitious, magical, and animistic (Freud, 2003). Freud's list of uncanny events—including doubles, dreams, magic, and inescapable fate—reads like a list of Borges' common tropes. Nevertheless, Freud would likely deny that Borges' fictions are uncanny because Borges' fictions, like the fairy tales that Freud discusses, make a magical world their home. Similarly, Rodríguez-Luis denies that Borges' fictions are fantastic. He thinks they, like Kafka's tales, belong instead to the category of the marvelous. Rodríguez-Luis also denies that Borges' stories are fantastic because so many of them clearly suggest allegorical readings of themselves. In particular, Rodríguez-Luis claims that Borges' stories deny reality in order to suggest a metatext (about artistic creation during the demise of the West) (1991: 34–46, 104).[40]

Rodríguez-Luis admits, however, that suggestions of a metatext may be fantastic if the metatext points to yet another hidden meaning (and so on?), if, that is, the metatext fosters multiple interpretations (1991: 116). Rodríguez-Luis offers Thomas Pynchon's *Crying of Lot 49* (1999) as an example. The near revelation of a hidden plot involving the Tristero, the Shadow Adversary of the U.S. Mail, haunts this novel and its protagonist, Oedipa Mass. Unfortunately, Oedipa does not know whether clues about

---

and myth (1985: 53–75). Aichele, i.e., sees Borges as a more "fantastic" author than Rodríguez-Luis does. The analysis here relies heavily on Aichele's work.

40. Cf. Sturrock, who thinks that all Borges' fictions are about fiction and its making (1977: 3).

this plot or coincidences fill her life, whether the Tristero exists or she merely fantasizes it. The novel ends with "the crying of Lot 49," the offering for auction of a misprinted stamp, which may prove the existence of the Tristero. Consequently, the novel ends before the reader learns Oedipa's fate.[41]

For Rodríguez-Luis, the novel also ends before one can learn whether supernatural agencies are involved in Oedipa's fate. The supernatural is crucial to Rodríguez-Luis's analysis because he assumes modern materialists no longer believe in it. Thus, the modern fantastic presents the sacred as a near revelation, "not as a presence, but rather as a determinate, marked absence at the heart of the secular world." The result is a world "forever suspended on the point of meaning."[42] But, such interpretative suspense precisely depicts the effects of Borges' fictions and resembles his conception of the near revelation of aesthetics:

> Music, states of happiness, mythology, faces belabored by time, certain twilights and certain places try to tell us something, or have said something we should not have missed, or are about to say something; this imminence of a revelation which does not occur is, perhaps, the aesthetic phenomenon. (Borges, 1964: 188)[43]

Despite Rodríguez-Luis' objections, then, Borges' fictions are fantastic because they generate an interpretative play of possible meanings.

Borges' fictions resist certain meaning—notions of the real and realism—by calling attention to themselves as fictions.[44] Borges' fictions live in, thrive on, and generate metaphysical uncertainty—an uncertainty not unlike that of Freud's uncanny or of Todorov's fantastic. In this, Borges' fictions are parabolic, rather than mythic. Thereby, Borges' fictions challenge dogmatism and totalitarianism intellectually and artistically. They

---

41. Borges tells a similar story, "The Approach to Al-Mu'tasim" (1962: 37–43), in a predictably shorter form. Umberto Eco's *Foucault's Pendulum* (1990) is another similar story. For discussion of the latter, see Chapter 3.

42. Frederick Jameson, cited in Rodríguez-Luis, 1991: 119. For modern materialists, this possibility is horrible as it suggests supernatural forces beyond and threatening to modern individuals. It may be the example of the uncanny in modernity. For discussion, see Chapter 5.

43. Crossan also cites this passage from Borges (1976: 169–70). He uses it to clarify his own notion of "comic eschatology," which denies the finality of the normal constructions of reality without resorting to the terror and certainties of the "final solution" of apocalyptic eschatology (1976: 30–33).

44. Semiotic play, self-reference, and subversion of genre/reality/ideology are characteristics of fantasy for Aichele, 2006: 31–58. For a detailed discussion of the fantastic's capacity to subvert genres, see Rabkin, 1976: 8–12, 29, 189–227.

1 *From the Gospel to Borges and Back Again* 17

rely upon or incite a reader's horror at totalitarianism, at the *pars* masquerading as the *totum* or at the *pars* subjecting the *totum*.

Borges' fictions are not flights from reality as much as they are disenchantments with human constructs presented as the true representation of reality.[45] They are not fantastic if one understands the fantastic to be the hesitation between two genres or ideologies. They are fantastic in that they generate hesitation about the absolute truth of any construct, system, genre, ideology, or interpretation of Judas. They are fantastic as they introduce a gap between any construct and ineffable reality.[46]

Borges' fictions call attention to the ironic disjoint between mysterious reality and the human quest for reality. This aesthetic perspective is not unlike Albert Camus' notion of the absurd, the dilemma caused by the conjunction of meaningless reality and meaning-seeking humans (Camus, 1991: 21).[47] Because of this viewpoint, Borges refuses to allow any assertion or system—even one that he has just articulated—to stand unchallenged. This position leads him to disrupt systems—like the canon—by elevating a subordinate part of that system—like Judas in "Three Versions of Judas"—to preeminence. Moreover, this stance leads him to embrace

---

45. Cf. Aichele, who defines genre as a method of locating a literary object in the space of the real world and, then, lists three genres: (1) deceit; (2) bad faith, thinking that one's understanding of reality reflects objective reality; and (3) good faith, recognizing story as story as well as the necessity of a story, i.e., a representation of reality (1985: 92, 100–101, 122, 137). For Aichele, fantasy and parable belong to the third category, which is comic and amoral, and to what, following Todorov, he sometimes refers to as "nearly ... believing" (Todorov, 1973: 31).

46. Borges has a tendency to marvel at unknowable reality and an aesthetic curiosity in the metaphysics and theologies that try to plumb it. Finally, however, Borges prefers mystery to any solution. His description of his own character Dunraven expresses his own aesthetic awe: "Dunraven, who had read a great many detective novels, thought that the solution of a mystery was always a good deal less interesting than the mystery itself; the mystery had a touch of the supernatural and even the divine about it, while the solution was a sleight of hand" (1999a: 260). By the way, critics often sort detective fiction into two categories: (1) those that present an intellectual puzzle to be resolved; and (2) those that present an injustice to be righted. If so, Borges and his Dunraven represent a third category, a reveling in mystery itself. That attitude is reminiscent of Poe and Lovecraft, both of whom Borges admired greatly. It also suggests what some aesthetic critics have called the human response to the negative sublime or what Rudolf Otto termed the "numinous" (1958: 12–40). In Borges' case, the awe is irreligious.

47. Like Borges, Camus recommends aesthetics, or absurd creation, as one appropriate response to that dilemma. For a comparison of Borges and Camus, see McMurray, 1980.

multiple perspectives.[48] For Borges, fantasy is important because certainty about or obsession with reality, truth, and metaphysical systems is deadly.[49]

The fate of the character Borges in "The Zahir" is illustrative (1964: 155–65). He receives a coin in change, and, soon, he fixates on this particular coin until he can think of nothing else. Gradually, he believes that the coin is the Zahir, "Notorious" or "Visible," one of the ninety-nine names of God. Unfortunately, as a book on various Zahirs informs him, the unforgettable Zahir ultimately drives one mad.[50] As the story ends, Borges wonders if this madness has not already come upon him. He has exalted one piece of reality at the expense of all others, so his fate is certain. The metaphysicians of Tlön, who seem to speak for Borges, know this to be the secret failure of all systems, and the ruin of those who bow to them.

Matters differ significantly in "The Aleph," a companion piece to "The Zahir" (1999a: 274–86).[51] In that piece, a pedestrian poet takes the character Borges to his basement and shows him a mysterious Aleph, a point in space that contains all points, an unconfused perspective on infinity. The Borges of "The Aleph" survives the consuming lure of this Aleph only when he imagines (another) the true Aleph—the En Soph or hidden name of God—to be enshrined in a column in a mosque, which he has

---

48. See the various stories in which he uses tales within tales to create a certain unreliability about the tales' narrations (e.g., "The Immortal" [1964: 106–18]; cf. the narrators of almost all the stories in the collection, entitled *Brodie's Report* [1999a: 343–408], who raise some doubt about the story's accuracy) or the various stories to which Borges appends notes or postscripts that deflect or subvert the tenor of the tale narrated (e.g., "The Approach to Al-Mu'tasim" [1962: 37–43]; cf. the effect which "The Two Kings and the Two Labyrinths" [1999a: 263–64] has on the preceding tale, "Ibn-Ḥakam al-Bokhari, Murdered in his Labyrinth" [1999a: 255–62]). In all these cases, the effect is a multiplicity of stories, rather than one canonical tale. The style resembles the multiple versions of events that Herodotus presents in the name of history.

49. See the discussion of the priest in "The God's Script" (1964: 169–73) above as well as the fate of the detective Lönnrot in "Death and the Compass" (1962: 129–41). Intriguingly, Lönnrot himself does not think the story over as he nears his death. Instead, he imagines a kind of ongoing semiotic play.

50. Even here, Borges cannot resist the play with multiplicity. A coin has a meaning only as a medium of exchange. The Zahir is one of many Zahirs. God has many (99) names. Borges also sets up a corrosive parallel between the narrator's obsession with the Zahir and that of the now deceased Clementina Villar, who seeks the absolute in transient fashion (1964: 157).

51. Both "The Aleph" and "The Zahir" originally appeared in a collection, entitled *The Aleph*. Wheelock makes these two stories the key to Borges' fiction (1969: 12–26). See n32.

never seen, and by beginning to forget the Aleph he has seen. Borges survives by accepting his human limitations vis-à-vis infinite reality.[52]

In sum (see Table 1 below), Borges does not deny that reality, something like Kant's noumena or the mystic's infinite, exists nor does he disparage the human attempt to navigate it by creating language, meaning, metaphysic, theology, art, and so forth. His fictions simply call attention to the constructed, partial nature of all these human creations vis-à-vis reality. These constructs become dysfunctional and deadly only when humans assume some one of them to be *the* depiction of reality. Accordingly, Borges' art is a prophylactic against such metaphysical certainty. Borges' fantastic fictions cause one to hesitate before all systems, to live with near belief or near revelations. They force one to recognize the gap between reality and the fictions of human systems. They leave one with play and uncertainty. In Borges' aesthetic world, characters come to a bad end when they believe in a human system too devoutly or when

Reality	Constructions	Ethic (Negative)	Ethic (Positive)
Infinite	Finite		
Divinity	Humanity		
"No one"	Individual		
Chaos	Meaning	Metaphysic	Fantasy
No syntax	Language	Theology	Ethic
	Art	(Psychological) Novel	Magical plots
		True belief	Near belief
		Truth	Fiction
		Solution	Awe, mystery
		Realism	Metalepses
			Self-referential play
		Canon	Heresy
"Funes, the Memorious"		Priest in "God's Script"	
"The Immortal"		Narrator of "Zahir"	Narrator of "The Aleph"
		Lönnrot	Librarian in "The Book of Sand"
		Runeberg	

Table 1. *Borges' Aesthetic Worldview.*

52. The librarian in "The Book of Sand" survives his encounter with infinity similarly by intentionally losing the infinite book that has come into his possession (1999a: 480–83). Forgetting—or rather the vagaries of memory—is also the key to the narrator's survival in "The Other Death" (1999a: 223–28). As discussed above, Funes cannot forget and, thus, cannot think, loses his humanity, and ultimately dies.

they obsessively pursue reality, truth, or God. Runeberg is one example. Characters do as well as humanly possible when they turn their back on claims to know unknowable reality and accept their human finitude. Borges is an example.

Three Versions of Judas and the Gospel Again

If one approaches Judas from Borges' aesthetic perspective, one will abandon the finality of the canonical Judas (as Runeberg does); forego the pursuit of the one, true Judas (as Runeberg disastrously does not);[53] and revel in multiple Judas stories, particularly those that offer heretical departures from the Christian classic, the gospel (as Borges does).[54] To make Borges' perspective on the interpretation of Judas clear, one need simply recall his view that "every writer creates his own precursors" and modifies, thereby, a reader's view of the past (Borges, 1964: 201). For Borges, then, interpretation *creates* the gospels and the canonical Judas as its precursor. It does not uncover the true gospel or Judas.

Using Borges as a lens and reading the gospels as his precursors provides no avenue to the real (historical) Judas. Using Borges as a lens does to the reading of the gospels what reading Kafka does to reading Browning and what Menard does to reading generally:

> Menard (perhaps without wishing to) has enriched, by means of a new technique, the hesitant and rudimentary art of reading: the technique

---

53. The pursuit of the one, true Judas is most obvious in historical critical studies, the quintessentially modern approach to the Bible. For differing appraisals of the historical Judas, see, e.g., R. Brown, 1994: 2:1394–1418; and Crossan, 1995: 66–81. Klassen (1996) is the most widely read attempt to reconstruct a positive, historical Judas since Thomas De Quincey. Gary Greenberg (2007) offers a more imaginative historical reconstruction, which has not proved as popular. For a critique of the historical critical approach to Judas, due largely to the absence of evidence, and a corresponding defense of fiction, see Saari, 2006. While literary critics seem well positioned to accept Judases, some also make monolithic assumptions. Thus, Kermode argues that the gospel Judas originates in the plot function "betrayal" (1979: 75–99). Paffenroth (2001) is a refreshing exception to the interpretative drive to the one, true Judas.

54. Several caveats are in order. First, Borges does not demand the end of systems. To live in a "system" or "construct" is part of human finitude. Borges simply calls for agnosticism in the face of these systems. One might compare his attitude to that of Nietzsche, who calls for temporary habits, as well as the courage to change one's convictions (cf. 1996: I, 629–38). Second, Borges is no great defender of the certainty of personal identity. His sympathies sometimes lie with Funes and the Immortal. Third, to derive an ethic from Borges is like deriving an ethic from Nietzsche. It misuses, or creates, the precursor rather strongly.

is one of deliberate anachronism and erroneous attributions. This technique, with its infinite applications, urges us to run through the *Odyssey* as if it were written after the *Aeneid*, and to read *Le jardin du Centaure* by Madame Henri Bachelier as if it were written by Madame Henri Bachelier. (Borges, 1962: 54–55)

Like Menard's, such fragmentary reading is a deliberately anachronistic reading. It creates Judases different from the canonical Judas simply because it dwells in a different culture, that of modernity. Such reading creates the precursor, the canonical Judas, quite willfully.

Such reading is also willfully fictional. It acknowledges its limited perspective, rather than masquerading as theological, historical, philosophical, or artistic truth. It dwells in interpretation. Of course, reading the gospels as Borges' precursors transforms the canonical Judas into a fiction too. The clearest sign of the canonical Judas' fictitiousness is his Christianity. However damned or demonic Judas may be in Christian interpretation, the canonical Judas is always, rather anachronistically, a Christian insider; he is "one of the twelve" and "an apostle." He is—even if a historical person stands behind the character(s) of Judas in the canon—a creation of Christian discourse. Here, of course, is an anachronism or metalepsis worthy of Borges.[55]

Moreover, in light of Borges, the canonical, Christian Judas is simply *one* fiction's victim, scapegoat, or villain, and, in Borges, fiction is always *Ficciones*. One can always tell other stories. In the Borgesian gospels, then, Judas inevitably becomes Judases.

After a (Borgesian) look at the canonical Judas, the following chapters use Runeberg's three Judases as vistas on the Judases of the gospels and interpretation: a Judas who is necessary to and cooperates with the divine plan; a Judas who is the determined outsider, yet necessary to the Christian myth; and a Judas who is supernatural, albeit demonic. Judas as fate, double, hero. Judas as victim, scapegoat, god.

---

55. This recognition renders all theological speculation about Judas' fate fantastic. Only Christians care if Judas is "saved" or "damned."

Chapter 2

The Canonical Judas: Oracular Betrayal

The Canonical Judas

Table 2 lists Judas' appearances in the canonical gospels: his introduction (all); the anointing complaint (John); the meeting with the priests about the betrayal and its fee (the Synoptic Gospels); the Supper prophecy of betrayal (all); the betrayal kiss in Gethsemane (Matthew, Mark); and Judas' subsequent fate (Matthew, Acts). While important differences are obvious, the gospels agree on four points: (1) a damning introduction; (2) a Supper prophecy of betrayal; (3) the betrayal itself; and (4) a final erasure.

Incident	Mark	Matthew	Luke	John
First mention of Judas	Mk 3:19 Betrayed Jesus	Mt. 10:4 Betrayed Jesus	Lk. 6:16 Became a traitor	Jn 6:64-71 The one without belief, a devil, known beforehand by Jesus; the one to betray him
Leaders' plot	Mk 14:1-2	Mt. 26:3-5	Lk. 22:1-2	Jn 11:45-53
Anointing	Mk 14:3-9 Some complain of waste	Mt. 26:6-13 Disciples complain of waste	-----[1]	Jn 12:1-8 Judas, a thief, complains of waste
Judas' meeting with priests	Mk 14:10-11 Priests offer money	Mt. 26:14-16 Judas asks for money. They pay thirty pieces of silver	Lk. 22:3-6 Satan enters Judas; Judas meets with priests; they agree to give money	Jn 13:2 Devil put into Judas' heart to betray; no recorded meeting with priests
Footwashing				Jn 13:10-11 The unclean Jn 13:18-19 The unchosen;

---

1. Luke contains a story of the anointing, but it appears in Lk. 7:36-50.

2 The Canonical Judas

Incident	Mark	Matthew	Luke	John
				Jesus predicts betrayal citing Ps. 41:9
Supper oracle	Mk 14:17-21 Jesus predicts betrayal by one eating bread with him. All say, "Surely, not I?" Jesus says "one dipping bread"; "Woe to him, better if not born."	Mt. 26:20-25 Jesus predicts betrayal. Others say, "Surely, not I, Lord?" Jesus says, "He who has dipped"; "Woe to him, better if not born." Judas asks, "Surely not I, Rabbi?" Jesus says, "You have said so."	Lk. 22:21-27 Jesus predicts betrayal by one with hand on table and pronounces woe on betrayer. Disciples ask themselves who it is. They quarrel over who shall be greatest	Jn 13:21-30 Jesus predicts betrayal. Beloved Disciple asks who. Jesus says, "One I give bread." Satan enters Judas with bread. Jesus says, "Do quickly." No one at table knew why Jesus spoke so. Judas goes out into night
Gethsemane	Mk 14:42 Betrayer at hand	Mt. 26:46 Betrayer at hand		
Arrest	Mk 14:43-52 Judas, one of twelve, arrives with crowd from leaders. Judas kisses Rabbi. Arrest, fight, flight	Mt. 26:47-56 Judas, one of twelve, arrives with large crowd from leaders. Judas kisses Rabbi. Jesus says, "Friend, what are you here to do?" Arrest, fight, flight	Lk. 22:47-53 Judas, one of twelve, leads crowd. Starts to kiss. Jesus asks, "Betray Son of Man with a kiss?" Fight, arrest	Jn 18:1-11 Judas, who betrayed him, brings soldiers and police from leaders with lanterns. Jesus asks, "Whom do you look for? I am he." Judas falls down with arresting party. Jesus says, "I am he. Let these men go." Fulfills "lost none of those given." Fight, arrest
Death of Judas		Mt. 27:3-10 Repents for having betrayed innocent blood. Returns money. Hangs self. Priests buy potter's field to bury foreigners	Acts 1:16-26 Peter: Scripture fulfilled. He got a Field (of Blood) as reward of his wickedness. He fell and burst, a penalty for wickedness. Judas turned aside; we will replace him	

Table 2. *Gospel Judases.*

That Judas has no significant role before Jesus' prediction of his betrayal—except for John's vilification of him as the one who objects to the anointing waste—is not surprising in light of the gospels' aesthetic mechanics. Readers of the gospels learn only incidentally about any character other than Jesus. Further, the only important issue about any of these characters is whether they stand with or against Jesus, so the only possible story lines for characters are conversion to Jesus and his cause or degradation, the failure to stand with Jesus. Judas' story is the premier example of degradation.

The gospels introduce Judas as if that degradation has already occurred.[2] Each of the canonical gospels introduces Judas more specifically and more dismissively than any other disciple. The reason for this damning introduction probably lies in the disciples' canonical role as the succession mechanism connecting later followers (and readers) with Jesus. The most significant gospel incident about the disciples, then, is their commissioning by the resurrected Jesus.[3] The gospels' introductions pointedly separate Judas from this authoritative group. From the very beginning, Judas is the traitorous apostle, the insider who becomes outsider, or the one who does not belong as John says more blatantly and more often than any other gospel (6:64–71; 13:11, 18–19). Consequently, Judas, alone among the apostles, has no authority. His final canonical appearance is his erasure from the apostolic band in Acts, but the gospel introductions have already accomplished this dismissal. Judas' canonical story is over before

---

2. Runeberg begins his reflections on Judas at this same place. Like the canon, Runeberg assumes Judas' degradation from the very beginning, so the degradation of each of Runeberg's Judases is certain before their stories ever begin. Here, the short story's epigraph insisting on the certainty of degradation is quite revelatory (1962: 151). Of course, this degradation applies to everyone in Borges' fictions, not just to Judas. It has to do with the corrosive effect of infinity, not ethics. See 1964: 202; and the conclusion to this chapter.

3. Matthew and Luke depict the disciples as Jesus' successors most clearly. If Mark ends at 16:8, as do the earliest manuscripts, then Mark differs significantly. Some interpreters (e.g., Weeden, 1971) have read Mark as a critique of the Twelve and of Peter. Mark 16:7, however, does suggest a future for Jesus and his disciples in Galilee, and later readers added endings to Mark (see Mk 16:9-20) to bring Mark into line with Matthew and Luke's commissioning of the apostles. John's Beloved Disciple may also imply a critique of Peter and the Twelve, but John's resurrection appearances do commission the apostles. The apocryphal gospels vary the line of authoritative succession quite dramatically. For discussion, see, e.g., Schaberg, 2004; Pagels, 2003; and Walsh, 2006b.

2 The Canonical Judas

it begins. Aesthetically, one might say that Judas' nefarious introduction is itself virtually oracular. .[4]

The second canonical incident about Judas is the Supper oracle about his betrayal, and it would hardly overstate the case to say that this oracle—combining allusion to scripture with Jesus' magisterial voice—creates the betrayer.[5] Around this oracle, the gospels struggle to tell a believable story about Judas. In particular, the gospels have difficulties outing Judas at the Supper. No other disciple appears to understand what transpires between Jesus and Judas. Except for John, the gospels do not mention Judas' departure from the meal, and no gospel records Judas' arrangement of the arresting party. The canon cares little about these lacunae. The betrayal's prediction by Jesus is the key point.

Not surprisingly, then, the canonical Judas has no motivation, except for John's slur about theft (12:6).[6] Curiously, Matthew, who alone mentions that Judas asks for a fee for the betrayal, says nothing specific about Judas' legendary greed (cf. Mt. 26:15 with Mk 14:10-11; Lk. 22:3-6). Furthermore, despite John's claim that Judas is a thief, John never says anything about a financial arrangement between Judas and the priests. John slurs Judas in order to dismiss his complaint about the wastefulness of the anointing. The judgment lingers in the background of the betrayal, but John does not carefully connect Judas' larceny with the betrayal. Instead, for Jn 13:2, like Lk. 22:3-6, Judas' ultimate motivation is demonic. Of course, this assessment is nothing other than the shadow side of the definitive oracle that creates Judas.[7]

The comment in Jn 13:30 that Judas left Jesus when "it was night" is ironic and theological, but it also aptly summarizes Judas' laconic canonical depiction. For the canon, Judas belongs to the dark as long as he is

---

4. But, see Klassen, who argues that the use of forms of παραδίδωμι in Mk 3:19 and Mt. 10:4 (and 1 Cor. 11:23) are not pejorative (1996: 41–61). See Chapter 3. Luke 6:16 and John 6:64–71 tolerate no such ambiguities.

5. But, see Kermode, who argues that Judas originates in the plot function "betrayal" (1979: 75–99, ptc. 84–86). Enslin claims that the seed of the story is the preparation for betrayal (Mk 14:1-2, 10-11) (1972: 126–27). While Judas' betrayal meeting with the priests precedes the Supper oracle in the Synoptic Gospels, the damning canonical introduction of Judas precedes both. Both Kermode and Enslin strive to penetrate the canon to find some Ur-Judas while the present discussion reflects on canonical aesthetics in light of Borges' fiction and, in particular, his notion of infinite books.

6. Brelich is eloquent on the canonical Judas' lack of motivation (1988: 15–42).

7. According to J. Robertson, if one omits prophecy, all that remains of the gospel Judas is Satan (1927: 16). See Chapter 5 below for more discussion of Judas' motivation.

not with or near Jesus. The canonical spotlight seldom strays from Jesus. Thus, Judas enters the passion narrative after his departure from the Supper again only when he reenters Jesus' ambit in the garden, and, in John, he arrives out of the gospel dark with lanterns and torches (Jn 18:3).[8] Moreover, when Judas returns to the fringes of the story, he is there only "to finger" Jesus.

Thereafter, Judas simply vanishes from sight. Having fulfilled his function as betrayer and not belonging to Jesus' succession, he is no longer of any interest in Mark, Luke, or John. Only Matthew and Acts detail his death. Acts, which delights wickedly in Judas' just desserts,[9] writes the canonical end to Judas, erasing him from the apostolic band, quite literally, by bursting Judas apart. By contrast, Matthew leaves Judas hanging as a kind of demonic doubling of Jesus' own hanging.[10] While Jesus' hanging ends with a respectful burial (and a triumphant resurrection), Judas is not

---

8. Caravaggio's *The Taking of Christ* nicely illustrates this Johannine motif of light (Jesus) and darkness (the world, the opposition). Except for Christ and Judas, illumined internally under a billowing red cloak, most of the light comes from the lantern that an onlooker (Caravaggio himself) holds. Moreover, mysterious light falls on the fleeing disciple to Jesus' left, while most of the right side of the painting—the opposition—is in darkness. Consequently, some critics claim that Judas divides the light and the darkness in this painting. This assertion makes sense if one compares it to something like Giotto's *The Kiss of Judas* in the Arena Chapel at Padua. There, the opposition and Judas' billowing yellow cloak engulf Jesus more completely. Jesus' disciples are pushed off-stage left except for Peter's sword-strike at Malchus. In this painting, too, the opposition carries the torches made necessary by the Johannine dark. Both works are easily accessible on the internet. For Caravaggio's *The Taking of Christ*, see, e.g., http://www.wga.hu/frames-e.html?/html/c/caravagg/index.html (accessed 7-26-09). For Giotto's *The Arrest of Christ* or *The Kiss of Judas*, see, e.g., http://www.wga.hu/index1.html (accessed 7-26-09).

9. Delight in the just, horrible end of Judas is quite prominent in later Christianity. See, e.g., the depictions in Papias and Dante. For discussion, see Paffenroth, 2001b: 17-32; and Zwiep, 2004: 111-20. Daube argues that the story in Acts is so dominant that most interpreters have read Matthew's account through its lens and, therefore, wrongly concluded that Matthew, too, sees Judas' end as his just desserts (1994: 95-108).

10. Christian art often recapitulates this double hanging. See, e.g., the ivory relief plaques from a casket (420-30 CE) in the British Museum. Photographs are available on the internet. See, e.g., http://www.britishmuseum.org/explore/highlights/highlight_objects/pe_mla/p/panel_from_an_ivory_casket_th.aspx (accessed 7-26-09). This reading contrasts with those who would read Judas' suicide in Matthew as a noble death. See, e.g., Klassen, 1996: 160-76; Droge and Tabor, 1992; Saari, 2006: 15-18, 77-98; and Whelan, 1993.

important enough to bury.[11] Judas remains hanging to continue pointing to Jesus' innocent blood/death. Other characters in Matthew's passion have similar roles (cf. Mt. 27:4, 19, 23, 24). Thus, Judas is in the Temple and on the tree in Matthew, as he was in the garden, simply "to finger" Jesus.

Magical Plotting: Kermode's Betrayal and Borges' Narrative Magic

With the exception of some very memorable flourishes (see below), the canonical Judas is erased apostle (or degradation), oracle, and the plot function of "betrayal." Frank Kermode has argued the last point forcefully (1979: 76–99). Ancient narratives do emphasize plot, rather than character.[12] Thus, in his discussion of tragedy, Aristotle famously says,

> the plot is the mimesis of the action – for I use "plot" to denote the construction of events, "character" to mean that in virtue of which we ascribe certain qualities to the agents, and "thought" to cover the parts in which, through speech, they demonstrate something or declare their views.... The most important of these things is the structure of events, because tragedy is mimesis not of persons but of action and life... (Aristotle, 1999: 6)

To this general observation about ancient narratives, Kermode adds the formalist analyses of fabula by scholars, such as Vladimir Propp (1968) and Anton Greimas (1984), who reduce stories to plot situations complicated by a mischief or lack, which are then resolved by a sequence of plot functions, such as dispatcher, hero, helper, villain, and false hero. In such analyses, characters become plot functions. Thus, in the passion narrative, Judas

---

11. Judas' non-burial is a significant problem for interpretations claiming that his death is noble. Contrast the careful burial of Jesus' body in all the gospels even though that burial is historically improbable given the normal practices of Roman crucifixion. The 2004 television movie *Judas* does bury Judas, but the motivation is the disciples' desire to do what Jesus would want, not the dignity of Judas. The issue is Christian ethic, not Judas.

12. The characters of ancient epics are essentially their epithets. See, e.g., wrathful Achilles, crafty Odysseus, or pious Aeneas. Judas is the "bosom enemy." See the discussion of Ps. 41:9 below. Paul Winter even thinks "Iscariot" an Aramaic word meaning "betrayal" (1974: 196, 198, cited in Kermode, 1979: 94). By the way, the canonical Jesus is also little more than an epithet. Only John is blatant on this point, depicting Jesus repeatedly as the one from above; nonetheless, for the Synoptic Gospels, Jesus is essentially the kingdom bringer. The absence of real character development—at least in modern terms—is evident in scholars' inability to agree on the meaning of this kingdom and in Bultmann's famous observation that the only thing the Johannine Jesus truly reveals is that he is the revealer (1955: 2:66).

is the adversary (or helper) who ironically fosters the plot.[13] As "Satan" is Hebrew for "adversary," Kermode wittily observes that when Satan enters Judas (Lk. 22:3; Jn 13:27) one has the "case of a character being possessed by his narrative role" (1979: 85).

Kermode supports this literary analysis with a discussion of the development of the passion traditions following Joachim Jeremias (1977).[14] Kermode's most important observations about that literary history are that the earliest mention of the betrayal occurs in 1 Cor. 11:23 and that the passage mentions no agent. One might also add that the construction in 1 Cor. 11:23 is passive—"on the night when Jesus was betrayed"—and that scholars like Jeremias have argued that such passives are often circumlocutions, which express divine actions while piously avoiding the use of the divine name (1971: 9–14). If so, one might translate the passage as "on the night when God betrayed Jesus." That translation, of course, would support Runeberg's assumption that Judas is part of the mysterious divine plan.

For Kermode, however, the issue is not theology but rather the literary development of the character of Judas, which begins with mere agency (1 Cor. 11:23) and moves through agency with a mere name attached (Mark) to the more developed stories in Matthew's thirty pieces, repentance, and suicide and in John's "outing" of Judas at the Supper. Theology, ritual inversions,[15] and interpretations of scripture provide the fodder for this development, but the canonical Judas remains, at heart, a plot function for Kermode.

Borges' Runeberg reasons similarly:

> To suppose an error in Scripture is intolerable; no less intolerable is it to admit that there was a single haphazard act in the most precious drama in the history of the world. *Ergo*, the treachery of Judas was not accidental; it was a predestined deed which has its mysterious place in the economy of the Redemption. (1962: 152)

Runeberg's reflections on Judas' place in "the plot," however, do not lead him to reflections on the literary development of character. Neither do

---

13. In plot function terms, it matters little whether Judas is adversary (as Luke and John state clearly and as Jesus' allusion to Ps. 41:9 suggests) or helper. See the discussion in Chapter 3.

14. In Jeremias' analysis, the Supper and the arrest are separate traditions, and the "betrayal," first mentioned in the context of the Supper (1 Cor. 11:23), eventually serves to connect the two traditions literarily. Kermode argues that this literary connection "bred the function of Betrayal."

15. The entry of Satan into Judas with the sop (Jn 13:27) and the betraying kiss are possible examples.

2 *The Canonical Judas* 29

they lead to Satan (the adversary) as the stories of Luke and John do. Instead, Runeberg's reflections lead to God as does the divine passive of 1 Cor. 11:23.[16] Nonetheless, despite their different interests in theology and literature, both Runeberg and Kermode trace Judas to something inhuman.

Like Kermode, Borges traces the determination (of characters like Judas) to literary concerns. For Borges, a deep narrative logic ultimately forms literary characters in the types of stories that interest him:

> the main problem of the novel is causality. One kind of novel, the ponderous psychological variety, attempts to frame an intricate chain of motives similar to those of real life. This type, however, is not the most common. In the adventure novel, such cumbersome motivation is inappropriate; the same may be said for the short story and for those endless spectacles composed by Hollywood with silvery images of Joan Crawford, and read and reread in cities everywhere. They are governed by a very different order, both lucid and primitive: the primeval clarity of magic. (1999b: 80)[17]

While causality is clearly a matter of plot and while plot interests Borges more than character, Borges' precise emphasis is on the differences in psychological and magical causality. Borges describes the deep logic of literary magic more precisely as "the law of sympathy, which assumes that 'things [not people] act on each other at a distance'" (1999b: 80).

---

16. To be more precise, Runeberg's reflections begin and end with God. Runeberg begins with a fascination with the infinite (book) and ends with the incarnate Judas. Theologians convinced of God's omnipotence have long spoken of Judas' role in salvation. For discussion, see Paffenroth, 2001b: 70, 135–42. In Morley Callaghan's novel, *A Time for Judas*, Judas cooperates with the betrayal necessary to Jesus' story (1984: 115–31, 185). While Judas reveals this secret to Philo (not the famous Jewish philosopher), his friend, he later asks Philo not to reveal the secret because that would ruin Jesus' story. Philo wrote, but buried the real story, and the novel's prologue details the discovery of Philo's manuscript. Callaghan's Judas, hero of a novel, muses more psychologically about his role in the story than the gospel Judas does. He does not wonder if he is plot helper or opponent, but he does wonder if he were chosen for the role because he is the best apostle or because he is flawed and, therefore, victim (1984: 129–33).

17. See Chapter 1 for a comparison of Borges' fiction to Irwin's description of the rhetoric of fantasy: "the persuasive establishment and development of an impossibility, an arbitrary construct of the mind with all under the control of logic and rhetoric" (Irwin, 1976: 9). As noted in that chapter as well, Borges' tropes resemble those elements that Freud lists as examples of the uncanny. Borges mentions some of these tropes in "Narrative Art and Magic" (1999b: 75–82), but he is discussing other authors. He offers a self-mocking review of his own similar conceits in the late story in which he meets an older, suicidal version of himself, "August 25, 1983" (1999a: 489–93).

His "The Encounter" illustrates this magic aptly (1999a: 364–69). Its narrator recalls a knife fight that he saw as a boy between two men with little training in such fights and even less reason to fight each other. In the fight, which seemed both like a chess match and a dream—a nice Borgesian combination of logic and unreality—one eventually killed the other in an act more senseless than criminal. Years later, the narrator tells this story to a retiring police chief, including an elaborate description of the two knives used. Bemused, the police chief tells the narrator about two earlier men—Almanza and Almada—who had two such knives and who were hated rivals. Fortune, however, prevented them from the duel they both desperately wanted. Reflecting, the narrator concludes that his story is actually the end of the police chief's story and that the knives of Almanza and Almada finally fought, using two later men as mere instruments: "Things last longer than men. Who can say whether the story ends here; who can say that they [the knives] will never meet again" (1999a: 369).

In a discussion of "The Encounter" and other stories, including "Three Versions of Judas," John Sturrock argues that Borges' characters are always plot rivals, not true characters (1977: 167–79). In fact, names are only loosely attached to them. Thus, the names of the men in "The Encounter," Almanza and Almada, are suspiciously similar, and people frequently confuse them. For that matter, so, too, are the names Jesus (Yeshua) and Judas (Yehuda).[18]

Borges even imagines an ancient sect, "The Sect of the Thirty," that worships Jesus and Judas interchangeably (1999a: 443–45). The sect follows the words of Jesus too literally, living in itinerancy, nakedness, and poverty, but, humorously, being unable to decide whether Jesus' words demand chastity or licentiousness.[19] Matters become far more serious, however, when the narrator reveals that the sectarians' lives climax in crucifixion because they believe the crucifixion to be the hidden reason for all of creation.

---

18. In fact, following these suggestions of Borges, one might argue that the names of these gospel characters are as determinative as oracles or magical knives. Could Yeshua (Joshua) be anything other than deliverer/savior? Could Yehuda (Judah) be anything other than he who sold his brother (as the story has already assigned the role of kingly deliverer that Yehuda might also imply)? The matter of these names might be quite similar to the function of epithets in ancient narrative. See n12. One might also wonder whether one named *Rune*berg could do anything other than look for a secret meaning.

19. According to some critics, some ancient gnostics were licentious and others were ascetic. In this short story, however, the humor ridicules the teaching of Jesus. Borges often challenges the teaching of Jesus. See his "A Prayer" (1999a: 339); and "Fragments From an Apocryphal Gospel" (2000a: 292–95).

They further believe that God designed everything in this secret drama—particularly the thirty pieces and the betraying kiss—to be emotionally wrenching and, therefore, unforgettable. Judas is absolutely necessary to the pathos of the drama of redemption.[20] By the way, the sect's conclusion is Runeberg's opening and quite orthodox assumption. The sect calls itself "The Thirty" after the number of the coins of the necessary betrayal in order to signify their knowledge of this secret drama and their commitment to its (only) two conscious participants: Judas and Jesus.

When Borges makes the canon his precursor in "The Sect of the Thirty," it becomes obvious that the thirty pieces, the betraying kiss, and Judas' suicide are the elements that do dramatically raise the level of pathos in the Judas story. They sear the Christian memory and figure most prominently, along with Jesus' oracle, in later Judas traditions. In fact, each of these items appears in "Three Versions of Judas" as well as in "The Sect of the Thirty."

Despite their subsequent appeal, however, these emotional flourishes are relatively insecure in the gospel tradition. Only Matthew mentions Judas' famous price (Mt. 26:15). Only Matthew and Mark have the infamous kiss. Luke reduces the kiss to a question on the lips of Jesus, and John features a theophany, rather than the kiss. Only Matthew has Judas' suicide by hanging. Acts imagines a different death. These emotional flourishes, then, are clearly less important to the canon than the oracles of the secret drama are.

Further, the coins and the kiss do not play the instrumental role in either Borges' short stories about Judas or in the canon that the knives do in "The Encounter."[21] For Borges and his Runeberg, the true agency in

---

20. For a novel built around Judas' necessity to the story, see Callaghan, 1984.

21. The famous thirty pieces do sometimes have an instrumental, determinative role, like that of the knives in "The Encounter," in some parts of the Judas tradition. See the discussion in Paffenroth, particularly, his discussion of the coins' role in "The English Ballad of Judas" (2001b: 76–79). The connection between the coins and degrading determination is also quite evident in Giotto's sequence of depictions of Judas in the Arena Chapel in Padua. The depictions begin with *The Payment of Judas* in which Judas accepts the coins from the priests (see the photograph on the cover of this book). Behind Judas, like a monkey on his back, is the tempting, if not determining, Satan (see Chapter 5 below for more discussion). Satan, of course, as J. Robertson has suggested, is simply the shadow side of the divine or, in the discussion here, of oracle (1927: 16). Next, is *The Arrest of Christ* or *The Kiss of Judas* discussed in n8 above. Finally, in *The Last Judgment*, Judas hangs (with usurers, other victims of greed) in hell for all eternity. For discussion, see Chapter 4 below. In the most succinct visual fashion possible, one has the canonical and Borgesian move from determination to

the Judas story is that of the oracles or the magical mentions of the canon (as infinite book). The coins, the kiss, and the suicide are subsidiary elements in the canon's narrative magic and part of its determinations.[22] As things are orchestrated at this miniscule level, human character does not matter. Thus, the Sect of the Thirty rightly knows the interchangeability of Jesus and Judas (cf. again the similarity between the names of Almanza and Almada).[23]

For Borges, Jesus and Judas, like Almanza and Almada, belong to the plot necessities of narrative magic (knives and oracles are interchangeable here), which he describes in his discussion of narrative art as "the crown or nightmare of the law of cause and effect, not its contradiction." In modernity, such magic smacks of the Freudian uncanny except in fiction: "This fear that a terrible event may be brought on by its mere mention is out of place or pointless in the overwhelming disorder of the real world, but not in a novel, which should be a rigorous scheme of attentions, echoes, and affinities. Every episode in a careful narrative is a premonition" (1999b: 81). In fiction's magical world, "every lucid and determined detail is a prophecy" (1999b: 82). Thus, all characters are little more than oracles.

In the magical canon, then, the betrayal takes place by Jesus' mere mention. Everything in the canon about Judas is "a rigorous scheme of attentions, echoes, and affinities," "a premonition," or "a prophecy." A magical fate determines the canonical Judas as surely as it does any novel's character. The canon, like Borges' fictions, is eerily providential.[24] More precisely, both fictions are fate-full and are uncanny, but neither is benign nor interested in human characters. In fact, in light of Borges, the canonical version is clearly quite deadly.[25]

Borges' "The Gospel According to Mark" illustrates (1999a: 397–401). The story's protagonist, Baltasar Espinosa, is a lazy, pliable, thirty-three year old medical student on vacation at a friend's ranch. While his friend is away on business, a flood leaves Espinosa stranded alone with the ranch foreman and his family, the Gutres. To pass the time, Espinosa

---

degradation. Photographs of these scenes are available on the internet. See, e.g., http://www.wga.hu/index1.html (accessed 7-26-09).

22. Borges also plays with the determined items in the passion in *"Biathanatos"* (1999b: 335–36).

23. Determining oracles either absolve Judas or damn everyone as Borges observes near the end of "The Sect of the Thirty" (1999a: 445).

24. The "providential," yet constructed nature of this causality is most clearly in view in Borges, "The Babylonian Lottery" (1962: 65–72).

25. See the discussion of "Gospels of Death" in Walsh, 2005a: 81–108.

2 The Canonical Judas 33

reads a gaucho novel to the illiterate family, but the foreman rejects this tale as too similar to his own life. Finding a Bible in English, Espinosa begins instead a dramatic translation of the Gospel of Mark. Enthralled, the family asks Espinosa, to whom they have begun to attribute miraculous authority and to whom they have begun to offer various sacrifices, to reread the gospel when he finishes, rather than to begin a new text. Eventually, the father asks Espinosa about the redemptive significance of Christ's death. Assured by Espinosa that salvation extends even to the crucifixion party, the family worships and crucifies Espinosa. At least, it seems that they crucify him. The story mercifully ends after they revile him and lead him out to their newly made cross.

Here, Borges does not read the gospel like Runeberg. Instead, he reads like Menard and changes the gospel, or reveals previously unnoticed features of it, by repeating it in a new situation. Among illiterate twentieth-century Americans, the gospel becomes a native legend or myth. One might imagine James Frazer happy reading it.[26] The gospel becomes a fiction, belonging to the unreality of art, to a magical, uncanny world, where things transpire by mere mention and according to a carefully plotted script.

The foreman's rejection of the too familiar, too realistic gaucho narrative, Espinosa's substitution of the fantastic gospel, and subsequent events create a narrative structure comparable to that of "Tlön, Uqbar, Orbius Tertius" (1962: 17–35). In both cases, someone introduces something unreal into the world, and the world capitulates to this unreality. The truth is that the Gutres' reality, like that of the narrator in "Tlön, Uqbar, Orbius Tertius," "hankered to give ground" (1962: 34). Nonetheless, the capitulation to Tlön or the gospel is horrible. As Borges' precursor, the magical gospel becomes a horrible fiction in which oracle determines (and kills) all.[27]

---

26. It is Frazer's notion of magic that Borges follows in "Narrative Art and Magic" (1999b: 80).

27. Borges' fictionalizing profanes the cross, but so, too, does his denial of the uniqueness of the crucified. See also Borges, "Christ on the Cross," where Christ's death becomes just another death, with no redemptive significance (2000a: 470–71). It is simply the third cross, rather than the sacred center. Christ's face is Jewish, not that of Christian art. The crowd treats him as any other crucified. Christ himself has no sense of the theologies, the sects, or the violence that will follow in his name. He knows only that he is a dying man. He whimpers in death. While Borges' Christ leaves behind some "splendid metaphors," his suffering is of no use to humans who continue to suffer. The gospel significations have vanished as they have in "The Gospel According to Mark." In "Christ on the Cross," however, the notion of the sacred, hidden drama is also absent.

Passover Plots[28]

Of course, the canon makes more providential claims. To do so, it often employs a fairly common narrative recipe: take an event, incident, or someone else's story, preferably one with disastrous consequences for the biblical community; then add God to this event, preferably as the agent of some mysterious good fortune for the community. The result is a secret drama. It is hardly historical. The providence enters at the level of interpretation or of story-creation. Providence belongs entirely to the magical causality of fiction.

Examples are rampant in the Hebrew Bible. The Former and Latter Prophets explain disaster after disaster—famine, war, and exile—as God's judgment, not as a mere natural disaster or as the militaristic actions of land-hungry empires on the make. The story pattern is so common that its absence—as in the book of Job—constitutes more than a little literary, as well as theological, shock.[29]

The canonical gospels handle Jesus' crucifixion similarly. The Roman Empire used crucifixion as a means of capital punishment for slaves and other non-citizens. The savage, tortured death of these miscreants displayed the power of the Empire. All the details of crucifixion—exposure, torture, non-burial, and so forth—intentionally shamed the victim in order to glorify Rome.[30] Not surprisingly, then, the canonical gospels speak about the details of crucifixion laconically (see Hengel, 1977). To dwell on the details could only glorify Rome. Thereafter, the gospels take even more aggressive measures to transform the imperial discourse that is their precursor.

First, the gospels minimize the cross's "shame" by handling the shame/mockery ironically. The one mocked as king and killed as king claimant is, in their view, actually God's king. For canonical discourse, Jesus

---

28. Fictions claiming that the canon or the institutional church has covered up the true story of the gospel are perennially popular (e.g., *The Passover Plot*; *Stigmata*; *The Da Vinci Code*). These fictions make the canon's own claims about cover-ups their precursor. The canon asserts that the secret truth has been covered up either by Roman imperial discourse or by the material horrors of crucifixion. See Walsh, 2007.

29. Notably, Borges prefers Job above all other biblical stories. See Borges, "The Book of Job," 1990: 267–75; and Aizenberg, 1984: 68–84.

30. For a discussion of capital punishment as a spectacle displaying the power of the ruler, see Foucault, 1979. For an application of Foucault to various New Testament documents, see S. Moore, 1996. For a discussion of the apocalypse as an imperial spectacle of power, see Pippin, 1999.

is hero, not slave nor criminal. Moreover, assuming the common dating trajectory of the canonical gospels, the gospels increasingly assert the innocence of the one crucified (Matthew; Luke) and eventually assert that the passion is an action completely under the apparent victim's control (John).[31] At the end of their narratives, the gospels further obscure the cross's shame by claiming that Jesus received a hurried, but respectful burial. The gospels refuse to leave Jesus' body as food for birds and dogs, which was the common lot for those crucified.

Second, and more importantly, the gospels transfigure—or obscure—Roman imperial discourse by depicting the passion as the prophetic fulfillment of various prophetic texts and as the fulfillment of prophecies by Jesus.[32] Thus, everything, including Judas' betrayal and Jesus' death, happens according to Hoyle (or the Septuagint), a hidden plan, or something quite like Borges' magical, secret drama. Ultimately, it is this literary device—the secret plot revealed by oracles—that transfigures the spectacle of imperial violence into a spectacle of divine providence. Following the pattern of the Former Prophets, the Latter Prophets, and apocalyptic texts, the gospels replace the nations—here Rome—with God as the effective actor.[33] The cross becomes hierophany as providence—rather than Rome's imperial power or the details of crucifixion—becomes the gospels' narrative focus. In this way, the canon turns attention from suffering to meaning.[34]

This focus on theodicy causes Judas to vanish from view; nonetheless, Judas is crucial to the story because the canonical gospels include two separate secret dramas: the plot of the religious leaders working behind the scenes to turn Jesus over to Pilate or to insert Jesus into Roman imperial discourse; and the divine providence plot of Jesus' suicidal mission. Judas provides the necessary lynch-pin between these two stories.[35]

---

31. Some scholars argue that the passion narrative builds upon earlier stories of the deliverance or vindication of the suffering righteous. See Nickelsburg, 1980: 153–84; and Crossan, 1991: 383–91. That may well be the case, but the providential storytelling style is even more basic to canonical aesthetics.

32. Patient Job, never knowing the reason for his suffering, stands in dramatic contrast to the gospels' all-knowing Jesus. Again, Borges' aesthetic sympathies lie with Job for whom the world is enigmatic, rather than with Jesus. See nn29, 61, 63.

33. Not incidentally, this replacement is far more important to the canon than the replacement that recent politically correct thinking obsesses about as it reads the gospels, i.e., the replacement of the Romans by the Jews.

34. Tilley claims that theodicy is the final insult offered to human suffering (1991).

35. Greenberg mounts a historical argument for Judas as go-between, negotiating

Mark clutches at the oracular Judas as a magical instrument like Borges' knives because Mark needs some device to unite the two plots. Mark needs something, like Descartes' pineal gland, to unite the spiritual and the material or the God/Jesus plan and the murderous intentions of Jesus' opponents. Judas, the disciple who hands Jesus over to his opponents, provides this link. He stands on the edge of both stories, uniting them (see Hughes, 1991: 223–38). After the gospel uses him to establish its providence story, Judas vanishes from view along with the glory-to-Rome discourse and the material realities of crucifixion.

John's arrest scene is particularly revelatory. Judas brings the arresting party out of the Johannine dark to Jesus with torches (Jn 18:3). Before the arrest can happen, Jesus takes control (18:4) and identifies himself with the language of and in the style of a divine self-revelation (18:5). The arresting party falls to the ground in the face of Jesus' theophany (18:6). Judas presumably falls with them. Nowhere else is Judas so clearly on the edge between the two stories or two discourses.[36] And nowhere else (with the possible exception of Acts 1:16–26) does Judas fall so precipitously by the wayside as he does here. On the edge, the lynch-pin between the plots, unfortunate Judas stands against God and necessarily falls.

For the canon, Jesus stands with and for God. As such, Jesus is a supernatural figure whom mere mortals should not or, rather, cannot overcome. For such a hero to fail, divine agency must come into play. Given canonical monotheism—despite Luke and John's flirtations with Satan as agent—it takes God to hand over, betray, or defeat Jesus.[37] Accordingly, Jesus—representing God—predicts Judas into existence and, then, dismisses him to degradation. For the gospels, this magical mention, not the action of Judas or of any of Rome's quislings, leads to Jesus' arrest and death. The predicted betrayal allows the (too) powerful Jesus to be taken by the opposition—his divine, providential intention all along.

This magical mention of Judas also allows the canon to shift focus from the hero's defeat, however temporary it may be, to the hero's betrayal by one who should be a loyal associate. The (traditional) hero's courage and integrity, whatever the circumstances, are givens. He is not a hero otherwise. The loyalty of his entourage is not a given. Accordingly, if one thinks of ancient literature like epics as using heroes to express a culture's

---

a deal with the leaders on behalf of Jesus (2007: 14–15, 264–71). Cf. Klassen, 1996: 57. Judas plays a similar role, though as a dupe, in Zeffirelli's *Jesus of Nazareth* (1977).

36. Christian art often visualizes Judas' edginess. See nn8, 10.

37. Once again, the passive form of 1 Cor. 11:23 may indicate divine agency. See Jeremias, 1971: 9–14; and Chapter 3 below.

2 The Canonical Judas

virtues, the attendant cast is a natural locale for the culture's vices. The canon's portrayal of the virtuous Jesus and the vile Judas fits this ancient context well.[38] Judas focuses the concern on whether Jesus' followers (including the readers of the canon) will be loyal or will turn traitor like Judas, not whether Jesus will be (or was) faithful or successful or not.[39]

The gospel protagonist's supernatural character requires the employment of yet another biblical pattern visible, for example, in biblical revisions of the Ancient Near Eastern conflict-creation myth.[40] In that creation myth, a god of order defeats a god of chaos to establish the world in which the tale's tellers live. Allusions to this tale appear in various biblical poets, and many think that the creation story in Genesis 1 is a revision of the Babylonian version of this creation myth. In Genesis 1, however, no divine conflict exists. God creates magisterially by magical fiat.

The ancient conflict tale appears nearer the surface in the story of the Exodus because Pharaoh is an Egyptian deity. For the biblical storyteller, however, Pharaoh is no god, so he cannot fight against YHWH. Accordingly, YHWH has to fight on both sides in order to create a story. The literary mechanism that achieves this divine self-conflict is the famous hardening of Pharaoh's heart.

In the gospel's passion, the Jewish religious leaders and Rome stand in for the ancient chaos monster or for Pharaoh.[41] Once again, God has to fight on both sides in order to create the appearance of conflict. Enter, now, the oracle that creates Judas.[42] In this analysis, the oracle-betrayal is a literary device, like the hardening of Pharaoh's heart, which resolves the

---

38. Mark casts all of the twelve in this mold. The other canonical gospels redeem the eleven and Peter, in particular, more enthusiastically. Many interpreters, however, have noted similarities between Judas and Peter. See, Telford, 2005. Cf. as well the portrayal in Zeffirelli's *Jesus of Nazareth* (1977), which in an important scene after Peter's denial segues from the running Peter to the fleeing Judas. The result visually morphs Peter and Judas into one character.

39. The Panteón Real in León, Spain is the resting place of twenty monarchs and the site of wonderful twelfth-century Romanesque frescoes. Those frescoes depict scenes from Jesus' passion and the final judgment. In the former, Peter's denial and Judas' betrayal are noticeably prominent. In private conversation, Jennifer Rohrer-Walsh has observed, "Oh, they've turned everything into a question of loyalty or betrayal [and, thereby, demanded loyalty to the king as to the divine]." Her remarks cast light on the canon's similar portrayal and use of Judas.

40. For a reading of Judas, as portrayed in John, in terms of this mythology, see Eslinger, 2000: 45–73; and Chapter 4 below.

41. The pattern is clearer in Revelation.

42. On this reading, Luke and John's satanic interpretations of Judas are vestiges of the ancient conflict myth.

dilemma for storytelling created by the notion of a divine sovereignty that is too powerful to brook any real rival.[43]

The fictional nature of such literary devices and of providence plots generally is obvious when they appear in a venue other than the canon. The film *Jakob the Liar* (1999), a story of a Jewish community's struggle for survival in a walled Polish ghetto during World War 2, provides an example. For Jakob (Robin Williams), the film's protagonist and narrator, the Jews survive Nazi oppression by telling dark jokes, dancing, and finding a little bit of news. The film itself is a dark joke. Because Jakob has a bit of news, his friends believe that he has a radio, a capital offense in the ghetto. Although Jakob denies the radio at first, he grudgingly acknowledges it when a friend who discovers it does not exist commits suicide. Trapped by his own lies/storytelling and his desire to help others, Jakob makes up news (often comically) in which his friends find some hope of survival. In one delightful scene, he improvises a speech by Winston Churchill broadcast by the imaginary radio for the waif who has come to share his life. Finding his old phonograph, he even plays some polka music and dances joyfully with the waif. In another comic scene, he predicts the liberating arrival of American tanks, replete with jazz bands atop them.

The jazz bands—like the oracle creating Judas in the canonical gospels—indicate the second-level story, the layering of a story of hope/providence over stories of death and imperial oppression. In the film's climax, Jakob surrenders himself to the Germans who are searching in vain for the non-existent radio and who are willing to kill everyone in the ghetto to find it. Despite torture and murderous threats, Jakob refuses to capitulate to the Germans' demands that he tell the ghetto members that there was never a radio. He leaves his fellow Jews their (illusory) hope. The German commander shoots Jakob on the gallows before the assembled ghetto and, then, sends everyone off to the (death) camps by train. The second-level story, however, is not over. The dead Jakob, still narrating the film, says that the members of the ghetto were never heard from again, but, then, he pauses and says maybe not. Then, he relates another ending that the audience sees in which the allies stop the train en route to the death camps with American tanks, topped with jazz bands.

Most critics panned the film, some claiming that comedy is an inappropriate genre for a Holocaust film[44] and others claiming an unsettling

---

43. According to Louis Marin, Judas solves an impossible problem—the death of God (cited in Kermode, 1979: 155n18).

44. Ironically, however, critics praised the comic *Life is Beautiful* (1997). The problem may well be simply that *Jakob the Liar* makes providence plots so clearly

2 *The Canonical Judas* 39

disjoint between the bulk of the film and its jazz band ending.⁴⁵ The ending does jar, but it would not if it were in the canon. After all, canonical providence and its oracular Judas are little more than a jazz band ending. Both are second-level stories riding on and remaking other stories.

According to Roland Barthes, such second-level significations are the sign of myth. In his classic example, the cover of *Paris-Match* shows a young African in a French uniform saluting the French flag. This picture obscures the biography of the young man by writing a second-level story, that of the French Empire, over it. The anonymous young man becomes the tool of French imperial discourse (1972: 117–31).⁴⁶ Something similar transpires in the canonical story. Judas (and Jesus for that matter) loses his particular identity, if he ever had one, and becomes a tool of the second-level providential story. Judas (and Jesus) becomes a cog in the divine machine.

For Jonathan Z. Smith, who has read his Borges, such work is the modus operandi of religion. Smith sees religion as a map, which depicts a territory, but is not the territory. The territory is something like Borges' mysterious reality, the world one attempts to navigate. The map is the constantly interpreted religious tradition. The interpretations span the gap between the tradition and the present and between the (interpreted) tradition and reality. Specifically rejecting Mircea Eliade's famous cosmogonic view of religion, Smith depicts religion as exegesis or theodicy. For Smith, religion always operates in a state of disjoint between world/

---

a matter of fiction. Yann Martel's *Life of Pi* (2001) provides another, but critically acclaimed example of a narrator providing two stories between which his audience must choose. First, in the bulk of the novel, Pi tells the story of his shipwreck and his improbable survival on a raft with menacing zoo animals. When interrogated by skeptics, he admits that one could tell a different "dry, yeastless, factual" story of his shipwreck and survival with a few other theomorphic humans (Martel, 2001: 302–16). When Pi points out that his investigators cannot prove the truth of either one of the stories and that the consequences for others are roughly the same in each (2001: 316–18), the investigators ultimately write a report supporting Pi's original story (2001: 319). The result is conscious belief in a constructed fiction. Such "near" belief is rather different than true belief in oracles and secret plots. See Chapter 3 for more discussion.

45. One can hardly quibble about the dead narrator, which has become rather commonplace in film. In addition to the classic *D.O.A.* (1950, 1988) (which is a slightly different matter), see, e.g., *Braveheart* (1995) and *American Beauty* (1999).

46. Barthes also uses the examples of sentences (e.g., I am a lion) losing their primary level of signification when they are employed as grammar examples or in grammar exercises.

tradition and interpretation or, better, between different stories that one could tell (Smith, 1978: 289–309).[47]

The Old Testament Judas: One Prophecy to Rule Them All, Ps. 41:9

Kermode argues that the character of Judas gradually emerges out of the plot function betrayal as story-tellers add materials based (among other things) on the interpretation of scripture.[48] As a result, the canonical Judas is essentially an Old Testament character.[49] The key passage is Ps. 41:9.[50] If one assumes the normal scholarly ordering of the canonical gospels, Mark begins the allusion to this text in its phrasing of Jesus' oracle at the Supper (Mk 14:18-19), but each of the gospels makes the connection to some degree even though only John quotes the psalm (cf. Mt. 26:23; Lk. 22:21; Jn 13:18).[51] That Mark does not specifically name its source may be for the best because Mark 14:1-21 reads Psalm 41 quite freely (see Table 3 below).

In the lament, the psalm's narrator declares his faith in a God who sustains those who remember the poor, locating himself implicitly in that

47. To illustrate these themes, J. Smith frequently refers to Borges, "On Exactitude in Science" (1999a: 325).

48. Some scholars argue that the passion narrative is essentially historical. See, e.g., R. Brown, 1994; and Meier, 2001. Others claim that it is primarily exegesis of scripture. See, e.g., Crossan 1995.

49. He is an Old Testament, not a Hebrew Bible character, because he belongs to the Christian canon and Christian discourse. That Judas is an Old Testament character also suggests his supersession by New Testament characters and story. See Chapter 4 below. Scholars frequently suggest that Judas represents Judaism. See Maccoby, 1992: ix, 5–9, 80, 101; and Crossan, 1995: 71. Even if one argues that the canon or an individual gospel does not make this equation, later Christians, like Jerome and Chrysostom, are not hesitant to do so. See Paffenroth, 2001b: 10, 37–57. Daube argues that one should refer to Mathew's Judas as Judah in order to avoid the negative Christian connotations of "Judas" (1994: 103).

50. Kermode calls Ps. 41:9 the "germ" of the announcement of the betrayal-scene (1979: 85, 88). He also observes that the evangelists use the Hebrew Bible for their story in much the way that novelists use the opening of their lengthy novels for later developments. Here, the Hebrew Bible becomes the Old Testament, the beginning of the Christian story (Kermode, 1979: 86–87; cf. Walsh, 2003: 96–102, 112–14). In Brelich's *The Work of Betrayal*, Jesus repeats the prediction of betrayal until the disciples can no longer avoid it. It becomes a fait accompli (1988: 1–6).

51. The logic of the secret divine plot bothers John and Luke, or, at least, their introduction of Satan into the Judas story makes it seem so (Jn 13:2, 27; cf. Lk. 22:3). Of course, such adaptations do not change the secret plot substantively. See J. Robertson, 1927: 16.

blessed group. Sick, with his enemy maliciously awaiting his death, and betrayed by his dearest, bread-eating friend, the psalmist asks the Lord to deliver him that he may repay his enemies. In fact, he knows that his God is pleased with him because his enemies have not yet triumphed. By contrast, in Mk 14:1-21, the religious leaders plot Jesus' death as Jesus is anointed and as Jesus rejects a concern for the poor. After Judas—the bosom friend—conspires with the leaders, Jesus makes preparations for the Passover and, at the meal, names his fellow bread-eater as his traitor with a double (?) allusion to Ps. 41:9 (Mk 14:18, 20).

Mark's changes are fairly obvious. First, while the psalmist depends upon God's protection of those who remember the poor, Jesus dismisses the disciples' concern for the poor and, presumably, the divine protection that accompanies such concern.[52] Second, while Jesus does pronounce a woe upon his betrayer (14:21)—like the invective in Ps. 41:4-10—the Markan Jesus never triumphs over his enemies as the psalmist hopes he will. Admittedly, Jesus' passion predictions do suggest an ultimate triumph, but it is in a future beyond death for an enigmatic Son of Man (Mk 8:31; 9:30-32; 10:32-34). Further, the subsequent Markan Gethsemane scene dismisses any hope of divine deliverance (Mk 14:32-42). Jesus' allusions to Psalm 41 in Mk 14:18, 20, then, do not constitute a prayer for deliverance like that in the psalm.[53] Rather, Mark's Jesus is as fated to die as its Judas is to betray. It is all written in the magical mentions of Jesus and of scripture.

Psalm 41	*Mark 14*
Lord protects those who remember poor (1-3)	Jesus dismisses disciples' concern for poor (4-9)
Enemies against me, wonder when I will die (4-8)	Leaders plot Jesus' death (1-2)
Bosom friend, who ate my bread, is against me (9)	Judas to priests (10-11)
	Jesus predicts bread-eater betrayal (17-21)
	Vv. 18, 20 allude to Ps. 41:9
Prayer for deliverance, triumph over enemies (10-12)	Woe to betrayer, but death on cross (21)

Table 3. *Psalm 41 and Mark 14:1-21.*

52. Greenberg argues that the historical core of Jn 12:1–8 is a dispute between Judas and Jesus over the poor, not a revelation of Judas' greed or thievery (2007: 146–47).

53. Similarly, Jesus' final cry (Mk 15:34) does not constitute a meaningful psalm of deliverance even though it alludes to one (Psalm 22).

Mark's strong misreading of Psalm 41 parodies the psalmist's hope. If one were to pursue the parody in the manner of Borges, one might arrive at a Jesus who condemns himself as he creates his betrayer. Thus, the Markan Jesus leaves the psalmist's realm of the good when he dismisses his disciples' concern for the poor. For the psalmist, the concern for the poor and hope for divine protection belong together. If one rejects care for the poor, then one also rejects hope for divine protection. When Mark alludes to Psalm 41, then, the gospel opens up the possibility not merely of naming the betrayer but also of finding a reason for the Markan Jesus' God-forsakenness. On this reading, Psalm 41 is the magical mention—or the Borgesian knife—that creates Jesus and Judas as suicidal rivals. Like Borges' knives, Psalm 41 waits in the world of the secret plot for foils to animate as betrayer and God-forsaken. It waits to act out an already plotted struggle between friends (or brothers as in Mk 13:12).

Such a reading is too Borgesian for the canon. In the canon, Mark's Judas simply incarnates Jesus' prediction of his betrayal. Even though Judas visits the priests before Jesus' oracle, Mark supplies no motivation for him. Judas is not clearly greedy nor is he disappointed in Jesus. Except for the fact that Judas is known canonically as the traitorous apostle, nothing explains Mark's Judas. Nothing explains Judas, that is, except for the secret plot. Nothing explains Judas, that is, except for Jesus oracle, amplified by an allusion to an older oracle (Ps. 41:9). While Mark's Jesus may not be the Johannine Logos, he does represent God. Thus, Mark's Jesus predicts his passion at least three times during his ministry with steadily increasing details (8:31; 9:30-32; 10:32-44). After the passion narrative proper begins, he predicts events with even more detail (e.g., the betrayal, denial, and flight of the disciples in 14:18-21, 27-31). As a result, the Markan Jesus not only knows all the details of the passion, he creates them. These details include Judas.

Through Jesus, the secret plot curses Judas, the chosen instrument of the betrayal (Mk 14:21). Ironically, the curse is remarkably like that which Job calls down upon himself after his own divine betrayal (see Job 3). The canon, however, does not allow Judas such a speech. Things do not speak, and oracle determines all: "There is not one lone guilty man; there is no man that does not carry out, wittingly or not, the plan traced by the All-Wise. All mankind now shares in Glory" (Borges, 1999a: 445).[54] Seen with Borges, this glory horrifies.

---

54. Paffenroth compares the oracular Judas to Oedipus (2001b: 70–78). He traces such comparisons to Origen's reflections on free will and prophecy (Origen actually mentions the Oedipus story) and finds its fullest form in *The Golden Legend*

Somewhat surprisingly, given Jesus' curse, Mark never narrates Judas' fate. Judas disappears after he has served his (secret) plot function. On the basis of Jesus' curse, one presumes that he comes to a bad end. Of course, in Mark, one never knows the fate of Jesus' other disciples either. One may presume (although some readers do not) on the basis of Jesus' definitive oracles (or the other gospels) that there is a reunion. Mark does not tell that story. Of course, Mark does not report what happens to Jesus after his burial either. One may presume on the basis of the words of a mysterious young man (or on the basis of the other gospels) that Jesus has risen and will return to his disciples. In short, Mark is simultaneously full of fate—the magical fate of secret plots—yet lacking in fate, a detailed narrative resolution for any character. It is no wonder, then, that Mark's Judas is enigmatic. All Mark's "characters" are enigmas.[55] What is clear in Mark is that someone—or something—had to betray and anyone could betray. Mark fills in the determined, necessary plot device known as Judas only by vague allusions to or, even, through a parody of Psalm 41. Mark says nothing else about Judas. Brother shall betray brother, indeed (Mk 13:12).

Psalm 41:9 and Jesus' curse are always there in the canonical Judas' background and, in effect, delineate the canonical Judas. While all the other canonical gospels use scriptural allusions to flesh out Judas, Matthew is the most creative. Thus, Matthew relies on scripture not only to create the friend's betrayal—Matthew even has Jesus refer to Judas as friend (26:50)—but also to create the infamous thirty pieces (26:15).[56]

(Voragine, 1941). The canonical Judas, however, is more similar to the caricatures posing as characters in Aeschylus' tragedies. Sophocles' tragedies, particularly *Oedipus Rex*, have more fully formed characters whose character is formed precisely by their response to (and resistance of) implacable fate. Incidentally, among the canonical gospels, it is Luke who most often forms characters similarly (but not as fully) by means of their response to the crisis brought about by Jesus' inauguration of salvation. If one wishes to pursue similarities between the canon and *Oedipus Rex*, one might better compare the canonical Judas to a peripheral character, like Laius, formed by an oracle. Incidentally, determining oracles also dominate Herodotus' *The History*, which modern historians disparage in favor of Thucydides' more rational *History of the Peloponnesian War*. Once again, oracle, when it appears outside the canon, seems uncanny to moderns.

55. Alter argues that allusiveness is the biblical norm in characterization (1981: 114–30). He uses this allusiveness to comment on biblical theology and anthropology and to read biblical characters as simulacrums of modern readers. That ability lies more in modern readers' ideologies than in Mark. See Kermode, 1979: 76–77; and Walsh, 2006b.

56. Some have seen Judah's betrayal and sale of his brother Joseph for twenty

Most critics see an allusion to Zechariah 11 in the thirty pieces although Matthew does not refer clearly to this text. Once again, the lack of precision may be fortuitous because the story in Zech. 11:4–17 has little in common with Matthew's paid, repentant Judas (see table 4 below).

In Zechariah, God appoints a prophet as shepherd of a doomed flock. After some shepherd in-fighting, the prophetic shepherd, apparently rejected by his sheep, foregoes his task and leaves the sheep to their fate. Demanding his wages from the sheep merchants, the prophet-shepherd receives the "lordly" price of thirty shekels of silver, which the Lord commands him to throw into the treasury in the Temple. The "lordly" is, of course, ironic as thirty shekels is the price of a slave (Exod. 21:32).[57] The merchants do not highly esteem the Lord's shepherd.

While several of these details appear in Matthew's account of Judas, Matthew's Judas hardly seems Zechariah's prophet-shepherd. Instead, Zechariah's prophet-shepherd is a better precursor for Matthew's Jesus. In fact, Matthew 26:31 (cf. Mk 14:27) has Jesus depict himself as Zechariah's stricken shepherd (Zech. 13:7).[58] If Matthew is creating Judas in light of Zechariah 11, then, one might well imagine Borges as the author of Matthew. As in a Borges' fiction, the identity of the divinely chosen actor (Matthew's betrayer) and the identity of the betrayed (Zechariah's shepherd) become interchangeable or, at least, hopelessly intertwined. One needs a scorecard to keep up with the identity of the players.

If Matthew alludes to Zechariah 11 with its thirty pieces, then Matthew names Judas as divinely appointed. Moreover, like Zechariah's shepherd, Matthew's Judas is a divinely appointed agent of destruction. Thus, while it is not as obvious a connection as the thirty pieces and the Temple toss, the motif of the impending destruction of the people also connects Zechariah and Matthew. Zechariah's chosen/rejected shepherd is a prelude to the rejection and destruction of the chosen people. The chosen/rejected shepherds of Matthew's passion narrative are as well (see Mt. 27:25).

---

pieces of silver as an important precursor of Judas (Gen. 37:26–28). See n18; and Enslin, 1972: 123–41.

57. In William Rayner's novel, *The Knifeman*, Judas asks for thirty pieces because it is a "ritual" sum and, therefore, gestures at the plan that he and Jesus have devised to overthrow the Romans (1969: 41–43). I.e., it takes both Jesus and Judas to realize Zechariah 11 in Rayner's novel.

58. Interestingly, Zechariah 13:6 refers to prophets with wounds received "in the house of my friends."

Zech. 11:4-17	Mt. 26:3-5, 14-16; 27:3-10
God appoints prophet as shepherd of doomed flock (11:4)	Religious leaders plot Jesus' death (26:3-5); Judas has no clear motivation (26:14)
Shepherd quits and demands wages (11:9-12)	Judas asks for money to betray (26:15)
Leaders name his wages, thirty shekels of silver (11:12)	Leaders offer thirty pieces of silver (26:15)
At Lord's command, shepherd throws silver into temple (11:13)	Repentant Judas casts silver into temple (27:3-5)
People ruled by worthless shepherd (11:15-17)	Leaders buy "field of blood" with money (27:6-10)

Table 4. *Zech. 11:4-17 and Mt. 26:3-5, 14-16; 27:3-10.*

Matthew's reference to Jeremiah in Mt. 27:9-10 also points in this direction. While scholars have not found Matthew's exact scriptural source, they frequently refer to Jer. 18:1-3 and 32:6-15.[59] Given Matthew's lack of precision, perhaps one should read Jeremiah more freely. In Jeremiah 18, the Lord instructs Jeremiah to go to the potter's house, which leads to divine instructions depicting Israel as mere clay with which the potter-God can act as he wishes as well as a warning of the judgments soon to fall upon faithless Israel. Mysterious opponents plot against Jeremiah who, then, asks God to destroy his enemies and their families. In Jeremiah 19, Jeremiah predicts that the coming divine destruction will cause the Valley of Hinnom to be renamed the Valley of Slaughter and that there will not be enough graves for the dead. To illustrate his point, he breaks a potter's jug (Israel). As a result, a priest has Jeremiah placed in stocks from which Jeremiah predicts the exile (Jeremiah 20). Later, however, when the Babylonians lay siege to Jerusalem, Jeremiah purchases family land in Anathoth (for seventeen shekels, not thirty) and has Baruch place the deed in a (potter's) jar to symbolize the return of the people's normal commerce to the land after its destruction (32:6–15).

If Matthew 27:9-10 did not specifically name Jeremiah as the source for the purchase of a potter's field, now called the Field of Blood, for thirty pieces of silver, few would have found Jeremiah 18-20 and 32 behind this eerie story.[60] The price is wrong and the land that Jeremiah buys is not

---

59. Kermode assumes that Matthew employs these two texts (1979: 87). See also Stendahl, 1968: 120–27; and R. Brown, 1994: 1:652. Paffenroth (2001b: 116–17) calls these connections possible, but prefers Jeremiah 19 as the source, following Gundry, 1967: 124–27.

60. As noted above in n56, some trace the story of Judas' betrayal to Judah's sale of Joseph. Others trace the story of Judas' betrayal and suicide to that of Ahithophel's

called the potter's field. Both Jeremiah and Matthew do, however, focus on a burial ground. Jeremiah's oracle expects the Israelite dead to be so numerous as to be left without burial (Jeremiah 19). By contrast, Matthew's far more optimistic leaders intend to bury foreigners. Matthew itself is hardly so optimistic given later passages like Mt. 27:25. More obviously, Matthew does not pick up on the hopefulness of Jeremiah's purchase of land in Jeremiah 32. While Jeremiah's action predicts the end of a disaster already happening, Matthew's Field of Blood writes a tragic finale to the fateful thirty pieces (cf. Paffenroth, 2001b: 115–17). It is as if Matthew wishes to bury that oracular money as soon as it has done its fateful work. Otherwise, the words are a strange coda to Judas' suicide (27:5). Of course, the coda also serves to reconnect Judas and the religious leaders. In short, Matthew's treatment of Judas is a part of Matthew's larger rejection of the Jewish leaders (see Matthew 23). That Judas remains unburied in Matthew is a further haunting note, particularly if Matthew does connect its Judas story with Jeremiah 18–19, with a story in which there were too many Israelite dead to bury. Matthew's disastrous story does not end with Judas. It moves on to blood on the people's hands and a Field of Blood. Regardless, then, of the precise connections with Jeremiah, Matthew's Field of Blood is a very bleak scenario. It is far bleaker, indeed, than Jeremiah's hopeful purchase of land in the midst of political upheaval. Matthew's bloody field is the "price" of Jesus' innocence.

Jeremiah 18-20; 32	*Mt. 26:3-5, 14-16; 27:3-10*
God sends Jeremiah to the potter's house for lessons in divine sovereignty which calls Israel to repentance or divine rejection (18:1-11)	Judas goes to the leaders and becomes part of their plot against Jesus (26:14-16)
Leaders (?) plot against Jeremiah (18:18)	Leaders plot against Jesus (26:3-5)
God sends Jeremiah to buy and break a potter's vessel as a sign of coming destruction. In the valley of Slaughter, there will be no room left to bury (19)	Judas hangs himself, but is not buried (27:5)
Jeremiah is arrested (20)	

betrayal of David and subsequent suicide (2 Sam. 16:20–17:23). Kermode notes that many thought that David, the Psalmist, referred to Ahithophel's treachery in Ps. 41:9, the oracle that generates the Judas story (1979: 155n21). Paffenroth once thought the two suicide stories connected (1992: 78) and calls it the majority opinion, but now thinks differently (2001b: 114, 171nn20–22). Incidentally, Ahithophel's advice to Absalom in 2 Sam. 16:21 echoes Nathan's judgment oracle delivered to David in 2 Sam. 12:11–12 so that determining oracles entangle Ahithophel, as well as Judas.

Jeremiah 18-20; 32	Mt. 26:3-5, 14-16; 27:3-10
God tells the imprisoned Jeremiah to buy land (for seventeen shekels) as a sign of Israel's post-destruction recovery (32)	Leaders buy "field of blood" with thirty pieces of silver to use to bury foreigners (27:6-10)

Table 5: *Jeremiah 18-20; 32 and Matt. 26:3-5, 14-16; 27:3-10.*

Infinite Books

Judas' fate in the canon and in Borges' "Three Versions of Judas" is remarkably similar to that of Baltasar Espinosa in "The Gospel According to Mark." An older, magical book spells their ends. One thinks again of the haunting possibility of the divine passive in 1 Cor. 11:23. The canon operates as magically as one of Borges' fictions. In fact, Borges' ideas about the magical causality of fiction, including the mere "mention" of things and the action of things upon each other at a distance, describe concisely the canonical gospels' exegeses of the Hebrew Bible/Old Testament.[61] Accordingly, the absurdly literal readings of Borges' Runeberg hardly differ from those of Mark and Matthew. Where the canon spins tales of providence, however, Borges finds the enigmatic, corrupting infinite:

> The Kabbalists believed, as many Christians do now, in the divinity of that story, in its deliberate writing by an infinite intelligence.... This premise (which was the one postulated by the Kabbalists) turns the Scriptures into an absolute text, where the collaboration of chance is calculated at zero. The conception alone of such a document is a greater wonder than those recorded in its pages. A book impervious to contingencies, a mechanism of infinite purposes, of infallible variations, of revelations lying in wait, of superimpositions of light.... How could one not study it to absurdity, to numerical excess, as did the Kabbalah?" (1999b: 85–86)

In the form of a malleable book, the infinite is particularly hard for an obsessive to release and is, therefore, particularly damning.[62] It is no wonder, then, that Borges' *Rune*berg searches the gospels so obsessively for the secret meaning that makes Judas' betrayal sensible. The follower of the Kabbalah similarly searches for the true divine order of the Torah

---

61. See Borges, 1999b: 81–82. See the discussions of the connections between typology and providence in E. Auerbach, 1968: 73–74; and Frye, 1982: 78–82. Aizenberg claims that the fantastic Bible is the point of departure for Borges' entire aesthetic worldview (1984: 68–84). She has Job, in particular, in mind. See nn29, 32, 63.

62. See the discussion of "Funes, the Memorious" (1962: 107–15); "The Zahir" (1964: 156–65); and "The Aleph" (1999a: 274–86) in Chapter 1.

assuming the present combination of twenty-two Hebrew letters to be out of order.[63]

Similar motifs dominate Borges' famous "The Library of Babel" (1962: 79–88).[64] There, a weary, nearly blind, dying librarian serves in the infinite hexagonal galleries of the labyrinth library with numerous other librarians. The library, which contains a (duplicating) mirror in its entrance hall, is no less than the universe itself. The librarian himself thinks of the library in terms of mystic metaphors normally reserved for God as "a sphere whose consummate center is any hexagon, and whose circumference is inaccessible" (1962: 80).[65] The library/universe is a divine work while the imperfect, human librarian "may be the work of chance or of malevolent demiurges" (1962: 80–81). Matters turn Kabbalistic when the librarian observes that the books of the infinite library combine and recombine twenty-five orthographic symbols—adding the space sign, the period, and the comma to the twenty-two letters—thereby creating all possible books.[66] In the face of this infinity, the librarian despairs, for "the certainty that everything has been already written nullifies or makes phantoms of us all" (1962: 87).

In a concluding note, the narrator observes that the notion of a vast library is superfluous. A single, infinite book—like the book that the canonical gospels and Runeberg read—would have the same effect. Borges imagines such a book in "The Book of Sand" (1999a: 480–83). A vague, gray seller of Bibles visits the tale's bibliophilic narrator, who already possesses several rare Bibles, but the peddler has a sacred book from India, with arbitrarily numbered pages, for sale. This diabolic book is infinite like the sand of the desert. Its reader can never find the same page again or the book's

---

63. Speaking for himself, Borges makes similar observations about enigmatic reality in reflections on the whirlwind and the mythological beasts in "The Book of Job" (1990: 271–74).

64. Borges was director of the National Library of Argentina and blind in later life. Umberto Eco features a blind librarian in charge of a labyrinth library, named Borges, in *The Name of the Rose*.

65. Borges plays with similar phrasing as a metaphorical description of God in "The Fearful Sphere of Pascal" (1964: 189–92).

66. In closing an essay on metalepses—like Don Quixote reading *Don Quixote*—Borges observes, following Carlyle, that humans write and try to understand history and are, at the same time, written in it (1964: 196). See the discussion in Chapter 1 above; Borges, "On the Cult of Books" (1999b: 358–62); and Borges, "The Total Library" (1999b: 214–16). In the last essay, infinite chance creates a library inhuman and horrible, the work of something like a "delirious god" (1999b: 216). De Man observes that Borges' God is on the side of chaotic reality and of death (1986: 27).

beginning or end. Intrigued, the bibliophile trades his entire pension and a valuable black-letter Wyclif Bible for the Book of Sand. Obsessed, the bibliophile spends all his time scanning the Book of Sand, becoming himself more and more monstrous, until he realizes that the book is monstrous. To avoid being lost completely in the book, the bibliophile discards the book by hiding it on an inconsequential shelf in the National Library.

"The Book of Sand" warns of the dangers of the infinite book.[67] In Borges' world, the infinite is monstrous and inhuman. Obsession with it is deadly. In fact, as the Babylonian librarian observes, the infinite book turns everyone into phantoms. Not just Judas, but everyone becomes someone else's dream or creation. One soon becomes lost in infinite books. Furthermore, as the order of the infinite book—if there is one—is unknown and unknowable, fate is not meaningful. It is equivalent to chance, an idea that Borges plays with overtly in "The Babylonian Lottery" (1962: 65–72). In that story, the Babylonians invent and, then, subject themselves to the lottery. Over time, the lottery begins to decide all "fates." Further, in the course of time, the Babylonians invest the chance of the lottery with the character of an ineffable divine providence. More precisely, the Babylonians invest the Company, which runs the lottery, with a silent, secret functioning similar to that of divine plots.

Unlike Judas' canonical story, this story ends with a Babel of competing opinions—including heresies—about the company. The last opinion is the story's last sentence: "A conjecture no less vile argues that it is indifferently inconsequential to affirm or deny the reality of the shadowy corporation, because Babylon is nothing but an infinite game of chance" (1962: 72). One might restate the quoted sentence without its introductory valuation: it is inconsequential to affirm or deny providence because life is nothing but an infinite game of chance. Despite the narrator's apparent dismissal of this view, the lengthy description of the development of the lottery and the Company makes this position virtually inescapable. The narrator's introductory valuation, then, seems ironic. Read so, the conclusion asserts the lack of meaningful difference between an unknowable fate and chance. Infinity equals chance. Borges' fate, then, is never providential and infinity holds for him an existential horror (Should one compare infinity's effect to that of the negative sublime?). Read as Borges' precursor, the canon—the infinite book in the Western world—leads one to similar reflections and to the degradations of Judas (Jesus), Runeberg, and everyone else.

67. Borges does, however, often remark on the human need for the supernatural or for the mythic. See, e.g., Borges, "A History of Angels" (1999b: 16–19); and Borges, 2000b: 53–55.

The canonical Judas is a victim of an infinite book, a victim of fate. While many others have noted this mysterious fact in reflecting on the drama of salvation (and even noted its apparent unfairness), Borges' fiction makes it inescapable. Quite simply, the canonical Judas is oracle. As such, the canonical Judas is no more than a cog in the divine machine (of providence/fate). He resembles those interchangeable characters taken over by the mysterious knives in Borges' "The Encounter." Such "things" are the property of books. More precisely, such things are the property of fiction, for, as Borges astutely observes, fate is part of the magical causation of plotted fiction, not of readers' everyday "reality." Moreover, such "things" are mere phantoms in someone else's dream. In Judas' case, he is an object constructed by true believers from mere mentions in what they take to be an infinite book. The canonical Judas is a Christian fiction.[68] The canon reduces Judas to instrumentality and to silence. Those who cooperate with the canon, who are true believers in the plots of the infinite book, humiliate themselves likewise. The next chapter explores this topic more fully.

---

68. Origen was one of the earliest Christians to reflect on the problem of free will with respect to Judas; and he argues that Jesus' oracle (and scripture) did not "force" Judas' betrayal. See Paffenroth, 2001b: 70–82. The theological point, which defends human freedom and responsibility, is salutary, but the canonical Judas has no such freedom. In fact, the canonical Judas is simply not a serendipitous place to reflect on free will. He does not form his identity vis-à-vis fate, as, e.g., Sophocles' Oedipus does. Later Judases, like Origen's, are a different matter although in Origen's interpretation divine grace is ultimately dominant. See Paffenroth, 2001b: 118–19, 140–42. Perhaps, then, theology is not the best place to reflect on free will either?

Chapter 3

THE COOPERATIVE JUDAS: TRUE BELIEVER,
PHANTOM OF THE INFINITE

Runeberg's First Judas: Sacrificial Christ and Superior Apostle

Like the infamous Judas of some of the gnostics, Runeberg's first Judas is the one apostle who understands Christ's identity and sacrifice.[1] While Runeberg sees the incarnation itself as a degradation (cf. Phil. 2:6-8), the crucifixion climaxes Christ's sacrifice. As informer, Judas cooperates with Jesus' deadly plan by bringing him to the enemy. Those who know this plan see the incarnation and crucifixion as a divine suicide and Judas as some ancient Dr. Kevorkian.

A similar idea appears in Borges' essay on De Quincey's reading of John Donne's *Biathanatos* (1999b: 333–36). Donne contends that some suicides are not mortal sins. His argument depends largely upon John (10:15, 18)[2] and upon the notion therein that Christ "gave up the ghost." Borges, however, discovers a deeper "esoteric argument beneath [Donne's] obvious one" in the Christian idea that the life and death of Christ center history:

> the centuries before prepared for it, those after reflect it. Before Adam was formed from the dust of the earth, before the firmament separated the waters from the waters, the Father knew that the Son was to die on the cross and, as the theater of this future death, created the heavens and the earth. Christ died a voluntary death, Donne suggests, and this means that

---

1. See Chapter 5 for a discussion of the Gospel of Judas, which was published only in 2006. Previous knowledge of the gnostic Judas who had superior knowledge and betrayed Jesus in light of this mysterious knowledge depended upon Irenaeus, *Against the Heresies*, 1.31.1; and Epiphanus, 1990: 133–35. Pyper discusses modern fictional versions of the Gospel of Judas (2001: 111–22). Paffenroth discusses the gnostic Judas and fictional versions of the obedient, cooperative Judas (2001b: 60–69).

2. John is the appropriate gospel for this argument because its Jesus is actor, not victim, in the passion, determining its hour (e.g., 12:23, 27; 13:1; 17:1; contrast 2:4; 7:30; 8:20) and its end (19:30).

the elements and the terrestrial orb and the generations of mankind and Egypt and Rome and Babylon and Judah were extracted from nothingness in order to destroy him. Perhaps iron was created for the nails, and thorns for the mock crown, and blood and water for the wound. This baroque idea glimmers behind *Biathanatos*. The idea of a god who creates the universe in order to create his own gallows. (1999b: 335)[3]

All of creation, then, down to the minutest details exists only for the divine suicide. The divine suicide confers meaning upon the world.[4]

While Jack Miles does not go quite so far, he also finds a divine suicide at the heart of the Christian Bible. In a first volume on the Hebrew Bible, Miles reads that text as a literary whole, rather than the fragmented narrative that most scholars find. His interpretation transforms the Hebrew Bible into the biography of a psychologically fragmented God, who is creator, destroyer, patron deity, and warrior (1996: 93).[5] While this deity acts powerfully and willfully in his youth, he belatedly discovers that he intends humans to become his image. Thereafter, the quest for this image becomes God's "career" and, thus, the Hebrew Bible's plot (1996: 87, 99, 250–51). The climax occurs in God's dialogue with Job, who is God's true image because he also searches for God. The encounter with Job reveals his ambiguities to the aging God. Thereafter, God ceases to speak, and active humans (like Nehemiah) replace him (1996: 325–29, 402–406).

Miles' *Christ: A Crisis in the Life of God* appends a reading of the Gospel of John to this biographical interpretation of the Hebrew Bible. Christ emerges from God's inactive silence with loquacious reflections on his identity and death. Gradually, Christ-God undertakes a divinely (and self-) appointed mission. Specifically, Christ commits suicide.[6] For

---

3. Cf. as well the structure of John Milton's *Paradise Lost*, where the divine council determining the future, sacrificial role of the Son (in Book 3) precedes the story of the fall of Adam and Eve (in Book 9).

4. Borges' musings here and in his Judas short stories are a dark play with or parodies of the argument from design and, by anticipation, its recent progeny, the intelligent design furor.

5. This divine fragmentation is even more obvious when Miles playfully reads the Hebrew Bible as if it were a polytheistic myth (1996: 398–402).

6. Miles discusses Christ's death as "suicidal" at length (2001: 160–78). His Christ deliberately provokes murderous hostility against himself. Cf. Lk. 4:16-30. In *God*, Miles compares God and modern individuals, for whom God is mythic model, to Hamlet (1996: 398, 407–408). *Christ* contains only passing references to *Hamlet*, but one is crucial: "Left alone, God Incarnate, like Hamlet in the "To be or not to be" soliloquy, ponders the scarcely comprehensible death that awaits him" (2001: 47).

3 *The Cooperative Judas*   53

Miles, this suicidal mission coheres with Christ's (distinctive) teaching on non-retaliation and, more importantly, atones for God's twofold guilt. The divine death responds to the Edenic curses, to the fact that the human condition and the world are a divine punishment, by taking the curses upon God himself (2001: 12, 24–25, 51, 211).[7] The suicide also responds to the divine inability or unwillingness to keep his covenant promises to protect Israel. Acknowledging his failure to reenact the Exodus, Christ-God elects to share Jerusalem's fate and entices Jerusalem to deliver him to the Romans (2001: 108–109, 151, 180). Thereby, the Lord of Hosts becomes the Lamb of God. For Miles, this divine repentance constitutes the plot of the Christian Bible (2001: 244, 312–17):

> The Gospel story, a story in which the Jewish God is condemned, tortured, and executed by the foreign oppressor of the Jews, is a particularly violent and dramatic way to announce that that God is no longer a warrior prepared to rescue the Jews from foreign oppression but, rather, a savior who has chosen to rescue all mankind from death. The New Testament story as a whole – combining the Gospel story with the story of the early church – is a particularly radical and disruptive way to announce that God has exchanged warfare on behalf of the Jews for missionary teaching through the Jews. (2001: 207)

"Repentance" names this action well because it continues the story of the divine warrior of the Hebrew Bible in a most peculiar manner. While Christ's sacrifice promotes the psychic integration of Miles' tortured God, it does little for his people. Rome remains in control. In God/Christ's biography, others cease to be important. God/Christ simply removes himself from his people's story and, then, reemerges only to resolve tensions within his own character.[8]

Of course, this individualistic depiction of God provides an apt mythic model for equally individualistic moderns:

> Other things being equal, protracted exposure to a God in whom several personalities coexist and alongside whom no other god is ever portrayed even for the folkloric fun of it must foster a way of thinking of the self as similarly composite and similarly alone. (1996: 407)

---

7. The curses of Eden are quite extensive (see Gen. 3:14-19). Is one to see Christ's sacrificial death as the divine response to the *extensive* pain of childbirth, to patriarchy, and to hard labor, as well as to death? Runeberg probably would not. He sees Jesus' suffering as that of a mere afternoon (1962: 155).

8. Miles' reading of the Christian Bible amounts to a Christianized version of Nietzsche. Cf. James Morrow's fantasy trilogy in which God dies, in the opinion of one theologian in the novels, to make way for human maturity and creativity (1994; 1996; 1999). For discussion, see Walsh, 2000.

With God as precursor, modern Westerners are ambiguous, fragmented gods. Somewhat surprisingly, given this tortured mythic precursor, Miles does not see Christ's suicide as similarly exemplary for moderns. Although he phrases it as a question, Miles uses Judas to prohibit Christian suicide: "Or was the ignominious suicide of Judas, Jesus' betrayer, added to the Gospel story precisely as a reminder that a chasm separates ordinary human suicide from the suicide of the God-man?" (2001: 170).[9] Although a question, it continues the orthodox animus to suicide and the canonical perspective on Judas.[10] Two hang, as in Matthew, but one is virtue and one is vice.

Borges' Sect of the Thirty read the gospel story of Jesus' death more relentlessly and (mytho)logically. For them, Jesus' death is mythic model. Seeing suicide as Christianity's foundation, they worship Judas, who assists Jesus' suicide, along with Jesus. Their beliefs (and actions) also imply that Judas' own suicide is part of what makes Judas into Jesus' first and best follower. Borges' Runeberg brings the matter to the forefront: Judas' consciously chosen self-destruction mirrors Jesus' sacrifice (1962: 153). Logically, the sectarians also seek to end their own lives in self-crucifixions (and Runeberg wallows in degradation).

While many early followers of Jesus, like Ignatius, sought martyrdom to complete their Christian discipleship (cf. Phil. 1:21-24; Mk 8:34-35),[11] Constantine's conversion changed the possibilities for Christian martyrdom quite dramatically, and Augustine thereafter enunciated the classic Christian position that suicide is a sin and a homicide. For Augustine, Judas demonstrates the essential "wrongness" of suicide:

---

9. The tone is not unlike Augustine's. See below.

10. Miles' brief mentions of Judas include other canonical traces as well. While musing on John's idea that Satan possessed Judas, Miles resorts to Judas' instrumental role in the secret plan and concludes that Christ must have tricked Satan into seducing Judas for the larger, later good of human redemption. Judas is an acceptable loss/sacrifice. Interestingly, DeConick argues that such ideas emerged as an orthodox response to gnostic reflections about Judas' role in salvation (2007: 133–38). Judas also provides a site for Miles to reflect on Christian lessons about loving those who betray one (2001: 216). The lesson is repeated with Peter (2001: 218). Miles, of course, is deliberately engaging in a literary reading of the Christian canon (2001: 247–53), not expressing an opinion on Judas nor constructing a theology. That Miles produces a quite canonical Judas, then, hardly surprises.

11. On Jewish and Christian discourse about martyrdom, see Boyarin, 1999. For a reading of Paul's gospel as a call to self-destruction, see Walsh, 2005a: 81–108. On Christianity itself as suicidal, see Nietzsche, 1974: 131; and Camus, 1991: 28–50.

3 The Cooperative Judas

> We rightly abominate the act of Judas, and the judgment of truth is that when he hanged himself he did not atone for the guilt of his detestable betrayal but rather increased it, since he despaired of God's mercy and in a fit of self-destructive remorse left himself no chance of a saving repentance. (1984: 1.17)[12]

For Augustine, as for Miles, Judas hangs to erect a boundary between the meaningful death of Jesus Christ and the meaningless death of those outside.[13] It might not be too much to say, then, as A. M. H. Saari does, that the hatred of Judas founds the Christian animus to suicide (2006: 76). This hatred also saves Christians from the brutal logic of Borges' sectarians and his Runeberg.[14]

Modern scholars challenging the allegedly monolithic Christian rejection of suicide have argued that some ancients saw suicide as noble and have drawn cautious connections between suicide and martyrdom. They have also pointed out that Matthew's story of Judas' suicide does not explicitly condemn him for this act (Droge and Tabor, 1992; Saari, 2006). William Klassen rehabilitates Judas even more forcefully:

> We could say that Judas was the first and the strongest witness to Jesus' innocence, making his confession to the highest authorities in the land. *He could well have been the first to die with Jesus.* Thus, in solidarity with Jesus, he would have died for what he believed: that Jesus was a good man, innocent of death, deserving no evil. (Klassen, 1996: 174, emphasis added)

Klassen's words come quite close to Runeberg's claim that Judas' self-destruction is discipleship.[15]

---

12. On Augustine as the significant moment here, see Droge and Tabor, 1992; Whelan, 1993; and Saari, 2006: 15–18, 59–76. Subsequent theologians were often even less charitable to Judas. Theophylactus argues that Judas shrewdly tried to commit suicide in order to arrive in hell before Jesus and to gain salvation from him there. He failed when the tree refused to bear him. On this and later legendary developments, see Paffenroth, 2001b: 120–25; and Zwiep, 2004: 111–20.

13. See, again, the contrasting hanging deaths of Jesus and Judas on the ivory relief plaques (420–30 CE) in the British Museum. Photographs are available on the internet. See, e.g., http://www.britishmuseum.org/explore/highlights/highlight_objects/pe_mla/p/panel_from_an_ivory_casket_th.aspx (accessed 7-26-09).

14. Saari rethinks suicide in light of his brother's suicide and his own subsequent conversion to Christianity. For Saari, Judas' many deaths are all Christian fictions and Christian, not divine, judgments on Judas (2006: 115–16, 126–27).

15. Even the recently published Gospel of Judas does not pursue this idea. It ends abruptly with Judas' betrayal of Jesus to the authorities. See Chapter 5 below.

In Christian discourse, however, Judas and suicide belong together and outside the frame of Christianity. Jesus and noble, redemptive death similarly belong together. Christian discourse will not allow one to mix and match. One leaves Christian discourse behind if one speaks of Judas' noble death or of Jesus' suicide. Thus, even those rethinking the Christian stance against suicide speak of Jesus' death as a suicide only in the form of carefully nuanced questions. Correspondingly, Hyam Maccoby claims that only the rejection of the Christian notion of Christ's redemptive death will ever redeem Judas (Maccoby, 1992: 22–33, 166–67). Jesus' nobility and Judas' villainy create and reinforce each other.

Despite conservative hostility to the film, Martin Scorsese's infamous *The Last Temptation of Christ* (1988) does not depart from Christian discourse on this point.[16] It ultimately affirms Jesus' noble, redemptive death. Before arriving at that rather orthodox conclusion, however, *The Last Temptation of Christ* features a remarkably human Jesus who struggles to escape the God who torments him and then tries desperately to understand God's plan. Further, the film uniquely invites the audience to share Jesus' halting progress toward the secret divine plan through a series of troubling visions.[17] More pertinently, as in the heretical tradition and in Borges' short stories about Judas, only Judas shares Jesus' growing knowledge of this secret, so the film becomes a "buddy film," the only one in the Jesus film tradition (see Walsh, 2003: 27, 36–37; Staley and Walsh, 2007: 112–14). Judas is literally Jesus' bosom friend. They are frequently alone together at night. In one important scene, the troubled Jesus sleeps on Judas' bosom. In the garden, Judas' betraying kiss is fully on the lips.

As the film opens, Jesus tries desperately to escape God by making Roman crosses and by assisting in the crucifixion of messianic claimants. Angry with this collaborator, the Zealots dispatch Judas to assassinate Jesus. Jesus avoids their plot because Jesus convinces his friend Judas to go with him on his search for God. In the interim, Jesus places himself in Judas' hands, inviting Judas to kill him whenever he will. Reluctantly, Judas becomes Jesus' first disciple; however, he promises to kill Jesus if Jesus swerves from the revolutionary path.

---

16. The film begins with titles acknowledging Nikos Kazantzakis' novel of the same name as its primary source. The disclaimer did not satisfy the religiously conservative. For a theological defense of the film's focus on Jesus' humanity, see Stern, Jefford, and DeBona, 1999: 265–95.

17. Young's 1999 *Jesus* also lets the audience share Jesus' visionary world in an opening sequence and in the Gethsemane scene, but this Jesus is far less troubled than Scorsese's.

3 *The Cooperative Judas*

While Jesus wanders the wilderness seeking the precise divine plan, Judas shepherds the other disciples. When Jesus returns and announces that God's plan is the axe (revolt), Judas—not Peter—confesses him as Lord (Adonai). To spark that revolt, Judas accompanies Jesus to the Temple to announce its destruction. Jesus, however, has yet another epiphany, foregoes revolt for his own sacrificial death, and co-opts Judas for this plan as "traitor" by speaking of Isa. 53:3-5, 7 in oracular terms.[18] In a cinematic innovation, Scorsese offers the conversation—the last temptation of Judas—by which Jesus seduces Judas, the strongest of his friends, to his new plan. Jesus appeals to Judas' integrity by reminding Judas of his murderous promise and by forcing Judas to admit that Jesus has left the revolutionary path.[19] When a reluctant Judas asks Jesus if he could betray his master, Jesus admits he could not and appeals to Judas' manhood by telling him that he, the stronger one, has the more difficult job, the role of betrayer.[20]

If this Judas betrays Jesus (to the quisling authorities he despises), it is only as he cooperates with Jesus' understanding of the secret plan.[21] In fact, Judas risks murderous Zealot ire by not assassinating Jesus and, despite Jesus' revolutionary failures, never fulfills his murderous promise. In fact, Judas saves Jesus repeatedly from disaster. In striking contrast, Jesus clearly betrays Judas. Jesus promises Judas revolution, but does not deliver. Jesus uses Judas as a mere tool in his various versions of the secret plan. In fact, Jesus never explains to Judas why the secret plan requires Judas' cooperation as "traitor."[22] Jesus simply asserts this (new) plan. Everything is rhetoric, not explanation. Everything is designed to coerce Judas.

The film does, however, strongly connect Judas with Jesus' destined death. As the film begins, Jesus reveals his troubled visionary world in an interior monologue. Not knowing who or what the voices want, Jesus demands an answer. Shortly, thereafter, Jesus makes a cross and stretches

---

18. The audience sees Isaiah and Jesus read what appears to be a lamb skin, but no writing is visible. The visual captures the motif of the secret plot excellently.

19. After the first failed revolt in the Temple, Saul/Paul, the Zealot, upbraids Judas for not assassinating Jesus as the Zealots sent him to do.

20. Jesus here enacts the gospel role of John the Baptist, pointing out the stronger one, and Judas becomes the one who brings the kingdom or, at least, the divine plan to fruition.

21. Novelists frequently imagine a secret cooperation between Jesus and Judas. See, e.g., Callaghan, 1984; and Rayner, 1969.

22. The LXX of Isaiah 53 does use forms of παραδίδωμι (see Klassen, 1996: 49) to speak of the servant's fate, but the film does not quote these verses.

himself out tentatively upon it. Suddenly, Judas bursts into Jesus' room and asks Jesus if he is ready. Visually, at least, Judas is the answer to Jesus' prayers and from the beginning appears to ask if Jesus is ready to die. The arrest scene in Gethsemane (Jesus' place of prayer) provides the visual bookend for this scene. After Judas brings the arrest party, Jesus looks at Judas again and says that he is ready (to die). In between these two framing scenes, Jesus has learned that God intends for him to die and has co-opted Judas for that plan. Jesus has put together the visual puzzle of the first scene connecting cross, Jesus, and Judas. Judas has no educative visions of this nature. He is simply Jesus' aide.

In the course of the ensuing passion, Jesus has a death-throe fantasy on the cross in which he forsakes the divine plan. Satan, disguised as a little girl, offers Jesus a normal family life. In the fantasy, Jesus lives out this normal human life (in sexual detail) and finally nears death as an old man during the siege of Jerusalem. As Jesus lies dying, Judas arrives from the burning Jerusalem and castigates Jesus for betraying his messianic destiny. He tells Jesus that his place was the cross, dying as messiah to save the world. In Jesus' fantasy, then, Judas represents Jesus' death as messiah. Not surprisingly, Jesus leaves his fantasy behind, returns to the cross as Christ, prays for forgiveness, tells God that he wants to be the messiah, and dies smiling.

Here, Christian redemption and its story depend upon Judas, as (a John the Baptist-like) Jesus says to Judas in private and as the fantasy sequence appears to prove. Judas is Jesus' answered prayer and his deadly destiny. Judas incarnates the secret plan of Jesus' sacrifice.[23] As in the canonical gospels, Judas is oracular, but *The Last Temptation of Christ* visualizes Jesus' difficulty (not Judas') in accepting this oracle. Vis-à-vis this secret plan and the "manly" Judas, Jesus is a vacillating, weak figure, but he finally reaches his messianic stature. Scorsese's Judas, like the Judases of Runeberg and the sectarians, is Jesus' premier disciple, but, unlike those other Judases, he never really understands the divine plan or Jesus. Like the canonical Judas, Scorsese's Judas simply obeys Jesus' oracular demands. As in the gospel, the Jesus of *The Last Temptation of*

---

23. Incidentally, the Judas of *Jesus Christ Superstar* (1973) functions similarly. Despite railing against the noxious demands of God/Jesus and trying desperately to separate Jesus, the man, from the superstar-messiah myth, Judas eventually plays his canonical role. *Jesus Christ Superstar* visualizes this fated role with a song-and-dance addition to the passion narrative. After Judas' suicide and as Jesus proceeds to the cross, a white-clad Judas descends from heaven on a lighted cross singing the film's theme song with a heavenly chorus. Once again, Judas is Jesus' suicidal destiny.

Christ creates Judas. In fact, in the fantasy sequence, Judas is no more than a phantom in Jesus' dreams.

The cooperative Judas clearly has the potential to disrupt Christian discourse. As Borges' "The Sect of the Thirty" illustrates, Judas, the cooperative and premier disciple, can unsettle the myth that celebrates Jesus and abominates Judas, the myth that distinguishes Jesus' good death from Judas' despairing suicide. Such shifts might also lead one to reflect on whether true belief/discipleship is suicide as Runeberg and the sectarians presume. Such shifts might also lead one to wonder what such suicides, divine or otherwise, accomplish.

Nonetheless, while it may seem counterintuitive, the cooperative Judas does not necessarily vary canonical mechanics. Thus, Kermode has observed that at the level of plot functions it matters little whether Judas is adversary or (cooperative) helper (1979: 84). *The Last Temptation of Christ* also illustrates that the buddy Judas can coexist with canonical aesthetics. While the Jesus of that film may be more human and more modern than that of the canonical gospels, Scorsese's Judas is quite orthodox. Oracular magic and secret plots still determine everything. Scorsese's film, like Borges' short stories about Judas, simply depicts a Judas who, like Jesus, is a true believer in the secret plan. Somewhat surprisingly, however, Scorsese does not follow this true belief and the canon to Judas' suicide. Scorsese leaves that destiny for Jesus alone. Jesus' destiny completely subsumes Judas. Scorsese's Judas has no death of his own.

The Cooperative Judas in the Gospels

Not surprisingly, then, traces of a cooperative Judas appear in the canonical gospels themselves. Runeberg and the sectarians find this premier disciple in Matthew's suicidal Judas (cf. Klassen, 1996; Daube, 1994). Certain features of Matthew's story, however, make it difficult to see Judas' suicide as the noble death of Jesus' true disciple.

First, even though Matthew does not explicitly condemn Judas' suicide, the gospel does not tell the story of Judas' burial. In the cultural conventions of the era, lack of burial is humiliating; burial is respectful. Certainly, Matthew has other more important people (Jesus) to hang and bury, so it would be foolish to expect wasted remarks on Judas' fate. Yet, Judas' lack of importance is precisely the point. Matthew leaves Judas hanging because he is not important enough to bury.[24] Judas simply furthers the

---

24. The fate of Judas in Matthew is not unlike that of Stracci in *La ricotta*, Pasolini's contribution to *RoGoPaG* (1962). Chronically hungry, Stracci, a peasant extra playing

Matthean passion plot, which centers relentlessly on only one significant death.

Second, Matthew's story of Judas' suicide may be yet another indication of the oracular Judas. At the Supper, as discussed in Chapter 2, Jesus predicts the betrayer into existence (e.g., Mk 14:18-20) and, then, pronounces a woe upon that betrayer (e.g., Mk 14:21). The arrest in Gethsemane fulfills the prediction of betrayal, but no scene in Mark fulfills Jesus' curse. As a result, some redaction critics, assuming the Two Source Hypothesis, see Matthew's story of Judas' death as an attempt to fill in the unfulfilled prophecy of the woe (see Paffenroth, 2001b: 113–14).[25]

Thus, despite the interesting reflections of the sectarians, Runeberg, and Klassen, Matthew's story of Judas' suicide does not seem the best place to look for traces of a cooperative Judas. Klassen's argument about the translation of παραδίδωμι is another matter (1996: 41–61). While English translations of the forms of παραδίδωμι in Mt. 10:4 and Mk 3:19 routinely introduce Judas as the one who betrayed Jesus, Klassen has argued strenuously that no Greek text exists in which παραδίδωμι clearly means "betray" and that another Greek word, προδίδωμι, which appears in Lk. 6:16, does clearly mean "betray." In the canonical gospels, παραδίδωμι appears fifty-nine times in connection with the passion of Jesus. Thirty-two of those cases involve Judas, and English translations render the word "betray" in those cases (Mt. 10:4; 26:15, 16, 21, 23, 24, 25, 46, 48; 27:3, 4; Mk 3:19; 14:10, 11, 18, 21, 42, 44; Lk. 22:4, 6, 21, 22, 48; Jn 6:64, 71; 12:4; 13:12, 11, 21; 18:2, 5; 21:20). The other twenty-seven cases do not involve Judas, and English translations render the same word "hand over" in those cases (Mt. 17:22; 20:18, 19; 26:2, 45; 27:2, 18, 26; Mk 9:31; 10:33 (2); 14:41; 15:1, 10, 15; Lk. 9:44; 18:32; 20:20; 23:25; 24:7, 20; Jn 18:30, 35, 36; 19:11, 16, 30) (Klassen, 1996: 50–57; following Schwartz, 1988: 96–97). Accordingly, Klassen concludes that the translation "betray" is based on theology, not philology (Klassen, 1996: 48, 51, 55). He proposes, therefore, more neutral translations like "hand over," "surrender," or "deliver" in all cases (Klassen, 1996: 57).[26]

---

the good thief in a Hollywood-style biblical epic, gorges himself on ricotta cheese at the cast's buffet. Thereafter, he dies on the cross from complications of that overeating without being noticed. When he is found dead, the director (played by Orson Welles) remarks that Stracci had to die to be noticed. The comment drips irony as does the entire short film. Like Judas, Stracci is an expendable, who is beneath the notice of the "important." See Walsh, 2003: 105, 114; and Staley and Walsh, 2007: 46–47.

25. One of Paffenroth's important precursors here is Senior, 1974: 23–36; and 1982: 347–49.

26. Following Popkes, 1976: 218, Klassen suggests four possible interpretations

3 *The Cooperative Judas*   61

Further, many of the passages (eighteen in the gospels) employ a passive form of παραδίδωμι (as does, for that matter, 1 Cor. 11:23).[27] As discussed in Chapter 2, one might see (some of) these as divine passives and conclude, as Borges' Sect of the Thirty does, that God, Jesus, and Judas are the prime actors in the passion. In fact, one might read these passives as indicating that God and Judas perform the same action vis-à-vis Jesus, whether that is betrayal or handing over (cf. Rom. 8:32).[28] Here, then, is a Judas who cooperates with the divine plot. In fact, here is a Judas who is the divine plot incarnate. One thinks again of the visual connections between crosses, Judas, and Jesus' answered prayers in *The Last Temptation of Christ*.

Klassen further observes that the gospel Judas simply obeys Jesus' requests (one might more accurately say, "Jesus' demands") (cf., e.g., Jn 13:27-30) (Klassen, 1996: 45, 62–70, 73–74). David Greene's *Godspell* (1973) expands this obedience into the portrait of a reluctantly cooperative Judas. *Godspell*'s Judas plays, for most of the film, the role of John the Baptist and of Jesus' foremost disciple. John/Judas appears first in the film, dancing into New York City, pulling a circus cart, and alternatively humming circus music and singing, "Prepare Ye the Way of the Lord." This ringmaster calls disciples from the crowds and baptizes them in Bethesda Fountain before Jesus arrives. When Jesus begins to lead the

---

of Judas' handing over of Jesus: (1) Judas handed Jesus over to his death; (2) Judas surrendered Jesus to the authorities legally; (3) Judas informed on Jesus by reporting some infraction to the authorities; and (4) Judas betrayed Jesus, breaking faith with him. Klassen rejects the fourth and merges the first three to posit that Judas brokered a meeting between the Temple authorities and Jesus, believing that both wanted the meeting. Although Klassen admits that he does not know Judas' motives and that some base motives might have played a role as they do in all human actions, he argues for a Judas, the Jew, who acted faithfully both as a Jew and as Jesus' disciple (1996: 57). Greenberg also argues for Judas' role as intermediary between Jesus and the authorities (2007: 14–15, 264–71). Cf. also the portrayals of Judas in Rayner, 1969; and in Zeffirelli's *Jesus of Nazareth* (1977).

27. Because of this passage, the absence of references to Judas in Pauline literature, and Paul's "positive" remarks about the Twelve, Kermode (1979) suggests that the idea of Judas the betrayer developed after Paul.

28. One can easily imagine ancients telling stories about Jesus' divine betrayal. Gods in antiquity often care little for humans. See, e.g., *The Gilgamesh Epic* or Job. The notion of the divine betrayal would also provide an intriguing perspective on the cry of dereliction in Mark's passion (15:34). Cf. Schweitzer, 1968: 370–71. For a discussion of the trope of God's betrayal of the righteous in tales of innocent sufferers, see also Klassen, 1996: 52, 54–55. The psalms, of course, frequently lament divine desertion.

group, this premier disciple is the only character that offers Jesus any serious resistance. Thus, while objecting to Jesus' turn-the-other-cheek teaching, Judas receives a slap from Jesus for his troubles. In the enactment of the beatitudes, he is the only disciple to begin a beatitude that Jesus does not immediately complete (Mt. 5:11). Finally, in the passion sequence, John/Judas acts the role of the betrayer, but he does so in reluctant obedience to Jesus' command, the Johannine "do quickly."[29] Further, when John/Judas returns with the police, he is unable to carry through with the betraying kiss. Jesus takes over, kissing John/Judas twice and enjoining him again, "Friend, do quickly what you have to do." Thus, Jesus magisterially empowers the betrayal, and only then can John/Judas affix Jesus to the junkyard's chain-link fence (cross), humming once again the ringmaster's circus tune. While the tune suggests the divine orchestrations and secret plots of the canon once again, this Judas cooperates consciously and reluctantly with Jesus' plan. Only that visible reluctance—evident as well in the Judas of *The Last Temptation of Christ* (at least, in the portrayal of Judas before the final fantasy sequence)—separates this Judas from another mere incarnation of divine oracles. This Judas cannot easily abide the destruction of his friend.[30] He is a reluctant traitor, and he is a traitor only because he is a loyal, obedient disciple.

Godspell finds a reluctant traitor/disciple by reflecting on John. If one returns to John from *Godspell*, one can find other traces of a reluctant disciple there. John's Jesus does not empower Judas with a twofold kiss, but John's Jesus does empower him with ritual bread, accompanied sinisterly by the entry of Satan. As a result, John's Judas betrays Jesus only after Jesus (or the Johannine narrator) fills him with "the adversary." The scene amounts, as Kermode has astutely observed, to "a character being

---

29. Interestingly, while *Godspell* presents itself as a film adaptation of Matthew, the film turns to John here. Does John (the Baptist or the oracle) become John (the gospel narrative) through the film's Judas character? Does *Godspell*, i.e., reveal the crucial significance of Judas as lynchpin between oracle and gospel narrative? At the very least, here, as in *Jesus Christ Superstar* and *The Last Temptation of Christ*, Judas is again—now by his connection with John the Baptist—little more than oracle. In all three films, it is Jesus, not Judas, who catalyzes the Judas-oracle or Jesus' deadly destiny, and Judas who is a reluctant second or disciple.

30. The idea of a Judas who tries unsuccessfully to stop Jesus' suicide is not uncommon. See, e.g., Jeffers, "Dear Judas" (1971: 2:5–45). In *Lamb*, Christopher Moore also imagines a friend of Jesus that tries to save him from his suicidal death and, in fact, hatches an unsuccessful Passover plot-pretend suicide (2002; cf. Schweitzer, 1968: 38–47, 161–79; Schonfield, 1967; and Rayner, 1969). For Moore, however, this friend is Biff, not Judas. Moore's Judas has a more canonical role.

possessed by his narrative role" (1979: 85). It smacks of a character possessed by an oracle or of a character incarnating oracle. It resembles the transformation of John/First Disciple into Judas in *Godspell* at Jesus' demand and betraying kiss. Was John's Judas also a faithful disciple until that overpowering demon? Does John's Judas perform the mandated task only under "the (divine and demonic) influence?" Does Judas vanish here and does only the adversary remain? Compared to the Judases of the Synoptic Gospels, John's Judas is particularly demonic (cf. Jn 6:70), but does John's demonization of Judas contain the hint of a disciple who could not betray until supernaturally possessed and activated? What kinds of horrors lurk in these possibilities?

A reluctantly cooperative Judas may also haunt certain sections of Matthew. After Matthew's Jesus creates a betrayer by fiat (26:21), the disciples each ask if he is the one (26:22). The NRSV translation of their question nicely suggests the negative reply anticipated by the Greek phrasing: "Surely not I, Lord?" Jesus' enigmatic response to them names the one who dips as the betrayer and adds a woe upon him (26:23-24). Judas, then, replies either a second time or simply in his turn, "Surely not I, Rabbi?" (26:25). While Judas' response is almost synonymous with that of the others, Matthew isolates Judas by naming only Judas as Jesus' specific interlocutor, by describing him as the one who betrayed Jesus, and by having Judas address Jesus as rabbi, rather than Lord. As Matthean disciples regularly address Jesus as Lord, Judas' chosen address for Jesus may particularly alienate him. Nonetheless, Matthew's deliberate separation of Judas from the others betrays his fundamental similarity with them (cf. the tone of Klauck, 1987).

Matthew's Jesus, then, addresses this carefully isolated disciple with a specific, but enigmatic reply, "You have said so" (26:25). Some prefer to translate the reply as a question, "Do you say so?" (cf. Klassen, 1996: 100–102). The question form depicts a cooperative Judas, invited by Jesus to decide his own role and to elect to follow Jesus' commands. One might even see here a Judas who is Jesus' best disciple, the only one with the perspicacity to recognize that Jesus' enigmatic oracles are actually invitations for a disciple to accept a particularly onerous, but necessary task.[31] Such a Judas would be the precursor of Scorsese's manly Judas and of Runeberg's first Judas.

---

31. In *King Jesus*, Robert Graves depicts a Judas who is the one disciple who understands Jesus' words to be an order (1946: 363, 367). The Judas in Callaghan's *A Time for Judas* tries to convince himself that he is this one, strong disciple (1984: 125–32).

Matthew has only the merest trace of this buddy Judas, however, because Jesus favors two other figures in Matthew with a very similar reply, Caiaphas (26:64) and Pilate (27:11), neither of whom are disciples or insiders. Moreover, in the very midst of this conversation between Judas and Jesus, Matthew specifically brands Judas as "the one who betrayed him" (26:25), and Matthew's Judas has, in fact, already contracted to betray Jesus (26:14-16). Thus, even if Matthew's Judas elects to fulfill the proffered role, the story still determines in advance his role.

Another trace of the cooperative Judas appears in Matthew's arrest scene. After Judas arrives with the arresting party, he hails Jesus as rabbi and identifies him for the arresting party with a kiss (26:49). However, heinous it has become in the tradition, the kiss still suggests a Judas who cooperates with or who even loves Jesus.[32] Again, Jesus responds enigmatically, "Friend, do what you are here to do" (26:50). The English translation "friend" (ἑταῖρος) puzzles because the address is not friendly. At least, Matthew's other uses of ἑταῖρος occur in confrontational situations. In Mt. 20:13, the vineyard owner responds to a complainer, who has to settle for the same pay as others who have worked less, as ἑταῖρος. In Mt. 22:12, the king asks a ἑταῖρος how he came to be inside without a wedding robe before demanding that the interloper be thrown into outer darkness. These associations are ominous and do not suggest any cooperation between Jesus and Judas. Instead, they suggest divine determinations.

Nonetheless, Jesus' reply to Judas here, like that at the Supper, may be a question: "Friend, why have you come?" (cf., e.g., the KJV, RSV, and NEB[mg]). As a statement, Jesus' reply is peremptory, and it demands obedience to an irresistible oracle.[33] The question allows for a more cooperative Judas. One might paraphrase, "What will you do?" Matthew buries any signs of cooperation here again, however, by marking Judas as betrayer (26:48) and by discussing the arrangement of the betrayal sign (26:48) before presenting the kiss and Jesus' enigmatic response.

Despite intriguing traces, then, the canon is not a fertile place for depictions of a cooperative Judas. The canon privileges the magical mentions of oracle above such matters, and the canonical Judas necessarily obeys

---

32. The arranged sign of the "kiss" in Mt. 26:48 uses the word φιλέω, which can also be translated "love."

33. Pasolini's *The Gospel according to St. Matthew* (1965) displays the argumentative, confrontational style of Matthew' Jesus. In the Sermon on the Mount, Jesus repeatedly and aggressively says, "I say." The "you say so" or "do you say?" addressed to Judas, Caiaphas, and Pilate form an apt bookend. One might also consider the framing effect of the repeated and aggressive "they" and "you" throughout Matthew 23.

the oracles that define him. One can find traces of a cooperative Judas only if one reads willfully. Read with the sectarians and with Runeberg, for example, the canonical Judas' obedience may not be altogether determined. Perhaps, he rises reluctantly to the onerous task demanded by Jesus with the aplomb of a faithful disciple. On the edge of oracle, there may be the merest hints of cooperation. Many modern interpreters of Judas, like Klassen, Scorsese, Jewison, and Greene, want to think so. Such cooperation, however, is not necessarily a good thing.

Deliberate Disgrace or the Necessary Theological Humiliation of the Human

Runeberg's first Judas acts far more freely than the canonical Judas does. Runeberg's first Judas imagines for himself the contours of the role of faithful disciple. Having done so, he selects the deliberate disgrace of betrayal and of self-destruction. Runeberg, however, merely suggests this Judas' story. Instead of narrating this story in detail, Runeberg creates a cooperative Judas simply through comments upon the well-known gospel story.

Borges' "The Form of the Sword," however, tells an intriguingly similar story (1962: 117–22). Stuck in the country because of a flood, a guest asks his host to tell him the story of his scarred face. After some reluctance, the host agrees as long as the guest agrees "not [to] minimize the opprobrium it [both story and scar] calls forth …" (1962: 118). The host's story is about Irish revolutionaries and, in particular, about the host's mentor relationship with the arrogant and cowardly John Vincent Moon, who over-exaggerates the effects of an injury in order to avoid a crucial battle. Returning after several days of battle, the host hears the traitorous Moon arranging the Judas-price for his arrest as he crosses the garden. Chasing the traitor, his friend, through the house, the host cuts Moon's face with a sword before the soldiers arrest him. As the story ends, the reader realizes the scarred narrator is Moon, but the guest asks what happened to Moon anyway. The narrator responds by confessing his traitorous identity and by asking his guest (again) to despise him.

The allusions to the gospel Judas story are rather obvious: the arranged plot, the identification of a garden as a place for the arrest (with an allusion to another biblical garden as well), the reference to the betrayer as "friend," and the mention of the Judas-price. This piece differs significantly from the gospel, however, in its narration. Here, Judas/Moon tells his own tale.[34] Like Runeberg's first Judas, Judas/Moon wallows in his

---

34. Fictions often feature Judas as narrator. See, e.g., the works discussed in Pyper,

chosen degradation. Despite his initial deceptions, he tells his story as if inflicting the scar upon himself yet again.[35] He cannot or will not tell a different tale.

Runeberg's first Judas does not vary the degrading canonical plot either. Although the tone differs (far more than it does in "The Form of the Sword"), theology still determines matters. Runeberg's Judas, as the narrator remarks, responds metaphysically or theologically to the canon as infinite book. Runeberg and his Judas are true believers in that book. Further, Runeberg's Judas assumes neoplatonically that the earth imperfectly mirrors the heavens. The heavenly is ubiquitous, eternal, and blessed while the earthly is spatial, temporal, and mortal. This hierarchical theology—like the canon's irresistible oracles—humiliates humans. Accordingly, Runeberg's first Judas stands in awe of the divinity that guarantees his destruction. The divine glory still dominates the story even though Runeberg's Judas is a much more conscious, active character than the canonical Judas.

Matters are eerily similar in the quest for the historical Jesus. There, history (and the human) also often has a distinctly divine aura. Thus, despite the anachronism of the idea of religion as applied to antiquity, the historical Jesus is almost always a "religious" figure. More importantly, claims to historical truth in this research are often simply modernized forms of theological (or philosophical) claims.[36] Two examples will suffice.

2001; and the speeches of Judas in Jeffers, "Dear Judas" (1971: 2:5–45). Judas is not, however, the narrator of the recently published, ancient Gospel of Judas. See Chapter 5 below. Technically speaking, Judas/Moon is not the narrator of the "The Form of the Sword" either. The narrator repeats a story told him previously by Judas/Moon.

35. Cf. the Judas in Callaghan's *A Time for Judas*, who does not want his part in Jesus' secret plot revealed (1984: 185). He knows that his redemption would ruin Jesus' story. He accepts disgrace in order to make Jesus' story "work." Philo, to whom Judas tells his story and who sees Jesus' Roman trial, wonders if everyone there follows some hidden script (1984: 159–60). Philo ultimately accepts Judas' perspective and buries Judas' story so that he, too, will not betray the story (1984: 244–46). This Judas is cooperative to the point of death (and infamy). Cf. the protagonist of *Stranger than Fiction* (2006) who also elects the death scripted for him in order not to destroy the story. Borges imagines a similarly cooperative Judas and one whose betrayal increases the pathos of the story so that it becomes more compelling and memorable in "The Sect of the Thirty" (1999a: 443–45).

36. See Aichele, Miscall, and Walsh, 2009: 399–419; Blanton, 2007; and Arnal, 2005. For an attempt to write early Christian history without the premise of Jesus' uniqueness, which is, perhaps, the fundamental theological underpinning of the quest, see Crossley, 2006. Parenthetically, the notion of Jesus' uniqueness serves modern

3 The Cooperative Judas 67

First, after David F. Strauss reduced the gospels to myth, his conservative opponents responded with assertions about historical truth in the form of the Two Source Hypothesis and in the original quest for the historical Jesus. Second, when history of religions scholars denied the comfortable distinction that the quest and others had made between the historical truth of Christianity (and Judaism) and the myths of other (false) religions and when Rudolf Bultmann reduced the historical Jesus to a mere *Das*, Bultmann's students founded a New Quest (seconded quickly by the biblical theology movement), which reasserted the historical truth and, therefore, the uniqueness of Christianity. The New Questers in particular often argued that history was crucially important because it prevented Christianity from lapsing into mere myth and because it distinguished Christianity from gnosticism (a synonym for mythology for the New Questers) and fundamentalism (a synonym for dogmatic theology) (see, e.g., Käsemann, 1982: 15–47). In both examples, "truth" and "uniqueness" are religious and theological assertions made under the guise of history.

Furthermore, methodologically speaking, historical Jesus research is the obsessive, suspicious reading of the canonical gospels. As the gospels are primarily mythic, historical criticism necessarily reads the gospels suspiciously, striving to uncover some hidden or implied (historical) truth. Seen so, historical research is remarkably like Runeberg's reading[37] and even somewhat similar to gnosticism's claim to reveal secrets to the elite. At the very least, it is as theological a reading as Runeberg's as its aim makes quite clear. Specifically, historical Jesus research selects one figure (or text) out of all the figures (or texts) of history to investigate obsessively. The selection, as well as the predetermined result, apologetically renders this one figure (and Christianity) unique. Without the underpinning of Christian theology, one wonders how one would arrive at such a conclusion or why one would even engage in the task.[38] Theology, then,

---

(individualistic) mythology as much as it does traditional Christian theology. See Walsh, 2005b.

37. Incidentally, Runeberg begins his quest for the historical Judas with the work of Thomas De Quincey, who was a pioneer in historical Judas research, and uses one of De Quincey's famous lines as an epigraph for his first volume on Judas. See Borges, 1962: 152. De Quincey finds a Judas who is a political revolutionary dissatisfied with Jesus' inaction on this point. See below and Chapter 4. Perhaps, it is no coincidence that H. S. Reimarus, who stands at the beginning of the quest for the historical Jesus according to Schweitzer, similarly finds a Jesus who is a political revolutionary. See Reimarus, 1985; and Schweitzer, 1968: 13–26.

38. On the Christian apologetics here, see Mack, 1988: 3–24; and Crossley, 2006: 1–33. The process founds a scholar's modern academic identity and, in most cases, a

justifies this quest for one ancient "human." One might best describe the historical Jesus(es) that results, then, as a human Christ(s). Jesus is not just any human. He is the human. He is the ideal religiously, ethically, or ideologically.[39] He devalues—at least, implicitly—all other humans. But, he himself is important only because he carries with him the shadow of the Christ (Walsh, 2005b: 161–65).

In Borges' language, the historical Jesus mirrors Christ. Runeberg's first Judas also reflects Christ, but far less clearly. Judas is not as unique as the Christian Jesus. Runeberg's first Judas is more human. Unfortunately, for him, the elevation of another human to uniqueness necessarily devalues and demeans him (and all other humans).[40]

Not coincidentally, the quest for the historical Judas is only a minor sidebar in the larger, more significant quest for the historical Jesus.[41] Moreover, even when the historical Judas becomes the subject of concentrated attention, the questions, tone, and conclusions are set by Christian theology. Thus, in an influential analysis of Judas as a revolutionary, De Quincey traces Judas' motive and actions to his mistaken belief that Jesus has an earthly kingdom in mind or, more simply and more theologically, to Judas' fundamental spiritual blindness (1897: 8:177, 181).[42] Judas fails

---

modern Christian identity. Non-Christians working in this research are still forming modern academic identity, and, as such, their work is still mythic or religious. The historical Jesus researchers engage in myth or, more precisely, the historical Jesus is a myth, "a strategy for dealing with a situation [modernity]." The historical Jesus deals with the incongruity between the tradition and the present. It adapts Jesus Christ, the supreme icon/ideal of Western culture, to modernity in order to negotiate a (modern, Christian) space to live. For a general description of this type of religious or mythic work, see J. Smith, 1978: 290–91, 299–302. For specific discussion of the mythic work here, see the references in n36 and the discussion in Chapter 6 below. Recent discussions of the mythic use of Jesus, as opposed to the institutional Christ, in American popular culture make similar comments. See, e.g., Prothero, 2003; Fox, 2004; and Walsh, 2003: 173–85.

39. The famous analysis of the idealization of this figure is Schweitzer, 1968. Cf. Pelikan, 1985.

40. The most famous claim that the divinity of Christ demeans other humans is Emerson's "The Divinity School Address," (1998: 103–17).

41. Thus, R. Brown deals with the historical Judas in an appendix (1994: 2:1394–1418). Meier finds the historical Judas important primarily because he provides historical evidence for the Twelve (2001: 3:142–45).

42. See also n37. Although he is writing fiction in "Three Versions of Judas," Borges rightly observes that the scholars interested in the historical Judas before De Quincey were largely German. Klassen traces De Quincey's heritage to Friedrich Gottlieb Klopstock, *The Messiah* (1773) (1996: 20, 26n35). He also notes that the only full length

because he attempts "to forward the counsels of God by weapons borrowed from the armoury of darkness" or because he seeks to fulfill "his master's will, but by methods running counter to that master's will" (1897: 8:186, 194). Theology or spiritual matters are beyond the human Judas. Not surprisingly, Judas' death and eternal fate fascinates (the Christian) De Quincey more than Judas' motivation does (1897: 8:184). The issues De Quincey raises about Judas are those of Christian theology. Such theology demeans Judas to an inferior status simply because he is a human. On this point, Maccoby's thesis is compelling: the rehabilitation of Judas waits upon the dismantling of Christian theology (1992: 166–68).

Even in Klassen's compassionate reconstruction of the historical Judas, a Christian theology (or ethic) founds the work:

> we as individuals face the same test as Judas. How can the encounter with Jesus and the good news he proclaimed be transformed into action? How do we relate to those who once were faithful followers of Jesus who appear to turn against us when they or we leave our community? Such an examination brings us to the very heart of the message of Jesus. (1996: 24)[43]

Theologians have long used Judas so. Paffenroth observes that Judas has provided interpreters with lessons in sin, the wages of sin, evil, free will and determinism, trust, hope, forgiveness of self and others, and so forth. Accordingly, Judas is a Christian *object* lesson, a tool in Christian discourse.[44] Following Karl Barth, Paffenroth concludes that Judas provides lessons in Christianity's central paradoxes, particularly that of the incarnation (2001b: 139–42). Not incidentally, that is precisely the mystery that fascinates Runeberg's first Judas and leads to his self-destruction. Given Christian theology, Judas' fate is a fait accompli. His degradation is the logical conclusion of Christian metaphysics. Christian Judases are necessarily humiliated figures even if they are Jesus' premier disciple.

---

treatment of Judas in English before Hyam Maccoby's 1992 work was R. B. Halas, 1946 (Klassen, 1996: 59n19). Klassen provides a helpful review of recent German work, most of which takes a redaction history approach. Cf. also Klauck, 1987.

43. Cf. the ethical "message" of the 2004 TV movie *Judas*; or the collection of poems by Kennelly, *The Book of Judas*, which reflects on Judas and betrayal in order to unlearn hate. Kennelly claims that the (aesthetic) imagination is the most effective weapon against hate (1991: 9–11).

44. One of the points, if not the point, of Paffenroth's work is that Judas is as mysterious and complex as any other person and, therefore, beyond simple judgments (2001b: xii, 142–44). The structure of Paffenroth's work helpfully suggests many facets of this complexity; nonetheless, the subtitles of each of Paffenroth's chapters begin with "object of ..." The Judases, i.e., are creations of Christian discourse.

Mere Ideological Sign

A different kind of theology determines the Judases of the literary criticism of the gospels that aims at a holistic reading of individual gospels.[45] In such criticism, everything in the narrative, even insignificant details like Judas, "fits" the larger whole. This larger whole is the message or ideology that a particular reading attributes to a particular gospel. If these literary Judases are no longer cogs in the divine machine, they remain mere signs in a larger ideological system.[46]

Thus, in Mark, Judas is a device merging notions of the infinite book, the plot of the authorities, and the imperial discourse of Roman crucifixion into Mark's divine passion plot.[47] But, for apocalyptic Mark, Judas' betrayal is also a consequence of the general apocalyptic crisis engulfing everyone.[48] The apocalyptic failure of all humans allows Mark to leave Jesus heroically alone at the cross as God's only faithful representative even as the apocalyptic crisis leaves him God-forsaken. Thereby, Jesus models faithfulness for Mark's readers in similar circumstances (see Mk 13:20). Jesus alone accomplishes what others, like the sleeping disciples, twice warned to watch (13:32-37; 14:32-42), could not. Consequently, Mark's Judas does not differ noticeably from other humans. The only real

---

45. For a criticism of the implicit theology involved in what was then called narrative criticism of the gospels, see S. Moore, 1989. Arnal notes that some in the so-called Third Quest make similar assumptions about the coherence and reliability of gospel narration (2005: 42–44).

46. Historical criticism departs from the canon by looking for a history behind the text (or reads a text as historically, rather than divinely, determined). The resulting secret plots and the supporting notion of truth, however, differ from canonical readings imperceptibly. Literary criticism departs from the canon by reading one gospel instead of the fourfold Gospel, but when it uses holistic controls (i.e., when a text is made to harmonize with itself to the extent that the reading silences discordant elements in the text), one again finds only slight departures from canonical readings.

47. On these points, the canonical gospels agree. Paffenroth notes that the Judases of the Synoptic Gospels all fulfill scripture—i.e., they are all oracular—while individual gospels deploy Judas in terms of special ideological concerns: Mark and the failure of the Twelve; Matthew and the indictment of the religious leaders; Luke and the inevitability of just punishment; John and the evil world (2001b: 10, 12–13, 18–22, 33–36).

48. Literary readings of the gospels are legion. The discussion above adopts fairly common imputations, with no attempt to argue the case: Mark and apocalyptic; Matthew and Torah; Luke and history; and John and gnosticism. For supporting references, see Walsh, 2003. For a discussion of the literary search for the "character" of Judas implicit in such literary readings, see Walsh, 2006b.

3 The Cooperative Judas   71

difference, for example, between the Markan Judas and the Markan Peter is that Jesus predicts woe for one and a reunion in Galilee for the other. After all, God has handed over (betrayed?) everyone, even Jesus (15:34), to the apocalypse (4:10-12; 13:20). Everyone fails sans divine deliverance in Mark's misanthropic determinism (4:10-12). Mark does not care about any human, least of all Judas. Judas simply helps Mark to draw out its cross-martyr myth and ethic and to define its times as apocalyptic. Brother shall betray brother, indeed (13:12).

Matthew's Torah-ideology requires a more responsible Judas. Accordingly, Matthew's Judas suggests payment for his betrayal (Mt. 26:14-15). As discussed above, the Matthean Jesus' enigmatic responses to Judas at the Supper (26:25) and at the arrest (26:50) may also suggest a Judas who creates himself vis-à-vis oracle and Jesus' commands (or questions). The repentance of Matthew's Judas is also consistent with the notion of a responsible Judas. Moreover, as Klassen argues, this repentance may also cohere with Torah and Jewish customs (1996: 96-115; Unnik, 1974). Unfortunately for Judas, even if this is the case, he follows the wrong Torah. Matthew's Jesus has established a new, messianic Torah, different from that of the scribes.[49] In this context, Judas' address of Jesus as "Rabbi," rather than "Lord" (26:25, 49), "outs" him. Matthew's Judas is simply not a "doer of the (messianic) word" (7:21-27; 25:31-46). Instead, he symbolizes the fate of those who reject Matthew's Jesus. They build their house upon the sand. They bring innocent blood upon themselves. Their actions are suicidal. For Matthew, Judas is a sign of this opposition, of innocent blood, and of the messianic Torah.[50]

As Conzelmann notes, Luke's Jesus parts the ages as the moment in salvation history that fulfills previous oracles and extends God's beneficence to the Gentiles (1961). Jesus wrestles with Satan in the wilderness before his ministry begins (4:1-13) and effectively banishes Satan (4:13) from the divinely favored time of his healing ministry (4:16-30). In fact, while there are demons and those who "test" Jesus in his ministry, Satan does not return until he enters Judas in the passion narrative to facilitate the opposition's plot against Jesus (22:3). While Luke is somewhat paratactic in the passage (22:1-6), Satan's arrival connects the religious leaders' search for a way to dispatch Jesus with an otherwise unmotivated disciple who betrays Jesus. Satan's possession of Judas transforms

---

49. For a discussion of the problems a contemporary Jew has with the Torah of Matthew's Jesus, see Neusner, 1993.

50. For Matthew, Judas points to Jesus' innocence. He also points, however, to those guilty of Jesus' innocent blood, i.e., to the religious leaders. See Nortje, 1994.

him into Jesus' adversary and brings about Jesus' trials (πειρασμός; cf. 4:13; 22:28).[51] While Luke does not carefully distinguish between Jesus' various adversaries, Luke does distinguish Judas from the other disciples. Only Judas falls to Satan's sifting (22:31). Jesus protectively prays for the other disciples, particularly Peter (22:31-34), and repeatedly encourages the disciples to pray that they may not enter into trials (πειρασμός; 11:4; 22:40, 46).[52] Instead of these supportive prayers, Judas receives a damning oracle (22:21-22). Supernaturally determined by both Satan and oracle, the Lukan Judas is an acceptable loss. He is so far away that he cannot even complete the betraying kiss. The Lukan Jesus stops him with a peremptory question (22:48). Lost, Judas is soon horribly destroyed. Thereby, Judas reveals the fate of the wicked (Acts 1:18; cf. Lk. 19:41-44; 23:28-31; Acts 12:23) and the ultimate triumph of God's salvation. Accordingly, Judas is easily replaced (Acts 1:20) as are all others who will not accept God's salvation in Jesus (Acts 7:1-8:4; 13:46; 18:6; 28:23-28).[53]

John's Judas signifies that gospel's metaphysical judgment upon the world's spiritual blindness.[54] Luke's Judas "becomes a traitor" and is possessed by Satan (Lk. 6:16; 22:3). John's Judas is a devil from the beginning (Jn 6:70-71). He is also one who does not believe (6:64) and the one who has not been chosen (6:65). John repeats the same themes in the foot washing scene. The devil controls Judas (13:2, 27). Moreover, Jesus describes Judas—apparently to his face—as not clean, not blessed,

---

51. Luke never makes Judas the agency of the testing (πειρασμός) of Jesus. Judas is merely the agent of Satan, who is responsible for Jesus' testing (4:13). Cecil B. DeMille's *The King of Kings* (1927) imagines Judas as tempter more directly. When DeMille's Jesus arrives triumphantly in Jerusalem, DeMille interlocks scenes in which Judas and, then, Satan tempt Jesus with kingly power in the Temple. In dramatic contrast, DeMille's Jesus stands in the Temple holding a sacrificial lamb. The editorial cuts merge Judas and Satan (cf. Lk. 22:3) and depict Judas as Jesus' tempter. Ray's subsequent *King of Kings* (1961) eliminates Satan from its story, but its De Quincy Judas also "tests"—the word is used by the film's narrator—Jesus with the offer of monarchy.

52. Judas is presumably present on the first occasion, but not the second, as he would have been arranging Jesus' arrest.

53. This Judas is also a sign of the apostolic church's move to the Gentiles. See Chapter 4 below.

54. Here, John has clear affinities with neoplatonism and gnosticism. Orthodox theologians would, of course, argue that notions of creation and incarnation (see, ptc., Jn 1:1–18) separate John from the gnostics. Nonetheless, John's ethical, metaphysical dualism sounds more like (the gnostic) Runeberg's reflections than any of the other gospels and more like the devaluation of this world that many critics associate with Christianity generally.

and not chosen (13:10-11, 18). As in Luke, Jesus does not protect or pray for Judas. Instead, Judas is the one destined to be lost (Jn 13:18; 17:12). Appropriately, when Judas leaves Jesus, he hurries into the night or away from the Johannine light (13:30). Accordingly, John says nothing about Judas until he returns from and in the dark, with torches, to arrest the Johannine light. The KJV rendering of Jn 1:5 captures John's ideological point succinctly: "the light shone in the darkness and the darkness comprehended it not" (1:5). The darkness has no chance. Even with torches, the arresting party cannot find Jesus until he reveals himself (18:5). John's Judas is a sign of that darkness and the sum of John's reflections upon evil: (1) those who oppose Jesus belong to the world and to Satan; they are evil; (2) those who oppose Jesus are not chosen by God; they are determined in advance; and (3) those who oppose Jesus are ethically suspect in every regard; they are wicked (cf. 12:6).

Conscious Judases? Belief, Resistance, and Horror

In this type of literary reading, the ideology that a literary reading imputes to a gospel forms Judas. He is a sign, for example, within and of apocalyptic fatalism, a Torah squabble, an emerging Gentile Christianity, or a sectarian hostility to the world. In an important sense, then, this ideological Judas differs little from historical or theological Judases. The ideology that creates a literary Judas is as hidden and as determinative as any providence. Unlike Runeberg's cooperative Judas, none of these literary Judases reveal any consciousness of their dependence on ideology. They are objects, signs in a discourse system, not humans. They do not have the "creature consciousness" that Rudolf Otto associates with human religious experience, the experience of creatures that recognize their finitude in the face of the overwhelming divine (or ideology) (1958: 12–40). If these Judases revealed such awareness, they would form better simulacra of modern true believers.

Of course, for moderns, the experience of human insignificance in the face of "reality" is not necessarily religious. According to Sigmund Freud, the basic human experience here is alienation or cosmic fear, not awe. And, for Freud, this fear is irreligious in the "truest sense of the word" (1989: 41-42).[55] For Albert Camus, this basic human alienation arises

---

55. For a fiction exploring this cosmic terror, see Lovecraft, 2005. Cosmic terror is a quite secular take on Otto's religious awe even though Lovecraft populates this novel and other fictions with ancient deities. Lovecraft advocates flight from, not

from the disparity between an irrational world and the human desire for meaning. For Camus, this absurd situation is so dire that one must consider whether to commit suicide or not. Camus ultimately rejects suicide in both its physical and philosophical forms. The latter handles the dilemma of the absurd by sacrificing human reason in favor of a belief in (irrational) mystery (or some secret plot). For Camus, such suicide abases the human and deifies the absurd.

True believers are such suicides. They willingly give themselves up to the theological abasement of oracles and the secret plan. Canonical and literary Judases may not have enough consciousness to cooperate in their self-destruction. The Judases of *The Last Temptation of Christ* and of *Godspell*, who submit reluctantly to irresistible oracles and/or Jesus' commands, better exemplify such suicidal cooperation. The Judases of Runeberg and the Sect of the Thirty are, of course, the premier disciples of such degradation.

For Camus, the "better" response to the absurd is revolt, a conscious acceptance of the inevitable, unceasing tension between the meaningless world and meaning seeking humans (1991: 28–50, 119–23).[56] As discussed previously, such revolt resembles Borges' ethic (or aesthetic) of near belief quite closely.[57] Unlike John Vincent Moon and Runeberg's Judas, some Borgesian characters come close to a fictional liberation from the degradations of true belief only to fall short.

The librarian in "The Library of Babel," for example, knows that the infinite library evokes a veritable Babel of ethical choices, some of which he catalogues (1962: 79–88). The first response is joy because all the librarians feel themselves in charge of a secret treasure. Then, belief develops in the Vindications, the prophecies that justify the world and every individual human. Consequently, some librarians spend their lives searching for their specific vindicating book, falling into murderous violence and madness in the search because they forget that the odds of finding that one

---

cooperation with, that which evokes cosmic terror. The canonical and literary Judases have no such option. They are trapped in theological/ideological worlds.

56. Camus illustrates such revolt with happy Sisyphus. He asks his readers to consider Sisyphus, the Titan condemned to roll a rock up a hill repeatedly throughout the ages, happy in the very moment when he begins the trudge down the hill to begin the task again. The choice of this example is apropos because it corresponds to Camus' opening description of the absurd, which is a description of a day in the banal life of a modern. Camus' ethic resembles Nietzsche's call to *amor fati* in the face of the eternal return (1974: 276, 341).

57. See Chapter 1 for a comparison of Borges and Camus and a discussion of Borges' fantastic fiction.

book in an infinite library are virtually zero. A general depression follows in which various heretics try to recreate the meaningful book through dice and luck. Thereafter, purifiers try vainly to eliminate all useless books while yet others begin to believe in the divine Man of the Book who has himself seen the infinite book that others have not. Having wasted his life in similar adventures, the librarian has become more reflective in his old age, but he still believes that the infinite book exists and that the world has a meaning more important than his existence. That fateful choice of cooperative belief renders all people mere phantoms; moreover, violence increases; suicides multiply; and the human race heads to extinction while the Library promises to last forever (1962: 83–87).[58]

The narrator of "The Babylonian Lottery" draws nearer to the aesthetic revelation, but only after he leaves Babylon. Then, he recalls that a relatively unsuccessful lottery (fate) gave way to a successful one when the Company took control, conducted the lottery in secret, and extended its control to everyone and everything (an enveloping secret plot). Moreover, the divine Company and its secrecy, like that of God, has generated all matter of opinions, including the "vile belief" that whether the Company exists or not matters little as chance rules all (1962: 65–72). Finally, however, even away from Babylon, the narrator simply cannot embrace such chance.

The narrator of "The Babylonian Lottery" and the librarian of Babel, like Runeberg and the sectarians, ultimately refuse to give up hope in the secret meaning. Borges, however, knows that such magic does not belong to his modern readers' ordinary reality (1999b: 80). For Freud, as well, such magic belongs to the uncanny, to rejected superstitions arising in the midst of anxious times. For these moderns, the true believers' secret providence plot is nothing less than horror.

The protagonist of Richard Fleischer's 1962 film, *Barabbas*, based on Pär Lagerkvist's novel by the same name, lives consciously in this horror. The film opens with Barabbas languishing in a dungeon during Jesus' Roman trial. Fatefully, Barabbas is set free and leaves prison with Jesus' blood literally on his hands because he has stumbled blindly against the post where Jesus has been scourged. While everyone knows Barabbas has been chosen to live in place of Jesus, Barabbas never understands the reason for this choice nor can he escape this fate despite a life that includes debauchery, banditry, imprisonment in sulfur mines, a stint as a gladiator, and a failed attempt at initiating the Christian apocalypse. At the end of his life,

---

58. One might read the entire story as an allegory of the history of religion or of the history of responses to the infinite book.

Barabbas dies alone on a cross in the growing dark, gasping, "Darkness … I give myself up into your keeping." The words are perplexing. Does "darkness" (followed by that long pause) simply refer to the lighting of the scene? Does the pronoun "your," then, refer to something like the Christian God? Is this a conversion at death's door? Or, does "darkness" name that to which Barabbas finally capitulates? Does it matter? Either option deifies mystery. In either case, Barabbas commits philosophical suicide. Barabbas' "darkness" does, however, name a modern outsider's recognition of the horror of secret providential plots and his inability to escape them.[59]

Throughout the film, Barabbas lives in the dark. Released from the dungeon at the film's beginning, Barabbas sees Jesus as a shadow in brilliant sunlight. He sees Jesus similarly during the eclipse at the cross. He arrives too late at the tomb to see the resurrected Jesus and judges the apostles' claims to be talk about shadows. Paired with blind men throughout the film and repeatedly in the dark underground—the mines, the arena, the catacombs—Barabbas repeatedly laments that God should make himself "plain." God never does. Thus, *Barabbas* begins and ends in something like the Johannine dark that finally envelopes Judas. *Barabbas*, however, concentrates on the one left outside, so one can see what Judas' story might look like if he were conscious of his forced cooperation with the secret plan. Here is what it means to know oneself damned by magical mentions and fate. Here is what it means to be an outsider trapped in a religious story (see Walsh, 2008a: 113–29).

While *Barabbas* reveals the horror implicit in the secret plot, it fails to teach methods of resistance. For that, one needs a character as aware and as verbose as Job. Despite the frequency of stories presuming Judas to be Jesus' intimate, premier disciple, Job-Judases are quite rare.[60] The Judas in Norman Jewison's *Jesus Christ Superstar* (1973), however, comes quite close.[61]

---

59. Lagerkvist has Barabbas speak directly to the darkness (1968: 148–49).

60. Paffenroth mentions only two possibilities, *Jesus Christ Superstar* and Topping, *Jewish Flower Child* (1970) (2001b: 85–99). Both Judases curse God and die. Thus, their stories end more abruptly than Job's. Many of Judas' speeches in Jeffers, "Dear Judas" (1971); and Kennelly, *The Book of Judas* (1991), have a Jobian quality as their Judases lament their scripted fate. In fact, every character in Jeffers, "Dear Judas," laments the "net" in which they are caught and their "dupery" by God. More horribly, the poem imagines the characters as remnants haunting a garden and repeatedly reenacting the same story. Only the Jesus-remnant betrays any consciousness of this reiterated fate.

61. On a more canonical reading, Judas, who wears distinctive red clothing, might be the film's Satan, testing Jesus.

3 The Cooperative Judas

Throughout the film, which is based on an earlier rock opera, Judas' voice competes with Jesus'. As the film begins, the troupe disembarks their tour bus and dons costumes for a passion play. Judas walks away alone before the music for "Jesus Christ Superstar" begins. Alone in the wilderness, Judas' first song expresses his repeated theme that Jesus is "just a man."[62] Unfortunately, the film's Jesus believes he is what "they" say he is—Savior, Messiah, or Superstar. "They" represents the fans and media, very modern versions of the infinite book, which produce Jesus' celebrity.[63] Judas desperately wants to strip "this myth" from "the man" Jesus because he fears it will destroy his friend and his people. Instead of trying to force Jesus toward political revolution (as De Quincey's Judas does), this Judas, like Caiaphas (in John and in this film), tries to stop Jesus from going "too far" and bringing political destruction upon them all.[64]

Judas' opposition is unsuccessful. His opening song ends with a repeated, plaintive appeal, "Listen to me." Jesus does not. In fact, in that opening sequence, Jesus strides purposefully past the anguished Judas, trailing an entourage. Nonetheless, Judas does not relent. Unlike the canonical Judas, this Judas has a strong, persistent voice. The film as a whole privileges his perspective, rather than Jesus'. The film begins and ends with Judas, so that Judas thoroughly encloses Jesus.[65] In fact, Judas so dominates the film that rumors still circulate that the filmmakers toyed with naming their project *The Gospel according to Judas*.

As Jesus' popularity and threat grows, Judas makes a deal with Caiaphas, whom he calls "friend." Judas wants no reward; he simply wants the authorities to tell him that he will not be "damned for all time."[66] The

---

62. This idea also appears in Mary Magdalene's more famous song, "I Don't Know How to Love Him."

63. *Monty Python's Life of Brian* (1979) and *Being There* (1979) are other films, that investigate the human production of messiahs.

64. One might read Judas' struggle as an attempt to "keep" religion out of politics and in its proper modern place, the subjectivity (or spirituality) of the individual. See the discussion of spirituality in Chapter 4.

65. One might read this enclosure as depicting a Judas that determines Jesus, rather than vice versa. Cf. the discussion of Scorsese's "buddy" Judas and that of the ringmaster Judas in *Godspell* above. Roger Young's 1999 *Jesus* portrays a Judas that tries to force Jesus (cf. the De Quincey Judas). In that movie, Jesus refuses to force humans to his will, believing that they deserve the freedom to accept God or not. By contrast, Judas and Satan try to force others to their will. The binary creates a clear ethical stance although the ethic is modern, not canonical.

66. This Judas seems to know his Christian mythological role all too well. Cf. the Judases in Jeffers, 1971; Kennelly, 1991; and Rayner, 1969.

conflict between Jesus and Judas climaxes at the picnic-like Last Supper. A despondent Jesus laments his disciples' general ignorance and lack of concern for him as he builds to the oracular betrayal. That scene devolves into a shouting match between Jesus and Judas with Jesus calling Judas "a Judas" and Judas wondering aloud how it would affect Jesus' ambition if he did not betray him. Jesus, then, chases Judas away "to do his job." When Judas pauses, Jesus follows haltingly and angrily insists on Judas' mission even though Judas denounces it. Lamenting that Jesus has no plan, Judas runs away through disturbed sheep.

After Judas' betrayal sets the passion under way, Judas repents. He complains again that Jesus does not listen to him, that he has only followed Jesus' directions, that he will be saddled with Jesus' innocent blood, and that he will be dragged through the slime and the mud. Once again, he complains that the does not know how to love Jesus, who is just a man. He also wonders whether Jesus loves and cares for him. Receiving no replies to his heaven-directed queries, he decides he has been used by God for bloody and mysterious divine crimes. Railing against a silent God whom he declares his murderer, he hangs himself.

But, Judas' story is not yet over. Instead of the Via Dolorosa, the film offers a transfigured Christ welcoming a white-clad Judas who descends from the heavens on a lighted cross. This Judas, like that of *The Last Temptation of Christ*, is Jesus' deadly, heavenly destiny. While still questioning Jesus, Judas is now part of the heavenly chorus singing "Jesus Christ Superstar." While questions remain, this adoring chorus overwhelms any opposition. Even here, however, Judas' story is not over. In the final scene, as the troupe, now finished with its passion play and out of costume, boards the bus, Judas lingers looking at something in the distance. A final shot shows the audience what Judas has seen: an empty cross on a hill with the sun setting behind it. Once again, Judas is little more than Jesus' cross.

While the film flirts at length with a railing Job-Judas, the penultimate Superstar scene undercuts Judas' questions and complaints. The adoring chorus effectively absorbs Judas' dissenting voice. Moreover, despite the opposing voices of Judas and Mary Magdalene, the film's plot is quite canonical. Jesus and Judas play their fated roles.[67] Nonetheless, Judas' strong, dissenting voice almost escapes the myth, the fate of the infinite

---

67. In an important scene, Pilate refers to Jesus as an innocent puppet. Judas descending from heaven on a lighted white cross in an elaborate song-and-dance routine well summarizes the divinely determined nature of both the Judas and the Jesus of this film.

book. In one dramatic moment, Judas asks, "What if I don't [betray you] and ruin all your plans?" What, indeed? Unfortunately, for those with desires for fictional liberation, Judas falls back into the secret plot and sighs, "I must betray you."

For moderns, this retreat may resemble Job's final and rather disappointing repentance. Many moderns desire a Job who holds his own vis-à-vis the divine whirlwind without repenting.[68] A Judas-Job who resists Jesus' oracular demands or simply "cuts and runs," walking off the murderous, suicidal divine job, should be as appealing to moderns. As discussed above, Scorsese's *The Last Temptation of Christ* (1988) imagines such a fantasy for Jesus, albeit temporarily, but not for Judas. Several moments occur in that film, however, where one might imagine a less oracular Judas. What if Judas simply rejects Jesus' multiple seductions?[69] What if, when Judas arrives to threaten Jesus the cross-maker early in the film, he ignores Jesus' whining about a divine plan and either kills him there or simply walks away? What if Judas manfully stands by his initial threat and kills Jesus when Jesus deviates from revolt? What if Judas simply walks off the Jesus-job? What if one imagines Judas married with children, instead of Jesus?[70] What kind of fantasy would that be? It would certainly be one further from Christian discourse than the fantasy that Scorsese offers at the end of his film.

Borges never imagines Judas walking off the divine, mythological job either; nevertheless, Borges refuses to bow before the fate that he plays with in his fictions. Instead of submission, in a rewriting of the Lord's Prayer, he calls for reason and justice on the part of humans: "The designs of the universe are unknown to us, but we do know that to think with lucidity and to act with fairness is to aid those designs (which shall never be revealed to us)" (1999a: 339).[71] Despite the tentative "aid those

---

68. As noted in Chapter 2, Borges' own sympathies lie with Job. True believers often excuse Job's repentance by arguing that he has no other choice in the face of the divine sovereignty. Some ancient societies, however, imagined trickster figures, like Prometheus, who successfully resisted divine plans. The biblical Jacob might be a similar character, and some interpret Job's repentance as an ironic attempt to humor a petulant deity. See J. Williams, 1971; and D. Robertson, 1973.

69. Jesus predicts betrayal so often that the disciples ultimately feel it a fait accompli in Brelich's *The Work of Betrayal* (1988: 2–6).

70. Paffenroth ends his work delightfully with such a fantasy for Judas (2001b: 143–44). In one of the poems in Kennelly, *The Book of Judas*, Judas laments that others think him divine or devil, instead of just a man (1991: 299).

71. Similarly, in "Fragments of an Apocryphal Gospel," Borges rewrites the teaching

designs," the repeated references to mystery ("unknown to us"; "never be revealed to us") dominate. The result is an ethic of present responsibility, not one of commitment to some secret plan.[72]

Fictional Lessons: Rejecting Secret Plots

The rarity of trickster Judases is unfortunate because true believers are as common in modernity as in antiquity. The quintessentially modern form of secret plots is the conspiracy theory.[73] Umberto Eco's *Foucault's Pendulum* nicely displays the fictional and deadly nature of such beliefs.[74] In the novel, a group of intellectuals who work for the same publishing firm create a secret Templar Plan (always capitalized in the novel).[75] Unlike Runeberg, Casaubon, the novel's protagonist, is skeptical of the Plan and is contemptuous of those who believe that the world has a hidden meaning. His best friend, Belbo, also repeatedly cautions against such prideful pretensions to knowledge by saying, "Take out the cork" (1990: 48, 418, 493).

Nonetheless, the friends' experiences in publishing occult books and with a game they play inventing a meaning for a secret message of the Templars leads them to believe in the Plan. Belbo, like all true believers, forgets that the Plan is their fiction. Casaubon himself laments that his friends have lost their sense of metaphor, a Borgesian awareness of the distance between language and reality. Unlike Runeberg's Judas, Casaubon remains aware that the world is actually a harmless enigma made terrible by one's insistence on a secret truth (1990: 81). He is also aware, as are

---

of Jesus in order to deny providence in favor of human action, justice, and present—not other-worldly—happiness (2000a: 292–95).

72. Borges' rewritings of Jesus' sayings also routinely deny ethical calculus. One must invest in the present because one does not know enough to judge future or final results. Cf. the rejection of the world of grace in Camus, 1956; and the ethic imagined in Camus, 1991: 117–18.

73. Conspiracy theories may be endemic to the modern mythology of the individual. At least, modern individualism seems to be built to a certain extent on a desperate rebellion against the ubiquitous, inescapable System (whether it is spelled empire, bureaucracy, capitalism, or otherwise). See Cohen and Taylor, 1992; and Walsh, 2007.

74. Eco has read his Borges. Borges is the name of the murderous librarian in Eco's first novel, *The Name of the Rose*. In his second novel, *Foucault's Pendulum*, Eco makes reference to Borges' "Funes, the Memorious" (1990: 152–53). Eco also structures this novel in a Borgesian fashion according to Kabbalistic notions about the Tree of the Sefirot.

75. The Templars are perennial favorites of conspiracy theorists. See, e.g., D. Brown, 2003.

3 *The Cooperative Judas* 81

other characters, that the only secret the Templars—or any other secret group—possesses is that there is a secret (meaning).[76] Casaubon also has the good fortune of relationships with various women who immerse him in daily life, rather than in the Plan. The most important of these women is Lia, who bears his child. At one point, Lia also offers an important, alternative interpretation of the secret message of the Templars, reading it simply as a pedestrian laundry list (1990: 438–45). She also resolutely insists that Casaubon's carnal life with her is all there is to life. There is no secret meaning beyond the mundane. In the last part of the novel, Casaubon increasingly realizes what he has lost by valuing the Plan over Lia and wishes (vainly?) that he could be with her again.

Unfortunately, as Casaubon remarks, if one acts like the Plan exists—that is, if one is a true believer—it does exist.[77] Fortuitously, for Eco's readers, Casaubon also reveals the human reason for creating such Plans. Secret Plans save humans from their frustration with their life by attributing their ills to some hidden plotter. But, Casaubon also knows (and relearns) that humans have a choice (not a fate) in life: one either invents a plotter (secret plan) or one takes responsibility for one's own life (1990: 511–513). Unfortunately, such earthly wisdom comes too late for Casaubon. As he hides in a museum, Casaubon sees Belbo killed by a secret society when he refuses to reveal the non-existent secret.[78] Casaubon, waiting for the society to find him at the novel's end, intends to resist them heroically as well. As he waits, he reflects upon the beauty of the life he has lost (in a pastoral scene) by creating the Plan.

The end is more hopeful than some of Borges' fictions, but it is not as hopeful as the end of *Candide*, to which Casaubon's pastoral fantasies allude. Candide rejects the secret Plan (specifically Leibnitz's idealist notion of the best of all possible worlds) in order to tend his garden. What would it hurt to imagine Judas' bloody field (Acts 1:18–19) as such a garden?[79] What it would gain is the near belief, the hesitancy, at which Borges' fiction always gestures. It would gain Casaubon's awareness of

---

76. Cf. Borges' delightful "The Sect of the Phoenix" (1962: 163–66); and Chapter 5 below.

77. Cf. Pascal's famous remark that the cure for unbelief is to participate repeatedly in the Mass. Cited in Pojman, 1994: 116.

78. The novel begins with Casaubon hiding in the museum and most of the novel is, thus, a flashback detailing how Casaubon came to this place. The flashback gives the novel a sense of inevitability similar to that created by the canon's oracles.

79. For a story of Judas' acquisition of this field and death there, which avoids the calumny of Acts, see Rayner, 1969: 196–98.

metaphor. It would gain an awareness of the danger of the human tendency to true belief and the possibilities of fictional liberation.[80]

To realize the worth of this life, one needs to give up true belief in secret plots (cf. Walsh, 2007). In order to avoid philosophical suicide and the acceptable losses of the un-chosen, one needs to abandon election. China Miéville's *Un Lun Dun* plays with such possibilities. The story opens in typical *Alice in Wonderland* or *Chronicles of Narnia* fashion with children going through a fantastic portal to a fantasy world (Un Lun Dun, i.e., not London). There, things turn messianic because Zanna, one of the child travelers, has been chosen as the One, the Shwazzy, to deliver Un Lun Dun from the Smog that threatens to destroy it. Given the messianism, Prophetseers naturally play a major role. They include the personified Book, Mortar, and Lectern. Matters become more intriguing, however, when Zanna fails to fulfill the—admittedly rather confused—prophecies about her victory over the Smog. In fact, she is injured in her opening battle and taken back to London by her funny sidekick, Deeba. Meanwhile, the Prophetseers and the Book are horrified that things did not go as written. The Book, in particular, lapses into a funk of despair and self-doubt (2007: 103–106).

Back in London, Zanna recovers, but remembers nothing. When Deeba, however, learns that the Un Lun Duners rely upon traitors in London, she deciphers a page of the Book given her as a parting gift and returns to Un Lun Dun to join their fight against the Smog. Part of her successful struggle includes the rehabilitation of the now, quite moody Book. Deeba needs the Book, knowing that it contains useful information, even though it is also often wrong. Despite her youth, Deeba knows (the Borgesian lesson of) the difference between language and reality. Accordingly, Deeba interprets the Book quite freely, even dismissing major steps in a long quest that the Book says are necessary (2007: 212, 222–28, 272–75). Lacking time, Deeba simply jumps to the end and, then, uses her ability to interpret the Book to convince others to go along with

---

80. Borges' own, less hopeful version of this story is "Death and the Compass" (1962: 129–41). Its protagonist, the detective Lönnrot, refuses to believe the murder of a rabbi a coincidence and studies rabbinic books obsessively until he deduces that the crime was an attempt to reveal the secret, four-letter name of God. Moving through the epiphany of each letter in a new murder, Lönnrot finally finds himself the captive of the criminal Red Scharlach and his men. Scharlach, having learned of Lönnrot's obsession and desiring revenge on Lönnrot for his role in Scharlach's brother's arrest, has built the whole plot, with Lönnrot's cooperation, upon the absolutely coincidental murder of the rabbi. Lönnrot, then, helps create the secret plot that brings him to his fate. An acceptance of coincidence might be healthier.

3 *The Cooperative Judas*   83

her made-up-as-she-goes plan. By far, the biggest change, however, is the fact that Deeba, the Un-Chosen, is now the messiah or, more accurately, is part of the group that saves Un Lun Dun. In one of the most amusing scenes, Deeba denies her destiny as the "funny sidekick" by saying that no one is just a sidekick (or phantom) (2007: 227–28).[81]

Further subverting the notions of infinite books, Deeba gains control of the hypostatic words spoken by Mr. Speaker. In fact, she escapes two dilemmas simply by convincing words that they do not have to follow the will of their creator. They have a life of their own. They can revolt (2007: 244–47, 374). Even more humorously and subversively, Deeba finally triumphs over the Smog when she realizes that what the Book and the Prophetseers think is a misprint is, in fact, the saving knowledge. The canonical interpretation says that the Smog is afraid of "nothing but the Ungun," but the Book admits that the text is really "nothing and the Ungun" (2007: 274–76, 407). A strong reader, Deeba fires the unloaded Ungun at the Smog and defeats it. In the finale, the Book itself converts to a belief in coincidence, opining in the spirit of the novel that destiny is bunk. Moreover, the Book forces the Prophetseers to change their name to Suggesters. Deeba, as everyone notes, is impressive and heroic simply because she is not fated to be the hero. As one character notes, "Where's the skill in being a hero if you were always destined to do it?" Conversely, where is the shame in being a traitor if you were always destined to do it?

Miéville's novel is a modern coming-of-age story and reflects the values of modernity, rather than those of the culture that created the canonical Judas or even the culture(s) that created the cooperative Judas. Modernity calls for Deeba-Judases (who are un-chosen heroes) who walk away from, resist, or revise secret plans and oracular destinies, rather than cooperate with them. Modernity prefers the resistance of Job and of Oedipus, however futile, to the cooperative self-destruction of Jesus and Judas. For modernity, the canonical Jesus needs a loyal, resistant friend, not someone who is mere tool or mere yes-man.[82] Jesus needs a friend like Deeba or someone like Frodo's friend Sam in *The Lord of the Rings*. Jesus-Frodo needs a Sam-Judas to help them both resist the seductive pull of infinite power in the rings or oracles that would rule them all.

Runeberg's first Judas is not such a figure. He remains merely the cooperative sidekick of the canonical Jesus. Runeberg's first Judas does,

---

81. As Deeba switches places with the expected messiah, the Shwazzy, she does something like what Runeberg ultimately does with his three Judases. On fictional rivals as reversible roles, see Chapter 4 below.

82. Biff plays this role in C. Moore's amusing *Lamb* (2002).

however, display the degradation, humiliation, and self-destruction that true belief in oracles or in the secret plots of the infinite book necessarily entails. Runeberg's first Judas also clearly defines the ethical options that the infinite book creates: the self-destructive cooperation of Jesus and Judas; or the resistance of Deeba, Oedipus, Job, and Sisyphus. Despite the protestations of many theologians, neither the canonical nor cooperative Judas truly invites reflections on free will (and determinism). Both canonical and cooperative Judases abandon the possibility of free will by deifying an (absurd) infinite. In Camus' language, they are tokens of philosophical suicide. It takes (the possibility of) resistance in order to allow an exploration of free will.[83] Finally, Runeberg's first Judas already suggests the unethical nature of the devaluation of the world in neoplatonism, gnosticism, and Christianity. The next chapter explores this issue more fully.

83. Cf. *The Matrix* (1999), whose hero, Neo, becomes the messianic One only after the Oracle tells him that he is not the One and that he will soon have to make a choice to save himself or Morpheus. By electing to save Morpheus, however, Neo becomes the One. Later, another character tells Neo that the Oracle told Neo what he needed to hear, not the truth. The subterfuge allows a modern space for the (illusion of) freedom of choice absolutely necessary to the modern myth of individualism. The plotting, however, also raises significant questions about free will, which subsequent installments in the trilogy pursue. The result helpfully exposes free will and resistance as modern conceits or myths before which moderns would do well to hesitate. See Chapter 1 for Borges' own reluctance about modern individualism.

Chapter 4

THE ASCETIC JUDAS: JUDAS THE SCAPEGOAT AND JUDAS THE JEW

Runeberg's Second Judas: Unworthy to be Good: Runeberg and John

When the orthodox theologians accuse Runeberg of various heresies because of his first Judas, Runeberg abandons theology for ethics. Noting that the gospels do not deny Judas full standing as an apostle during Jesus' ministry, Runeberg argues that one must assume that Judas proclaims the kingdom, cures the sick, raises the dead, cleanses lepers, and casts out demons, with all the other disciples (cf. Mt. 10:7–8).[1] Moreover, like De Quincey, Runeberg insists that one should attribute the highest motives to one specially chosen by Christ. Instead of cupidity, then, Runeberg claims that Judas acts from "an opposite moving force," that is, from ascetic motives. By his betrayal, Judas piously denies himself the spirit and goodness.

Despite the narrator's claim that Runeberg abandons theology for ethic, theology lingers significantly in the background in this second Judas' metaphysical assumptions. This Judas bases his ascetic ethic on the neoplatonic or gnostic view of this world's inferiority to the spiritual world above. Like Paul, Runeberg's second Judas decides that only an ethic of human degradation properly acknowledges the metaphysical disparity between God and humans (1962: 154). A footnote expresses the ethic's consequence provocatively, "[V]irtue was 'a kind of impiety almost'" (1962: 154).[2] In order to be a true believer, then, Runeberg's second Judas betrays Jesus.

Borges' "Unworthy" relates a similar story. An elderly Jewish bookstore owner, Jacob Fischbein, tells one of his customers, the unnamed narrator of "Unworthy," a story of his youth (1999a: 352–57). As a poor,

---

1. Many critics make this point. See, e.g., Klauck, 1987, the subtitle of which is "a disciple of the Lord"; and Anderson, 1991: 31.
2. See the story's epigraph as well. The narrator explains the ethic by reference to 1 Cor. 1:31.

redheaded boy living in a poor neighborhood on the edge of the city, Jacob Fischbein adopts the name Santiago in order to adapt. His boyhood hero is a young gang leader, Francisco Ferrari, who stands up to toughs and defends the honor of the women of Fischbein's family. Santiago reveres him as a god. When Francisco invites him to join him in a bar, Santiago feels it a command. While others treat Santiago with contempt, Francisco befriends him and trusts him. Eventually, Francisco decides to rob a warehouse on the edge of the city and designates the trusted Santiago as the lookout. Before the fateful Friday, Santiago, who feels unworthy of Francisco's trust and friendship, informs the police of Francisco's plans. In the subsequent police raid, the police shoot Francisco in suspicious circumstances. Later, newspaper reports transform Francisco into the hero that Santiago has dreamed him to be.

This tale has numerous connections with the Judas story. Like the Judas of some Christian art, Jacob/Santiago is redheaded.[3] Like the canonical Judas, Jacob seems a Christian (or, at least, a worthy disciple), taking the name Santiago (Saint James), but is not really. As Jacob/Santiago remarks, he could never do anything about the Fischbein. The story features a gang (disciples) led by a god-hero who is betrayed and killed in suspicious circumstances and then transformed by later reports into a hero. Unlike the stories of the canonical Judas, however, this traitor's story reveals his motivation: (1) he does not feel worthy of his friend or of his friend's estimation of him; (2) people treat him as a coward and as contemptible; (3) he believes that "we all come to resemble the image others have of us"; and (4) being treated and feeling unworthy, he becomes unworthy, without any remorse.

That complex motivation casts some light upon the mysterious actions of the Judas in George Stevens' *The Greatest Story Ever Told* (1965). In that film, Judas is Jesus' first disciple; nevertheless, the film frequently isolates Judas, separating him visually from Jesus and the other disciples.[4] For example, as the disciples prepare for the final Supper, Judas sits alone

---

3. Scholars frequently describe the Judas of Christian art as red-haired, but detailed studies point out that Judas is only occasionally so. See Baum, 1922: 520–29; and Mellinkoff, 1982: 31–46.

4. Christian art isolates Judas by portraying him alone in profile, without a beard, wearing a yellow robe, carrying the purse, or without a nimbus (or with a dark-colored nimbus). Artists sometimes depict him alone on one side of the Supper table or receiving a black fly or bird, representing Satan, with or instead of the Eucharist (Mellinkoff, 1982: 31, 38, 43). Mellinkoff's article contains supporting illustrations. See also Maccoby, 1992: 111–15; Schiller, 1972: 2:24–41, 51–56, 76–78; Jursch, 1952: 101–105; and Kuryluk, 1987.

at a table. When Jesus arrives, Judas slips into the dark streets where he almost collides with the Dark Hermit, Stevens' Satan character.[5] Hauntingly, the camera lingers upon the Dark Hermit, not Judas. These visuals associate Judas quite powerfully with the satanic opposition. In the next scene, in a room dimly lit by candlelight, one knows that the story and camera have followed Judas only when he announces himself to Caiaphas as the "friend of Jesus." As Judas negotiates Jesus' arrest, even these authorities wonder why Judas would deliver his friend and master, and if he is willing to hand Jesus over, why he would care what happens to Jesus thereafter.[6] Judas can only answer that Jesus is the "purest, kindest man I have ever known. I've never seen him do anything but good. His heart is gentle. Old people worship him. Children adore him. I love him."

Seen in isolation, this "motivation" is quite confusing. Read with Borges' Santiago, however, this Judas betrays Jesus simply because Jesus makes him feel unworthy. An earlier scene in the film, where Jesus visits with Lazarus, Martha, and Mary, corroborates this interpretation. When Jesus asks Lazarus to give up his wealth and follow him, Lazarus cannot.[7] Made anxious by Jesus and his demanding teaching, Mary worries as Jesus leaves their house that Jesus is "too good [for his own good]."

This sense of Jesus' ethereal goodness suits the film because its Pantocrator Christ comes from another world. In this film, one first sees Christ as a triumphant figure in the religious art of an apse dome as a voiceover recites part of John's prologue. The prologue continues as the film segues to the story proper. The mature Jesus of the subsequent film resembles that Pantocrator Christ. The film, then, brings church art to life, and church art stands in for the otherworldly neoplatonic heavens (or the church's mythic traditions).[8] Before this ecclesial, ethereal Christ, Stevens' Judas, like Runeberg's second Judas, deems himself metaphysically unworthy.

After arranging the betrayal, Stevens' Judas returns to the Supper. When Judas arrives, Jesus stares meaningfully at him, bows his head in

---

5. The Dark Hermit seduces various characters in the film. E.g., he tempts Jesus in the wilderness, inaugurates Peter's denials, and incites the crowds to cry out for Jesus' crucifixion. See Walsh, 2003: 149, 151, 167n18.

6. Everyone in the scene carefully avoids the word "betray," although Sorak, a character invented by Stevens, almost slips and says the ill-fated word.

7. Stevens' Lazarus combines several gospel characters including John's Lazarus and the Synoptic Gospels' rich young ruler. See Walsh, 2003: 149.

8. See Walsh 2003: 147–71, which compares this film, *Shane* (another of Stevens' films), and John. All have heroes who appear suddenly in the story from afar. Cf. Staley and Walsh, 2007: 51.

anguish, and then prayerfully announces that the hour of his glorification has come. After the oracles about betrayal and denial, words about his body and blood, and selections from John 14–17, Jesus imperially demands that Judas, identified clearly by Jesus' stare, "do it quickly." Judas leaves haltingly, overwhelmed by forces larger than himself. Jesus returns to the theme of his glorification. Stevens' Judas, then, is an instrument for Jesus' glorification, which is a Johannine synonym for the passion. Judas' alienation and degradation, like that of Runeberg's second Judas, glorifies the divine Christ by relief.

These metaphysically unworthy Judases raise serious ethical questions about the Christian worldview. In Christian theology, as in neoplatonism and gnosticism, humans are inherently inferior to superior, supernatural realities.[9] One can hardly expect such humans to act well, and one can damn them without other evidence. Among the canonical gospels, John makes this metaphysical damnation most blatant in its portrayal of the "world" outside the community: (1) they belong to Satan; (2) they are not chosen; and (3) they are capable of all manner of evil. Thus, John's Judas, who belongs to Satan and who is not chosen, is thief (12:6) as well as betrayer.[10] No evidence supports the narrative judgment. The narrator needs none other than the observation that Judas belongs to Satan/the world. That he is a thief follows from the metaphysical assumptions. The judgment simply reflects Judas' outsider and worldly status. It coheres with the other narrative judgments that litter Jn 6:64–71 and John 13 and declare Judas not chosen (explanation for evil #2) and a devil (explanation for evil #1).

Jesus' attack on the Jews (Ἰουδαίους),[11] who believe in him but do not understand his words, contains similar metaphysical slurs (Jn 8:31-47). According to Jesus, these Jews look for an opportunity to kill him because they do not accept his words. They do not accept his words because they are children of the devil (explanation for evil #1). The devil is a murderer and a liar, so they, his children, cannot appreciate the truth (explanation for evil #3). They are not from (chosen by) God (explanation for evil #2).

---

9. Cf. Nietzsche's famous critiques of Christianity for denying the value of this life and for hindering the development of aristocratic values. More concisely, for Nietzsche, Christianity is resentment. See Nietzsche, 1974; Nietzsche, 1966: 260; and Nietzsche, 1954: 1–7, 43, 53, 58. For a discussion of the ethical problems implicit in grace, see also Walsh, 2005a: 109–43.

10. By contrast, Matthew, which is the only gospel to say that Judas suggests a betrayal price (Mt. 26:14-16; cf. Mk 14:10-11; Lk. 22:3-6), does not offer such an explicit narrative judgment.

11. Judas is the similar Ἰούδας.

4 The Ascetic Judas

This diatribe hardly illumines evil. It reinforces John's sectarian boundaries and externalizes evil. Its critique of outsiders is a logical consequence of a theology that devalues the present world in favor of the divine (and the sect). For John, no meaningful difference can exist between the opposition to Jesus, the world, and Satan. Those who do not believe are metaphysically and ethically inferior. Runeberg's second Judas simply accepts this status as his religious duty.

Necessary Rivals and Narrative Perspective

While this metaphysical hierarchy fascinates Borges' Runeberg and motives the decisive actions of his first and second Judases, Borges himself does not have such theological certainty. For him, the disparity between the worthy Christ and the unworthy Judas is essentially a narrative matter. Jesus and Judas create themselves through their narrative rivalry.

Borges' "The Duel" illustrates (1999a: 381–85).[12] After her husband's death, Clara Glencairn becomes a painter, inspired by her friend Marta Pizzaro, a portrait and landscape painter. Deliberately contrasting herself with her friend, Clara becomes an abstract painter. Although she does not meet with success initially, her friend Marta champions her work. By chance, critical opinion changes, and Clara wins a prestigious award. Later, Marta receives a position that Clara covets. While they are jealous rivals throughout their careers, they also treat each other loyally:

> Clara Glencairn painted against, and in some sense for, Marta Pizzaro; each was her rival's judge and solitary audience. In their canvases … I believe I see (as there inevitably had to be) a reciprocal influence. And we must not forget that the two women loved each other, that in the course of that private duel they acted with perfect loyalty to one another….
>
> On February 2, 1964, Clara Figueroa suffered a stroke and died…. Marta realized that her own life now had no meaning…. She never painted again. (1999a: 384–85)

Without their rivalry, they have no identity.

The canonical Judas and Jesus similarly require and define one another. In plot terms, of course, the hero demands a villain and vice versa. In Christian discourse, which Runeberg unwaveringly accepts, Jesus is the hero. When Judas recognizes Jesus as the hero, he accepts his own relative

---

12. See also the discussion of Borges' "The Sect of the Thirty" in Chapter 2. *I Heart Huckabees* (2004) makes a similar point. In the film's denouement, hero and rival realize that they are locked in a swirling dance (and may have been so for eternity). Their rivalry defines them.

unworthiness. He can only be the disciple (Runeberg's first Judas) or the rival (Runeberg's second Judas).

Things change dramatically if one switches discourses. The medieval *Toledoth Yeshu*, popular among medieval Jews, provides a clear example.[13] In this story, Joseph Pandera tricks and impregnates Miriam, and Jesus is the illegitimate result. His illegitimacy has predictable effects, and Jesus becomes disrespectful of the sages and offers impudent interpretations of Torah. Inquiry about his origins forces him to Galilee. Soon, however, he learns the ineffable Name of God in the Temple, becomes a sorcerer, and gathers a large following. He claims to be the Messiah and the fulfillment of prophecies.

The authorities find a hero, Judas, to rival Jesus. Judas also learns the Name and sorcery. In a flying miracle match, Judas finally triumphs and defiles Jesus. The defeat causes Jesus to lose the powerful Name and allows the authorities to imprison him. When his followers rescue him, Jesus returns to the Temple and relearns the Name. Once again, Judas helps the Torah authorities arrest Jesus, who hang Jesus on a cabbage stalk. After Jesus' burial, a gardener (Judas in some versions) moves the body. When Jesus' followers claim he has been raised, the authorities produce the body and demonstrate that Jesus is a false prophet.[14]

The *Toledoth Yeshu* builds upon gospel and Talmudic materials to counter Christian claims about Jesus' virgin birth, source of power, relation to prophecy, integrity, and resurrection. Instead of Son of God, Jesus is a false messiah, a sorcerer, and a false prophet who leads the people astray. As such, he deserves to die:

> If prophets or those who divine by dreams appear among you and promise you omens or portents [sorcerers], and the omens or the portents declared by them take place, and they say, "Let us follow other gods" (whom you have not known) "and let us serve them," you must not heed the words of those prophets or those who divine by dreams; for the LORD your God is testing you, to know whether you indeed love the LORD your God with all your heart and soul. The LORD your God you shall follow, him alone you shall fear, his commandments you shall keep, his voice you shall obey, him you shall serve, and to him you shall hold fast. But those prophets or those who divine by dreams shall be put to death for having spoken

---

13. The *Toledoth Yeshu* appears in many forms. For an English translation, see, e.g., Goldstein, 1950: 148–54.

14. Jesus dies on a cabbage stalk because he has cursed any tree that would bear his body. In Goldstein's translation, the gardener is anonymous. In the denouement, the Torah authorities send Paul (Peter in some versions) as a secret agent to lead Jesus' followers to practices and beliefs that clearly separate them from the Jews.

treason against the LORD your God – who brought you out of the land of Egypt and redeemed you from the house of slavery – to turn you from the way in which the LORD your God commanded you to walk. So you shall purge the evil from your midst. (Deut. 13:1-5)

A tidbit from the Talmud draws precisely this conclusion about Jesus:

It was taught: On the eve of Passover they hanged Jesus of Nazareth. The herald preceded the execution of the sentence by forty days, proclaiming: "Jesus of Nazareth is being taken out to be stoned because he practiced sorcery and led Israel into the worship of false gods. Anyone aware of extenuating circumstances must come forth and make them public." But no such circumstances were found and he was hanged on Passover eve. Ulla (a 4th century Babylonian scholar) said: "Why should you think that we should seek extenuation? Jesus of Nazareth led Israel into worship of false gods, and Scripture (Deut. 13:9) prohibits even seeking extenuation."[15]

In the *Toledoth Yeshu* (and the Talmud's tidbits), Jesus, a Jewish deviant, rashly endangers his fellow Jews' association with God.[16] Its Jewish Judas successfully defeats Jesus, exposing him as a sorcerer, and finally delivers Jesus to the Torah authorities. As a result, Judas becomes the hero. He is the good Jew, doing his duty and bringing the deviant Jesus to the attention of the Torah experts so that they might handle this false prophet (see Klausner, 1944: 324–27; Maccoby, 1992: 99; and Klassen, 1996: 66–74, 194–201).[17] In short, Jesus and Judas swap places. The Christian traitor is the Jewish hero.[18]

The Scapegoat

Runeberg's second Judas does not replace Jesus in this fashion. He is Jesus' double or fraternal rival (the bosom enemy). The gospels include a

---

15. Babylonian Talmud Sanhedrin 43a, quoted in Sperling, 2001: 253–54. On Jesus in the Talmud, see Dalman, 1973; Klausner, 1944: 18–54; Sperling, 2001: 251–59; and Goldstein, 1950.

16. Cf. the attitude of the Nazareth synagogue worshipers in Lk. 4:16–30 or of Caiaphas in Jn 11:50.

17. Klassen argues that Judas brings Jesus to the authorities so that Jesus may personally confront those he has criticized (as Jesus' own teaching demands) (1996: 66–74, 194–201). Klassen's Judas, i.e., is a disciple of Jesus as well as a good Jew. For an attempt to explain why observant Jews cannot follow Jesus' teaching, see Neusner, 1993.

18. Klausner says concisely that the *Toledoth Yeshu* simply takes the gospel accounts and "changes evil to good and good to evil" (1944: 51). He also says that the *Toledoth Yeshu* illustrates how Christian truths looked to medieval Jews (1944: 53).

Thomas, whose name means twin.[19] The apocryphal Gospel of Thomas features Didymus Judas Thomas, which one might translate, "Twin Judas Twin," as Didymus (Δίδυμος) is Greek for "twin." As the Gospel of Thomas has affinities with gnosticism and as Judas Iscariot is the hero-apostle of some gnostics, one might merge these coincidences and conclude that this Judas Thomas is actually Judas Iscariot the twin.[20] Following Borges, one might go further and conclude that Judas is Jesus' twin.[21]

Such conjectures are, however, unnecessarily rash and, more importantly, uneconomical. If one follows Borges, it takes far too long to arrive at the point, which the gospels have already made, that Judas is Jesus' narrative rival.[22] In fact, the canonical Judas is actually more like Jesus than either of Runeberg's mirrors. Runeberg's first, cooperative Judas is only Jesus' near double, the human disciple of a divine master.[23] Runeberg's second, confrontational Judas is Jesus' necessary rival. By contrast, the canonical Jesus and Judas are the twin sacrifices of the passion (cf. Maccoby, 1992: 9, 41–48, 60).[24] They are the only two "insiders" who die.

19. In some texts of Mt. 27:16-17, Pilate offers the crowd a choice between Jesus Barabbas and Jesus Messiah. As "Barabbas" means "son of the father," Jesus Barabbas and Jesus Messiah become rather troubling doubles. Cf. the discussion of *Barabbas*, whose protagonist is an inverse double for Jesus, in Chapter 3.

20. In the Gospel of Barnabas 216–217, God transfigures Judas, Jesus' primary opponent, so that he looks and sounds like Jesus. This double, not Jesus, is then crucified.

21. In Mt. 13:55 and Mk 6:3, Jesus has a brother named Judas.

22. Aizenberg asserts that Cain and Abel is the biblical story that fascinates Borges more than anything other than Job and that his stories repeatedly revise the rivalry between Cain and Abel (1984: 108–48). Most of the Borges' short stories considered here as revisions of the Judas story (or as stories of rivals who create themselves) could also be seen as retellings of Cain and Abel. See, e.g., "The Form of the Sword" (1962: 117–22); "The Unworthy" (1999a: 352–57); "Theme of the Traitor and the Hero" (1964: 127–31); "The Encounter" (1999a: 364–69); "The Theologians" (1964: 119–26); "Death and the Compass" (1962: 129–41); and "The Duel" (1999a: 381–85). For a discussion of Borges' characters as little more than plot rivals, see Sturrock, 1977: 167–79.

23. On the failure inherent in such imitation, see Castelli, 1991; and Walsh, 2005a: 145–77.

24. For Maccoby, Judas represents the Jews and Judaism that Christianity creates and rejects as part of its self-definition (1992: ix, 1–21, 26–29, 80). From his perspective, the other sacrifice of the passion narrative is Judaism or the Jews. Cf. John's equation of the Jews with the world and Satan (e.g., John 8), the Synoptic Gospels' association of the passion with the destruction of Jerusalem (e.g., Mark 13; Lk. 19:41–44; 23:28–31), and Matthew's blood curse (27:25). For a psychological reading of Jesus and Judas as doubles, see Tarachow, 1960: 528–54. He depends upon the myth

Of course, the gospels carefully distinguish these twins, extolling and deifying one while reviling and demonizing the other.

The story of two sacrificial victims with disparate fates recalls the two goats the high priest sacrifices on Yom Kippur:

> He shall take the two goats and set them before the LORD at the entrance of the tent of meeting; and Aaron shall cast lots on the two goats, one lot for the LORD and the other lot for Azazel. Aaron shall present the goat on which the lot fell for the LORD, and offer it as a sin offering; but the goat on which the lot fell for Azazel shall be presented alive before the LORD to make atonement over it, that it may be sent away into the wilderness to Azazel. (Lev. 16:7-10)

William Tyndale, whose translation the KJV follows, renders Azazel as (e)scapegoat. Consequently, even today a scapegoat is one (s)elected to take the blame so that others may "get off scot free." Nonetheless, most scholars see "scapegoat" as a mistranslation. The NRSV, quoted above, avoids the translation difficulties by transliterating the Hebrew word "Azazel." Traditional Jewish interpretations understand Azazel as a reference to the mountainous cliff over which the second goat is driven to its death. More recent interpreters see Azazel as a reference to a wilderness demon.

The scapegoat-Azazel tradition makes an intriguing interpretative background for the canonical Judas. After all, Judas is the one who "takes the fall" for the passion of Jesus. When Judas takes the blame, everyone else, including a rather malign deity, "gets off scot free." Further, scapegoat Judas is the one driven out, or made outsider, by the passion narrative. Thus, in Mark, Judas (the scapegoat) disappears from narrative view after the arrest as Jesus (the sacrificial goat) is led to death. While Judas also disappears in Luke and John after the arrest, these gospels also specifically consign Judas to Satan, who is, at least in Luke, a wilderness demon, like Azazel.

Runeberg does not use scapegoat language for Judas. His second Judas sacrifices himself deliberately. Nonetheless, Runeberg highlights Judas' sacrifice, rather than Jesus'.[25] This focus departs significantly from Christian discourse, which relentlessly concentrates on Jesus' sacrifice while Judas wanders from view. René Girard's recent work on scapegoats reiterates the canonical focus.

In an early work, *Deceit, Desire, and the Novel*, Girard argues that the

---

work of Frazer and of Freud as well as upon J. Robertson, 1927. See also Dieckmann, 1991. He traces Judas as a scapegoat in medieval and subsequent interpretations. He ultimately rejects such externalizations of evil.

25. Cf. the focus on Judas' sacrifice in *Jesus Christ Superstar* (1973). See Chapter 3.

novel's basic structure rests upon "triangular desire," a phrase he uses to indicate the mediated quality of desire. One does not simply desire an object. Instead, one learns desire by imitating a mediator' desire. Desire is mimetic and triangular. It requires a mediator. In traditional times, the mediator was a god, but, in modernity, the mediator is another human and, therefore, a rival as well as a model. Accordingly, modern mimetic desire is synonymous with envy and violence. Moreover, Girard posits that moderns do not know that their experiences in this regard are universal and, as a result, falsely consider their rivals (the happy) gods. Incidentally, this description of desire forms a precise blueprint of the theologically unworthy Judas. Considering himself unworthy, or unhappy, in comparison with his mimetic, god-like rival, Judas acts violently against him. Runeberg's second Judas, of course, does this without rancor.

For Girard, the "luminous counterpart" of the novel's structure and its deviated transcendence is "Christian truth." Great novelists approximate this truth because they are not their heroes; they have been cured both of their heroes' desires and limited perspectives. Otherwise, they could not write about their heroes. The end of the novel, then, is the story of the hero's conversion, including the hero's repudiation of the mediator, of metaphysical desire (the desire that leads to conflict and death), and of pride (a false sense of autonomy). The conclusion reconciles the hero and the world, the human and the sacred, and it restores vertical (traditional) transcendence. Thus, for Girard, Christian symbolism—specifically, the move from pride/original sin to grace—explains the basic structure of the novel.[26]

In a subsequent work, *Violence and the Sacred*, Girard asserts again that humans—because of mimetic desire—are intrinsically violent. Society begins, not with a social contract, but with a murder that redirects communal violence toward one fringe person, who could be destroyed without incurring reprisal. By this means, Hobbes' war of all against all becomes a war of the all, less one, against that one, who becomes thereby the scapegoat.[27] The polemically created unanimity begins society, with its inevitable structure of differences. The community forgets the scape-

---

26. On mimetic desire, see Girard, 1965: 1–52. On pride and deviated transcendence, see Girard, 1965: 53–82. On the illuminating structure of Christianity, see Girard's opening comparison of Don Quixote's imitation of Amadis with the saint's imitation of Christ; and Girard, 1965: 256–314.

27. This scenario revises Thomas Hobbes' primal scene, set forth in *Leviathan* (1958: 106), in the direction of the primal scene of Sigmund Freud, set forth in *Totem and Taboo* (1950). Cf. also Burkert, 1983.

4 The Ascetic Judas

goat's innocence; remembers the murder as just, necessary, or even divinely directed; and deifies the victim for the benefits which he/she has brought through his/her death. The scapegoat, then, is both criminal and pillar of society.[28]

When subsequent crises threaten society's structure of differences, religion staves off the threat by replaying the original scapegoat scenario with surrogate victims. Religion's primary task is to keep the sacred—the absence of difference or mimetic desire and its violence—at an optimum distance (1972: 1–38, 89–118).[29] For Girard, myth is a story of the beneficial death of a scapegoat who, thereby, becomes the community hero. Properly understood, myths reveal "not suppressed desire, but terror, terror of absolute violence" (1972: 73, 87, 117).[30] Myths are violent fictions or even "persecution texts" which depict the victimization and divinization of the scapegoat. Most concisely, myths are scapegoat texts (1986: 24–44).

For Girard, the gospel passion narrative develops against this mythic background, but the passion narrative denies that the victim deserves to die.[31] Instead, Jesus is innocent; his death is not necessary or just; his death is the basic human crime. He is a(n innocent) lamb, not a scapegoat. Thereby, the passion narrative exposes the crowd (cf. John's "world") that stands collectively against and murders this lone innocent. By envisioning Jesus as innocent victim of the community and by shifting the narrative perspective from that of the community to that of the lone victim, the passion narrative reveals the hidden scapegoat mechanism. Thereby,

---

28. In Athenian society, the scapegoat was the φαρμακός, one kept richly at state expense and executed to deal with a crisis. The φαρμακός is the insider driven out in order to expel evil. Derrida makes much of the absence, yet trace, of the φαρμακός in Plato's *Phaedrus* in an essay on "Plato's Pharmacy" (1981: 63–171). The duality of the φαρμακός is evident in the related φάρμακον, which means both medicine and poison. One thinks of the duality of the sacred, of Girard's sacrifice, etc. For Girard's discussion of the φαρμακός, see 1972: 94–98, 296–97.

29. By contrast, Mircea Eliade sees the sacred (or hierophany) as that which creates the "world" of a community and religious institutions as vehicles designed to access that sacred (1959).

30. According to Rollo May, Oswald Spengler once remarked that death stood behind myth (1991: 217).

31. *Deceit, Desire, and the Novel* unites an analysis of mimetic desire with the Christian discourse that reveals and salves that desire. *Violence and the Sacred* roots mimetic desire in anthropological and sociological studies, but it does not illumine this mimetic desire with Christian discourse. Several subsequent works remedy that lacuna by turning to an analysis of biblical texts (1986; 1987a; 1987b).

the gospel becomes a demythologizing force, which Girard hopes will bring an end to violence, an end to the scapegoats that are the "foolish genesis of bloodstained idols and the false gods of religion, politics, and ideologies" (1986: 110–24; quote from 1986: 212).

When one focuses on Jesus as the innocent victim as Girard does here, the sacrifice of Judas and Judas himself vanishes.[32] The disciples become mere examples of mimetic action. As Peter's denial scene illustrates, they all succumb to the eternal temptation to side with the all against the scapegoat (1986: 149–64).[33]

Caravaggio's *The Taking of Christ* illustrates Girard's scapegoat mechanism by placing the betrayal at the center of a crowd. An enveloping red cloak above the duo's heads, the soldier's armored arm, and Judas' grasp enclose Jesus in the crowd's maw. Jesus' clasped hands depict his acquiescence as a frightened disciple flees on the edge of the frame. So far, everything fits Girard's analysis. A minor detail, however, separates Caravaggio's painting from Girard's argument. Caravaggio visualizes Judas at the very heart of the sacred drama. Judas' sacrifice does not escape Caravaggio's attention as it does Girard—and the canon.[34]

For Girard, as for the canon, a secret plot dominates everything. While the secret plot of the scapegoat mechanism differs from that of the canon's secret providential plot, its effect is the same. People still become phantoms, mere cogs in the machine. Now, Judas and the crowd vanish in the mechanisms of mimetic desire and sacred violence.[35] Even Satan becomes a mere symbol of the scapegoat mechanism, specifically of its violence and of Jesus' triumph over it, particularly in the gospel exorcisms (1986: 165–97). In short, for Girard, only the divine Jesus escapes the mechanization and dehumanization of the secret scapegoat plot.

---

32. One might catch a glimpse of the horror here by attending to what Matthew does with the motif of innocent blood in its passion narrative.

33. In 1986: 115, Girard does mention Judas, saying that nothing separates him from Peter. Once again, no one but the innocent victim Jesus matters.

34. The painting is available at http://www.wga.hu/frames-e.html?/html/c/caravagg/index.html (accessed 7-26-09). Perhaps, Judas does not vanish in Caravaggio's painting because Caravaggio identifies more closely with biblical misfits and villains than Girard does. He often paints himself with those standing against the saints. E.g., his features are those of the severed head of Goliath in his Borghese *David with the Head of Goliath*. He also appears with the soldiers in *The Martyrdom of St. Matthew* as he does in *The Taking of Christ* discussed above.

35. For Tarachow (1960), whom Maccoby (1992) follows, Judas becomes the ritual murderer or priest.

4 The Ascetic Judas 97

Incidentally, despite his attention to fulfilled prophecies, which reveal the scapegoat mechanism, Girard's secret plot is not divine (1986: 100–11). Fulfilled scriptures and the gospel now reveal the persistence of human violence and religion's obfuscating participation in this violence. Nonetheless, the aura of Girard's discourse remains quite like that of John and of Christianity generally. Girard's discourse remains revelatory, and it still demarcates clearly defined, ethically weighted borders. There are only two perspectives: that of the persecutors, which is bad and violent; and that of the victim, which is good and forgiving. Similarly, there is myth, which is bad and obscurantist; and there is the gospel, which is good and liberating. Like canonical mechanics, these polarities expel evil (as they create it).

Despite Girard's clarifying efforts, troubling confusions remain.[36] The sacred is both life-giving and death-dealing. It combines that which appears to be good and that which appears to be evil. Similarly, sacrifice is a sacred obligation and a criminal act. The scapegoat is (imputed) criminal and (imputed) pillar of society. Twins and fraternal rivals also confuse borders.

As Girard notes, religion navigates these dualities, and religion's theologians frequently clarify matters further with theories that remove evil from the gods who, thereby, become completely beneficent. On occasion, theology creates the idea of an evil monster to rival its god or villains to rival its god's heroic representative (1986: 42–43, 76–94; 1972: 1–4, 85–87, 250–73). Girard's reading of the gospels does not simply analyze this process. It continues it. Girard's analysis theologically purges evil. Both the gospels (myth) and Girard (the theologian) rigorously separate good and evil, gods (innocent victims) and monsters (persecutors).

As a result of Girard's theological revelations, Judas disappears. Or, more precisely, Judas becomes part of the evil crowd that persecutes Jesus, the innocent victim. Unfortunately, for Girard's analysis, the gospels (other than John) do not simply array "the all" against scapegoat Jesus. The gospels single out Judas and the Jewish leaders for particular damnation. They disappear, die, or await destruction. If one refuses to focus solely on Jesus' sacrifice, if one eschews the blinders of the canon and Girard, it becomes clear that the gospels scapegoat Judas and the Jewish leaders as they exalt Jesus. From this perspective, it takes the sacrifice of both Jesus and Judas to replicate the two sacrifices of Leviticus 16.[37] Incidentally, it

---

36. Derrida's reading of the φαρμακός/φάρμακον is also deconstructive of such clear binaries. See n28.

37. Elsewhere, Girard notes that twins obscure difference and, therefore, threaten

also takes both Judas and Jesus to complete Girard's own ideas about the scapegoat as both criminal (Judas) and pillar (Jesus) of society (see Tarachow, 1960).[38]

Unlike Girard and the canon, Hyam Maccoby is unwilling to ignore Christian discourse's sacrifice of Judas/Judaism:

> It may seem a strange coincidence that of all Jesus' twelve disciples, the one whom the Gospel story singles out as traitor bears the name of the Jewish people. The coincidence was not overlooked by Christian commentators, who saw it as a mysterious sign, by which the Judas-role of the Jewish people was divinely hinted at.... As the argument develops, the element of coincidence will tend to disappear, and it will become reasonably clear that Judas was chosen for a baleful but necessary mythological role precisely because of the name. (1992: ix)

For Maccoby, Judas reveals Christianity's mythic participation in human sacrifice (1992: 41–48, 59, 73). The Christian Judas is the priestly executioner common to myths of human sacrifice, who has an almost fraternal bond with his sacrifice, Jesus. Judas, then, is Jesus' inverse image. While Jesus submits to the death demanded by the divine father, Judas orchestrates that death. Jesus submits and Judas rebels. Judas' sadism mirrors Jesus' masochism. One loses his life; the other loses his soul.[39] The similarity to Runeberg's second, ascetic Judas is uncanny.

For Maccoby, these ethical polarities spiritualize Christ and Christianity and scapegoat Judas and Judaism. To justify this claim, Maccoby refers to Walter Burkert's "comedy of innocence" scenario in which a community disowns its part in the human sacrifice that founds their unity by disowning the executioner who is actually the public's servant. A review of the long history of the vilification of Judas and of the sporadic anti-Semitism in Christianity further supports Maccoby's claims (cf. Dieckmann, 1991). For Maccoby, the only escape from this vilification of Judas and the Jews is the rejection of Christian theology or, more specifically, the rejection

---

the return of primordial violence. To avoid such problems, primitive societies often simply rid themselves of twins (by exposing them) (1972: 56–67, 79–81, 158–68). Girard's analysis treats Judas, Jesus' fraternal rival in the gospels, similarly.

38. Girard claims that mythic confusions, like those created by Borges' "Three Versions of Judas," will reinstate primordial violence. Perhaps such fears are merely the nightmares of conservatives and of theologians (cf. Hobbes, 1958: 144–52, 169). Perhaps, instead, it is the certainties of mythological/theological binaries, which inevitably require a scapegoat, that justify and create violence. Perhaps, it is the willingness to consider such binaries artificial that will avoid primordial violence.

39. Maccoby relies here on his earlier work, *The Sacred Executioner* (1982); and on Tarachow, 1960.

of the Christian myth of spiritual redemption in Christ's death (1992: 1–21, 138–39, 149–52, 160–68). Not incidentally, for Maccoby, Judaism abstains from the human sacrifices in which Christianity glories.

Placed alongside each other, the analyses of Girard and Maccoby mirror one another. Both emphasize the duality of the sacred, sacrifice, and the scapegoat. Both trace religion to (justified) human sacrifice. Both combine psychological and anthropological theories to explain the origins of religion and myth. Both abhor violence and claim that one religion alone exposes the mythic and violent nature of all others. Only the names change. Reading Girard and Maccoby in tandem, then, is quite like reading "Three Versions of Judas" or "The Form of the Sword." It reveals the importance of mythic, theological, or narrative perspective in the matter of assigning clearly defined characters—or ethical valuations—to roles in stories. Gods and demons, as well as heroes and traitors, depend upon a narrative perspective.[40] They are, in light of Borges, fictional roles that define each other and to which one can attach any name.[41]

The Outing of Judas in the Gospels: The Frame

Discourse's construction of such borders is easier to see from outside the mythic community, with someone like the heretic Runeberg, than from the inside. Thus, Girard cannot see the gospel's mythic work while Maccoby has no difficulty at all. In the Christian mythic perspective, Judas, the fraternal rival of Jesus, necessarily disappears. In the gospels, his vanishing act externalizes evil.

Outing the insider who does not belong (the scapegoat, the bosom enemy, or the traitorous apostle) is a ritualistic performance. Accordingly, Judas' outing takes place in the context of the founding of the central Christian ritual. That outing's necessary context, however, raises the troubling possibility that Judas participates in the Eucharist (see R. Brown, 1994: 2:1398–99). Only John bothers to note Judas' departure from the Supper (Jn 13:30), but John does not narrate the Eucharist's establishment. The Synoptic Gospels, which have the ritualistic institution, obscure the issue of Judas' presence and participation. In Luke, Judas seems present because the institution words (Lk. 22:17-20) precede the oracle creating

---

40. In the film, *The Good, the Bad, and the Ugly* (1966), the Ugly repeatedly refers to the Good as either angel or demon depending upon whether the Ugly finds the Good useful for his purposes or not. Nietzsche, of course, explicates clearly the interested, political nature of ethical valuations (see, e.g., 1966).

41. Cf. the discussion of Borges' "The Encounter" in Chapter 2 above.

the betrayer (22:21-23). By contrast, the betrayal oracle (Mk 14:17-21; Mt. 26:20-25) precedes the institution words (Mk 14:22-25; Mt. 26:26-29) in both Mark and Matthew. Perhaps, then, Judas left the Supper before the Eucharist in Mark and Matthew, but these gospels fail to mention his departure.

In art, Judas is often present at the founding Eucharist, but he is symbolically alienated.[42] For example, Judas may lack a halo, have a black halo, sit alone on one side of the table, carry the purse, wear distinctive (often yellow) clothing, or have red hair. The visuals identify him as the outsider who does not belong. More tellingly, in some artists' renderings, Judas reaches for food or receives bread from Jesus as Jesus speaks the damning oracle. In even more damning scenes, Judas receives a satanic black bird or black fly with or instead of the Eucharist (see Schiller, 1972: 2:24–41).

Films often isolate Judas similarly (see Walsh, 2006a: 38–43). In DeMille's *The King of Kings* (1927), Judas holds the Eucharistic cup, but quails at the prospect of drinking. In effect, he outs himself. In Stevens' *The Greatest Story Ever Told* (1965), Judas, who has come and gone throughout the Supper, is present for the Eucharist, but it is not clear that he participates. The camera focuses on Judas as the cup comes to him, but quickly cuts back to Jesus as he imperially demands that Judas "do quickly" the destined deed. When the camera cuts back to Judas, he puts down the cup, stands, and backs out of the room in awestruck fear. At the heart of this scene is a crucial absence. One never sees Judas drink from the cup.

The question of Judas' participation at the Eucharist is important because ritual hollows out evil.[43] It creates a space without evil by expelling evil. The evil Judas should not be there as a participant. Hence, the outing oracle occurs at just that crucial moment. At least, so it seems in insider discourse. Kirk Hughes puts the matter more neutrally:

> On the edges of consecration is evil. Around the edges of the Last Supper we find Judas busily betraying. To the edge of the garden Gethsemane (at the garden wall?), Judas leads the priests. On the edge, Judas delivers Jesus to the priests. At the edge is the drama of deliverance.... The edge (you must have seen it by now?) becomes essential. It brings us right to the heart of the matter. The frame, frames, informs us. Dare we say that the fram(e)(s)(ing) (in)forms? (1991: 228–29)

Hughes plays with multiple meanings of "frame." As the scapegoat or expelled insider, Judas acts as the picture's frame, prescribing the correct

---

42. See the references in n4.
43. See the anxieties revealed by 1 Cor. 11:27–32.

4 The Ascetic Judas

view. Judas, along with the red cloak and the soldier's armored arm, functions in this way in Caravaggio's *The Taking of Christ*. Jesus rests passively and divinely in the hollow or frame created by evil (or its expulsion). However, Judas also "frames" Jesus in the sense that he betrays Jesus without just cause. Accordingly, Hughes moves away from the sacred center of the gospels' narrative painting, the founding of the Eucharist, to note that the stories of Judas' betrayal and the arrest frame the Last Supper, at least in the Synoptic Gospels (see Table 6 below) (1991: 224–25).[44] Hughes concludes, "Quite simply put, Judas frames Jesus." He also says, "Poised precariously at the periphery of Jesus' Last Supper (the first of Christian history's ever proliferating consecrations) looms the figure of Judas" (1991: 224).

Judas' Betrayal	Mt. 26:14-16	Mk 14:10-11	Lk. 22:3-6
Preparations for the Supper	Mt. 26:17-19	Mk 14:12-16	Lk. 22:7-13
The Supper	Mt. 26:20-35	Mk 14:17-31	Lk. 22:14-38
Gethsemane	Mt. 26:36-46	Mk 14:32-42	Lk. 22:39-46
The Arrest	Mt. 26:47-56	Mk 14:43-50	Lk. 22:47-54

Table 6. *Judas "Frames" Jesus.*

The result should create a space for the good, hollowing the sacred out of ever threatening evil. To do so, however, the sacred frames evil. Thus, Jesus/God frames Judas in the gospels. Numerous oracles predict Jesus' passion, and the vindicating resurrection provides a divine answer to the passion. The divine, then, frames Judas and all Jesus' opponents. If Judas is the frame, he is also in the (divine) frame. Troublingly, Judas is necessarily at the Supper precisely because Jesus' oracular words create Judas there (Mt. 26:21-23; Mk 14:18-20; Lk. 22:21). Moreover, Jesus' woe effectively delivers Judas to (divine) destruction at that ritual moment (Mt. 26:24; Mk 14:21; Lk. 22:22). The narrators of Luke and John add a handing over of their own as they deliver Judas to Satan (Lk. 22:3; Jn 13:2, 27). As a result, Jesus/gospel frames Judas as much as vice versa. Once again, the twin sacrifices of the gospel or its twin betrayals are in

---

44. Hughes plays with Derrida's notion of the frame. See Derrida, 1987b. Cf. also Aichele, 1985: 1–21. Hughes' article mimics the columned presentation of Derrida's *Glas* (1987a). The top of the left-hand column prints excerpts from *The English Ballad of Judas*. Below stand excerpts from various critics. The top of the second column has excerpts from a modern novel about infidelity. Below stands Hughes' own comments about Judas.

the frame.[45] The good and the evil are not clearly separated. Evil must be there at the ritual moment in order to be separated and/or expelled. Christian ritual, then, creates Judas.

All these frames and shifting perspectives leave one on the edge of the Borgesian infinite. Myth, ritual, and theology try desperately to domesticate this chaos. The crucifixion becomes a divine plot. One twin becomes spiritual and divine. The other becomes worldly and demonic. The mythic community lies between. Its rituals enforce these boundaries.

Not surprisingly, the gospels do not let the Eucharist stand alone in the marking out of Judas. They further demarcate Judas with his own inverted rituals. John, for example, adds something horribly like a Black Mass, a demonic inversion of the Eucharist. It is not grace or the divine that enters Judas with the bread. Instead, Satan enters him with the sop (Jn 13:27).[46] Similarly, Judas' betraying kiss in Mark and Matthew inverts the ritualistic kiss of peace.[47] This kiss betrays the brother. The ritual inversions mark Judas as the scapegoat or the φαρμακός. The inversions name him as the insider who no longer belongs. His outing creates and frames the borders of the true community.

Judas as Christian Fiction: Object of Christian Discourse

An object of Christian discourse, this Judas is a metalepsis worthy of Borges.[48] The ritual Judas intrudes Christianity into the gospel passion. For Maccoby, Judas also trails Judaism into these precincts because he represents the Christian attempt to supersede Judaism. Such theological insertions are clearly anachronistic, but these matters are present in embryo in the report of Judas' divine destruction in Acts. If the ritualistic metalepses suggest fiction, so, too, does the fact that the story of Judas' death in Acts differs so dramatically from Matthew's report of Judas' suicide.[49]

---

45. The betrayal of Judas by Jesus takes center stage in *Jesus Christ Superstar* and *The Last Temptation of Christ*. See the discussion in Chapter 3.

46. As noted, John does not institute the Eucharist during Jesus' last meal, but it includes what sounds like a homily on the Eucharist in John 6. Interestingly, John demarcates the demonic Judas for the first time at this very moment (6:64-65, 70-71).

47. Luke interrupts the kiss with Jesus' imperious question (Lk. 22:47-48).

48. See the discussion of Paffenroth and "object of" in Chapter 3.

49. See Saari, 2006. Cf. Zwiep, who concludes that the differing stories point to local rumors (2004: 105–21). A third prominent account of Judas' death in Christian discourse is that of Papias who claims that Judas dies a ghastly death after a tortuous, outcast life. See the discussion in Zwiep, 2004: 111–18.

4 The Ascetic Judas 103

The poetic, providential nature of Judas' death in Acts is yet another sign of fiction. This death is a divine "reward" for Judas' wickedness. He falls and bursts (Acts 1:18). The only other figure in Luke-Acts whose death is as macabre is that of Herod Agrippa, eaten by worms for usurping divine prerogatives (Acts 12:23). Of course, Luke also imagines the impending, just "death" of Jerusalem (see Lk. 19:41-44; 23:28-31) because she has rejected the prophets—Jesus, Stephen, Peter, and Paul. In this context, Judas' (or Judaism's) field is rather hauntingly named the "Field of Blood" (Acts 1:18-19).[50] For Acts, all these horrible deaths prove that a divine justice runs the world. Such melodrama is the result of Christian discourse about and judgment on outsiders. Judas signifies the horrible fate of those left behind God's salvation history.

Judas' just destruction is more popular than Judas' suicide in Matthew. While art or film often depicts Judas' hanging, they frequently do so in ways which import the divine-destruction ideology of Judas' death from Acts (cf. Daube, 1994: 103).[51] In Giotto's *The Last Judgment* in the Arena Chapel, for example, Judas hangs for all eternity in hell. It is his permanent fate.[52] Similarly, in film, Judas typically hangs as his "just" end.[53] In DeMille's *The King of Kings* (1927), Judas' suicide does not even end his unfortunate story. In the crucifixion's epic finale, which includes supernatural darkness and earthquake, Judas still hangs from the tree as it falls into hellish depths. The spectacle's visuals succinctly damn him.

The depiction of Judas' just punishment in *The Passion of the Christ* (2004) is even more horrific. Not interested in Judas' motivation in the least, the film concentrates on Judas' payment. Instead of separating the betrayal arrangements and Gethsemane with the Supper as the gospels

---

50. Zwiep argues that Judas' possession of his own field contrasts negatively with the depiction of communal wealth in early Christianity in Acts (2004: 166–68). Perhaps, such possessions are sufficient grounds for death in Acts. See the fate of Ananias and Sapphira in Acts 5. If so, perhaps Acts is the precursor of the depiction of Judas in Giotto's Arena Chapel and in *Jesus of Nazareth*. See below.

51. Cf. the discussion of theological attitudes toward suicide in Chapter 3.

52. Pictures of Giotto's *The Last Judgment* are widely available on the internet. See, e.g., http://www.wga.hu/index1.html (accessed 7-26-09). In some depictions of Judas' hanging, demons wait to grasp his soul. See Schiller, 1972: 2:77. Similarly, in Dante's *Inferno*, a three-headed, monstrous Satan chomps on Judas (and Brutus and Cassius) throughout eternity.

53. The hanging in *Jesus Christ Superstar* (1973) is the most positive in the Jesus film tradition as it is so quickly followed by Judas' heavenly transfiguration. The depiction in the 2004 *Judas* also ameliorates the hanging by having the disciples, motivated by Jesus' ethic, bury Judas with appropriate Jewish prayers.

do, the film cuts back and forth between Judas' arrangements and Jesus' tortured prayers in Gethsemane. The result contrasts Jesus and Judas in order to vilify Judas. To heighten the pathos, Judas receives the money in a slow-motion shot, spills the money, and grovels on the ground to collect it.[54] The next scene also shows Jesus kneeling, but in order to conquer. He prays and, then, rises to stomp the demonic snake's head. The visual connections suggest that Judas' head will quickly follow.

Thereafter, Judas' story is a descent into hell, a demonic nightmare visually extending the tradition begun by Acts.[55] After the betrayal, Judas loiters under the bridge from which the temple police toss a chained Jesus, who hangs face-to-face with a tormented Judas. Suddenly, a screaming ghoul (resembling the figure in Munch's *Scream*) darts out of the darkness at a terrified Judas and vanishes just as quickly.[56] The scene distorts cinematic reality and signals Judas' descent into the demonic. Soon, a quailing Judas hides from playing children who eerily "see" Judas' torments. Shockingly, the children suddenly morph into biting, reviling demons. Then, a hand-held camera follows Judas' whirling fall. In the next Judas scene, similar fury-like children and Satan chase Judas outside the city walls. Visually, Judas is driven into the wilderness for Azazel. Screaming, Judas holds his head as if trying to keep it from coming apart. Suddenly, the demons and Satan are gone, and Judas is alone beside a maggot-ridden carcass, whirling with flies (a suggestion, no doubt, of Beelzebub). Unable to hold his eroding reality together, Judas takes the rope from the carcass and hangs himself. The maggot-ridden carcass, which remains in the shot, depicts Judas' fate.

The death above a decaying animal doubles Judas and Jesus again as Jesus is the lamb slain to bear the world's sins (see the film's opening titles). More obviously, the presence of the androgynous Satan connects both deaths. Ultimately, however, Jesus' death defeats Satan as the opening Gethsemane scene promised. The visual climax of this triumph is a shot from above of Satan screaming alone, forsaken in a desolate, hellish landscape as Jesus dies. Judas has long departed, but the screaming Satan does echo Judas' similar screaming, forsaken end. Even though

---

54. One has to return to Olcott's *From the Manger to the Cross* (1912) or DeMille's *The King of Kings* (1927) to find comparable visualizations of Judas' greed. For a discussion of Judas' motivation in film, see Chapter 5. Incidentally, no gospel shows Judas receiving the payment.
55. For a discussion of this film's use of horror conventions, see Walsh, 2008b.
56. Recognizing the horror conventions, Tatum calls this figure a werewolf (2004: 213).

4 *The Ascetic Judas* 105

no longer present, Judas belongs with Satan in the blasted wilderness, and both are screamingly defeated as the betrayal-Gethsemane sequence foretold.

Ray's *King of Kings* (1961) doubles the deaths of Jesus and Judas more sympathetically.[57] That film pairs Judas' end with Jesus' by having Barabbas hold Judas' body after Jesus' crucifixion. The setting of the scene pathetically mirrors the Christian pietà. The ethical valuations are similar to those of Gibson's film and the canon. Jesus is heroic success; Judas is tragic failure. But the tone differs. The gleeful relish in the demise of the wicked evident in Acts and its successors is absent.

Judas is not only a sign of those left behind in Acts; he is also a sign of the divine establishment of the apostolic church. In Acts, nothing can stand in the way of salvation history. Judas' apostasy is as insignificant in this regard as Jewish unbelief and Roman prisons. Consequently, Peter quickly passes over the loss of Judas as part of the divine program foretold by David (Acts 1:16) in his hurry to reach his real point, the divine replacement of Judas (Acts 1:20b-26). The various references to the infinite book in the passage create yet another example of the oracular Judas.

Like Mark's version of that Judas, Peter's Judas relies upon a reading of the psalms, but Peter reads more carefully than Mark. At least, Peter begins better. First, he refers to Ps. 69:25 (in Acts 1:20) and follows the psalm's narration closely. The psalmist cries out to God for deliverance and for revenge against enemies. In Acts 1:20, Judas has become Peter's enemy and, therefore, Peter describes him as God's enemy as well. The conjunction is ethically troubling, but Peter's reading does not distort the psalm on this issue. Peter's second oracle, however, is Ps. 109:8, and the speaker there, whose words Peter adopts, is the wicked who beset the psalmist. In dismissing Judas, then, Peter speaks as do the wicked of the psalms.[58] Any troubling ethical concerns here are simply ignored. For Acts, the only significant issue is Judas' dismissal.

Acts eliminates Judas in order to clear the way for the ultimate divine (and Christian) victory. While Mark's oracular Judas stands between and

---

57. Christian art often contrasts these deaths. See, e.g., the ivory relief plaques (420–30 CE) in the British Museum. Photographs are available on the internet, e.g., at http://www.britishmuseum.org/explore/highlights/highlight_objects/pe_mla/p/panel_from_an_ivory_casket_th.aspx (accessed 7-26-09).

58. The psalmist quotes his enemies' curse in order to counter it and to return it against them (see Ps. 109:20). To find vengeance, Peter also abandons the Lukan Jesus' words about forgiveness (Lk. 23:34). Perhaps he read a Luke that did not contain them. Or, perhaps, the Lukan Jesus' oracles condemning Israel were more serviceable to him.

links the spiritual and material designs in the passion, the oracular Judas of Acts stands between Jewish rejection and gentile acceptance of the message about Jesus, facilitating the transition from the former to the latter (cf. Acts 13:46-47; 18:6; 28:25-28). As a result, the apostolic institution rises upon the burst body of Judas. By the end of Luke-Acts, particularly if one imagines the end predicted for Jerusalem, a field of blood is all that is left of those left behind.

The Golden Legend's Judas amplifies the replacement story in Acts. First, its version of Judas' death provides another example of the ideology of divine destruction and illustrates how this ideology can permeate interpretations of Matthew's hanging:

> Then he went and hanged himself from a tree, and burst asunder in the midst, and all his bowels gushed out. He did not vomit them from the mouth, because his mouth could not be defiled, having touched the glorious face of Christ. It was just that his entrails should burst forth, since it was out of them that his evil plan arose, and it was equally just that his throat, from which the betrayal issued, should be closed by the rope. And he died in mid-air, because he had given offense to the angels of Heaven and to the men on earth, and thus deserved to perish between earth and Heaven. (Voragine, 1941: 1:174)

Second, like Acts, *The Golden Legend*'s story focuses on Judas' replacement by Matthias. The story ends with a discussion of the providential control of the casting of lots (Acts 1:26), and it begins with etymological reflections on "Matthias" as "the gift of God": "Or, Matthias comes from *manu*, the good, and *thesis*, placing: the good that is placed instead of the evil, for Matthias was placed in the stead of Judas" (Voragine, 1941: 1:171). The story separates the good—Jesus and his followers—and the evil—Judas, the Jews, and Pilate (Voragine, 1941: 1:213). Accordingly, the Judas of *The Golden Legend*, like that of John, commits all manner of evil: murder; friendship with Pilate; patricide; incest; theft; and suicide.

The first four offenses appear in what the narrator admits is an untrustworthy legend in which Judas is an Oedipus figure.[59] Judas' mother receives a troubling oracle, which leads to Judas' exposure (the scapegoat motif again). Preternaturally, he returns to kill his father and marry his mother. In harmony with certain tendencies in the salvation history in Acts, however, the oracle that outs Judas does not specify patricide and incest. Instead, it predicts that Judas will be "so evil that he would be the downfall of our race!" (Voragine, 1941: 1:172). Here, then, Judas more

---

59. See Chapter 2 for a comparison of Judas and Oedipus. See also Baum, 1916: 481–632; and Paffenroth, 2001b: 70–78.

clearly symbolizes the Jews left behind than he does in Acts. Thankfully, the narrator claims that the story lacks credibility. Unfortunately, the narrator's incredulity does not stem from the oracle's damnation of an entire people. It arises from the oedipal story's conclusion, which asserts that Judas joined Jesus' disciples in order to repent (Voragine, 1941: 1:173). The narrator simply cannot imagine the thief and betrayer—stories which follow the alleged transformation—repenting.

Some film versions of Judas exacerbate these anti-Semitic tendencies. Thus, after the cleansing of the Temple in *The Gospel according to St. Matthew* (1964), Pasolini's Jesus curses a fig tree which immediately withers. Pasolini's Judas, but not Matthew's, remarks upon this miracle (cf. Mt. 21:18-22). Pasolini, that is, ties Judas to the withered tree far more obviously than Matthew. Between the leaders' plot to put Jesus to death (Mt. 26:3-5) and the anointing, Pasolini offers another shot of the withered fig tree. At the anointing, Pasolini's Judas, but not Matthew's, objects to the waste and, then, smilingly—to maximize the betrayal's perfidy—joins the leaders' plot. Later in the passion narrative, Pasolini's Judas hangs himself upon another withered tree (Walsh, 2003: 103–104). These repeated shots of withered trees visually connect Judas, the Jewish leaders, and destruction.

The end of Judas in *The Greatest Story Ever Told* (1965) is more concise. As Jesus is crucified, Stevens cuts repeatedly to the Temple where Judas drops the money and commits suicide. He does so, not by hanging himself, but by falling into the altar fire as Jesus is nailed to the cross. More than one critic has seen this fiery end as an allusion to the Jewish Holocaust. If so, the precise connection is ambiguous. Does the portrayal chasten Christian anti-Semitism by suggesting an intimate, unholy connection between the gospel and the Holocaust? Or does it suggest, more vilely and more canonically, a justification for the self-destruction of Judas and those Jews "left behind" in their rejection of the gospel salvation story? As Judas is the one figure in the film who judges himself unworthy of Jesus and as he bears a name so reminiscent of Judaism, the unexplained connection between Judas and fire in the Temple precincts is, at best, disconcerting.

The demise of Judas in Zeffirelli's *Jesus of Nazareth* (1977) also troubles. After Peter's denial, he runs through darkened streets. In a powerful cut, the movie segues smoothly to Judas running in the streets after his betrayal.[60] Thereafter, however, the movie follows Judas to his hanging

---

60. On the contrasting characterizations of Judas and Peter in film, see Telford, 2005.

suicide. This Judas does not repent. At least, he does not return the money. He dies with the spilled money bag beneath his feet. The movie lingers over this shot. Given the history of anti-Semitic slurs about Jewish greed, the visual disturbs.[61] Moreover, after the movie follows Judas to his suicide, it follows Peter to his transformation by the resurrection message into the apostolic leader of the church. The way of Judas leads to death. The way of Peter leads to resurrection life. The sequence succinctly realizes the triumphal ideology of Acts 1:16-26.

Spiritual Christianity and Worldly Judaism

In fact, the overall structure of Zeffirelli's *Jesus of Nazareth* supports Christianity's supersession of Judaism. While the first part of the movie sets Jesus' early life in the context of a lavishly recreated first-century Judaism, the emphasis is on the coming messiah, and the movie's first part climaxes in a synagogue as Jesus declares prophecy fulfilled in his ministry. The movie's second part depicts Jesus' ministry as the precursor of apostolic Christianity with a number of vignettes about various disciples. It ends with the successful apostolic mission and with the resurrection of Lazarus. The third part reinforces the apostolic (resurrection) message and mission by visualizing the redemptive death of Jesus. Nicodemus watches the cross from afar and intones, "Born again." The movies' third part ultimately climaxes with the resurrection, which transforms Peter into the apostolic leader and spokesperson of the church that has replaced the Judaism of the movie's first part (Walsh, 2003: 37-38).

While *Jesus of Nazareth* depicts a Roman crucifixion in, what was at the time, fairly gruesome detail (Staley and Walsh, 2007: 78, 198n23), Nicodemus' "born again" comment lays a spiritual, redemptive message over Jesus' suffering and death.[62] The emphasis upon the resurrection functions similarly because the movie's resurrection does not alter the world. The apocalypse, which resurrection augurs, does not follow. The colonized and imperial situations remain the same. Accordingly, the movie's

---

61. Giotto exploits these Christian biases in his Arena Chapel as he uses Judas as an example of the fate of usurers and the greedy. First, Judas takes money to betray his master at Satan's urging (see the reproduction on this book's cover). He, then, betrays his master with a kiss. Finally, he hangs in hell with usurers. See the discussion in Chapter 2 above. Photographs are available on the internet. See, e.g., http://www.wga.hu/index1.html (accessed 7–26–09). For more discussion of greed as a motivation for the betrayal, see Chapter 5.

62. See the discussion of the secret providence plot and myth in Chapter 2.

resurrection message is purely spiritual. *Jesus of Nazareth* and Acts, its precursor, agree on this point. The resurrection changes only the lives of those who believe. For both, Peter symbolizes this transformation.

Nicodemus' comment also writes a spiritual message over the Judaism portrayed so lavishly in part one of the movie. Unlike the Nicodemus of John, who thinks in terms of this world, the movie's Nicodemus "sees" the hidden, spiritual meaning of Jesus and his cross. Vis-à-vis Judaism (and Roman imperial discourse), Christian spokespersons, like this Nicodemus and Runeberg's second Judas, always speak spiritually, rather than literally.[63] Christianity necessarily does so. Spirituality is one of the few choices available in its struggle with Judaism. Any "literal" interpretation of the ancient texts favors Judaism. To compete, emerging Christians deny the letter in favor of the spirit. They write, that is, a second story over the literal, and over Judaism, which mythologizes the Hebrew Bible/Septuagint as an Old Testament and which then completes that Old Testament with a New Testament.[64]

Borges' Runeberg and his obsessive readings of the Christian Bible are similarly spiritual. In fact, such spiritualization seems a process endemic to infinite books and their secret plots:

> Since the events related in the Scriptures are true (God is Truth, Truth cannot lie, etc.), we should admit that men, in acting out those events, blindly represent a secret drama determined and premeditated by God. Going from this to the thought that the history of the universe—and in it our lives and the most tenuous detail of our lives—has an incalculable, symbolic value, is a reasonable step. (Borges, 1964: 209)

The infinite book and its secret plot reduce everyone to the blindness of the Johannine Jesus' interlocutors. Everything has a hidden, symbolic meaning known only to the illuminati. This enigma haunts Runeberg and his real world counterpart, Léon Bloy. The quote above comes from an essay in which Borges explores Bloy's life-long reflections on 1 Cor. 13:12, specifically upon *"videmus nunc per speculum in aenigmate."* For

---

63. Neusner argues that such spiritualizing is one of the fundamental contrasts between Judaism and Christianity. For Neusner, Jesus speaks about salvation in a future kingdom or world above while the rabbis and Torah sanctify this world (1993: 58–132). The contrast with the Gospel of John is palpable. Cf. Nietzsche's critique of Christian spiritualizing. See, e.g., the preface to Nietzsche, 1966, where he describes Christianity as Platonism for the masses.

64. Aichele aptly describes the Old Testament as the New Testament's spiritual colonization of the Hebrew Bible (2001: 138). This work (2001) by Aichele and its predecessor (1997) explicate the Christian investment in spiritual semiotics.

Bloy, like Runeberg and other theologians, everything is meaningful; yet, everyday life seems chaotic, not meaningful. Thus, one can know the secret meaning/plot only enigmatically. In fact, as the secret is known only "through a mirror in darkness," one may see things backwards. Finally, it becomes unlikely that anyone knows who they are or what their role is in the secret plan.

All of this starts with the simple—and basic Christian—assertion that matters are other than they appear. In fact, Borges specifically asserts, "I venture to judge them [Bloy's spiritualizing reflections] verisimilar and perhaps inevitable within the Christian doctrine" (Borges, 1964: 211). Furthermore, if one begins with "truth's" fundamentally symbolic or spiritual nature, one is not far from Runeberg's spiritually ascetic Judas. One is not far from the conclusion that one cooperates with the spirit by denying it. One is also not far from Runeberg's third Judas, from the Judas who is himself the incarnate one. After all, in the world of the secret, spiritual plot, known identities are not likely to be the truth. Intriguingly, and appropriately, Borges identifies Bloy as a definitive influence on the "Three Versions of Judas" (Borges, 1962: 106).

Scorsese's *The Last Temptation of Christ* (1988) never pursues the spiritual asceticism of Runeberg's second Judas.[65] Instead, the film celebrates the Christian exaltation of the spirit. In both Kazantzakis' novel and the film, the Zealot Judas represents the flesh and the mystic Jesus represents the spirit. A nocturnal scene in the film in which Jesus and Judas talk alone about different kinds of freedom exemplifies this point well. Judas demands a revolution that will lead to freedom from the Romans. Because Jesus knows that evil, not the Romans, is the problem and that political freedom will not free humans from the flesh, he talks instead about spiritual freedom. Given the huge gap between the spirit and the flesh in this neoplatonic world, neither really understands the other, and Jesus and Judas, despite their intimacy, work at cross purposes. Of course, the spiritual Jesus ultimately triumphs. The film depicts this spiritual victory in various ways.

First, Jesus' initial understanding of the divine plan leads him to forsake the sensual Mary Magdalene. In an early scene, Jesus visits her house, which has two serpents painted on the door, and waits in a queue for this prostitute's services. When her day's work is done, she angrily taunts Jesus to act like a man and to make love to her. Fleeing the carnal Magdalene, Jesus enters the wilderness where he is tempted by snakes, using the voice of the Magdalene. Rejecting love and family as temptations, Jesus begins

---

65. See the discussion of this film's canonical Judas in Chapter 3.

his ministry of love for all. Of course, love for all is a spiritual message compared to the material, fleshly love that the Magdalene demands from him. The film's infamous last temptation fantasy reprises this same temptation, the temptation to choose a normal human life of love and family over the secret plan of spiritual life through Jesus' death. Jesus chooses the spirit on both occasions.

Second, at two separate points, Jesus declares his superiority to Torah. At the wedding in Cana, a man objects to the polluting presence of Mary Magdalene. Jesus defends her by claiming that God has room enough in heaven for all. When the man objects that this attitude violates the Torah, Jesus replies that his heart (the spiritual center) overrules the Torah. Later, in the first Temple scene, when the priests defend the money-changers, Jesus horrifies the priests by claiming that he is the end of the Torah, God, and the saint of blasphemy. He also claims that God, the immortal spirit, belongs to the world, not Israel. Like love for all, a universal Torah is a more spiritual entity than the Torah that makes the Jews God's particular people.

Third, and most importantly, the film realizes the visionary world of Jesus for its audience. At first, Jesus simply describes this visionary world in an interior monologue, but gradually the film visualizes Jesus' wilderness visions. In the second of these scenes, Jesus talks with John the Baptist. Subsequently, Jesus and the audience learn that the Baptist is already dead when this happens. Without knowing it, the audience has come to share Jesus' visionary world as if it were (the cinematic) reality. In the same scene, Jesus shares his mission with his disciples by taking out his heart and extending it to them. The film has left normal reality behind and, from this point on, moves routinely back and forth between "reality" and Jesus' visions.

The grand finale operates similarly. Various techniques render the crucifixion an "interior," spiritual experience—an experience with Jesus—rather than an outsider's experience of an exterior, material reality. Eerie silences punctuate the scene. The audience hears Jesus' thoughts and heartbeat. The audience hears a mighty storm but sees blue skies. Then, in an eerie calm at the eye of the storm, Jesus faces the tempting young girl. The film portrays the ensuing fantasy far more "realistically" than it has the previous crucifixion scenes. When the temptation ends, the crucifixion visuals return, but the techniques creating an interior presentation do not continue. Now, one simply watches Jesus accept his messiah role. The spiritual interpretation that Jesus is messiah in his death has now become the exterior (cinematic) reality. Jesus dies smiling with keening, strobe lights, and church bells. Once again, and quite powerfully, the audience has been made privy to Jesus' visionary reality.

The scapegoat here is Judas because the triumph of the spirit depends upon Christ's manipulation and betrayal of Judas. Intriguingly, however, the flesh/Judas has to intrude into Jesus' death-throe fantasy to demand that Jesus be faithful to the spirit, to the divine plan. Consequently, the spirit relies upon the flesh (Judas) or makes the flesh its precursor. Not incidentally, Scorsese's Jesus is also the most human Jesus in the Jesus film tradition. If one accepts the spirit's victory in this film, it is only as this human Jesus comes to understand and accept the secret plan.[66] The spirit, then, is a visionary adjunct of the fleshly Judas and the human Jesus. Of course, one could similarly describe (spiritual) Christianity as a visionary adjunct of (material) Judaism and, possibly, (spiritual) Christianity as a visionary specter still haunting (materialist) modernity.

From Theology to an Aesthetic Ethic

Borges' narrator observes that Runeberg's second Judas forsakes theology for ethic. One can dispute that to a certain extent because of this Judas' neoplatonic assumptions; nonetheless, the narrator's claim is true in that Runeberg's second Judas asks what kind of life he should lead, not what he should believe. That this Judas chooses a life of spiritual asceticism makes him a potential analogy both for the Judaism superseded by spiritual Christianity (as in both *Jesus of Nazareth* and *The Last Temptation of Christ*) and for the development of materialist modernity, a culture that has rejected theology for psychology and the spiritual for the material. Not surprisingly, then, modernity, like Runeberg, is fascinated with Judas' psychology, with his motive for betraying Jesus.[67]

Runeberg rejects cupidity, Judas' traditional motive, in favor of spiritual asceticism as Judas' motivation. Consequently, Runeberg's second Judas inverts the traditional image of the greedy Judas as well as the image of the spiritual Christ. Instead of grasping, this Judas forsakes all that he thinks is truly important. He does not do this sinfully or mistakenly as theologians assume. He consciously sacrifices the spirit, which he values above all things,

---

66. The exaltation of the spirit (Jesus) over the flesh (Judas) is quite similar to the supersessionism of *Jesus of Nazareth* and the canon. Here, again, *The Last Temptation of Christ* is quite canonical.

67. See Chapter 5. Happel discusses modern criticism's move away from aristocratic virtue to (democratic) psychology to explain characters like Judas (1993: 110–12). In Brelich, *The Work of Betrayal* (1988), the detective Dupin argues that the fascination with Judas' (unknowable) motives has led interpreters down a dead-end road. Borges, who rejects the novel's subjectivity in favor of magical plots, would likely agree.

on behalf of God/Christ and to find true religious devotion. Judas, like so many other Borgesian followers of Christ, follows an absurdly literal and logical ethic (cf. Borges, 1999a: 443–45).[68]

Like Runeberg, many modern interpreters have abandoned the arena of theology to explain Judas. Since De Quincey, most have favored political explanations of Judas' actions.[69] As discussed in Chapter 3, De Quincey argues that Judas betrays Jesus in order to force Jesus to act to free Israel from Roman occupation and that this motivation is blind to spiritual matters (1897: 8:177, 181). Consequently, De Quincey's Judas, like Scorsese's, still belongs to spiritualizing Christian discourse.

Nicholas Ray's *King of Kings* (1961) modernizes the De Quincey theory.[70] Once again, the spiritual Jesus story rides upon a more basic story—here, the glorification of violence in a "sword and sandal" biblical epic. The film opens with a narrator (Orson Welles) recounting the long Roman oppression of the Jews and asserting that they survived through their hope for a messiah. Despite scenes about Jesus' infancy, the first messianic claimant is Barabbas, who successfully harasses Pilate's arriving army in the film's first epic battle. Significantly, the visuals pair Judas, Barabbas' lieutenant, with Barabbas. The subsequent baptism of Jesus is, by contrast with this battle scene, understated although it does feature a screen-wide close-up of Jesus' striking blue eyes.[71] As Jesus' popularity grows, Barabbas seeks to use Jesus for the revolt against Rome he desires, but Jesus' message is peace, love, and the brotherhood of man.[72] Judas stands between these two messiahs and has to decide, as the narrator opines, whether to follow the messiah of war or the messiah of peace.

---

68. One could also read this ethic as a logical interpretation of Mark 8:35. Cf. Walsh, 2008a.

69. In Jesus films, e.g., political aims at least partly motivate the Judases of *The King of Kings* (1927), *King of Kings* (1961), *Jesus Christ Superstar* (1973), *Jesus of Nazareth* (1977), *The Last Temptation of Christ* (1988), and *Jesus* (1999).

70. The Judas in *Jesus of Nazareth* (1977) may be even more modern as he believes political maneuvering can best realize Jesus' ideals. That movie deliberately separates Judas, as an intellectual, from the other disciples who represent good, common sense. Judas never understands Jesus' message, which is for the heart, not the head. Once again, this Judas is the product of spiritual discourse. See Walsh, 2003: 167n20.

71. One might see these eyes as indicative of a subjectivity of inner, divine depth.

72. An epic presentation of the Sermon on the Mount articulates Jesus' teaching at length. The film's advertising touted the epic Sermon extensively. It should be the epic counterpart to the battle scenes, but the film's generic context (the other biblical epics) overrides this possibility.

When Jesus arrives in Jerusalem in triumph and preaches in the Temple, the film offers its second epic battle, Barabbas' revolt in the Temple courtyards. The Romans crush this revolt and arrest Barabbas. Devastated by his friend's failure, Judas takes on the De Quincey Judas role and betrays Jesus to force him to revolt and throw off the Roman oppression (and, more importantly, to save Barabbas).[73] Judas, of course, is wrong and the passion ensues. Barabbas and Judas follow Jesus along the Via Dolorosa and watch the crucifixion from afar. After Jesus' death, Barabbas finds Judas hanging and brings him down to hold him in a bleak pietà, creating a pathetic parallel to the earlier scene in which a closely paired Barabbas and Judas watched Pilate's arriving army and, thereby, visually asserting the film's (semi-)pacifist message.

The film is slightly more modern than De Quincey's interpretation of Judas because the film does not require a commitment to traditional, neo-platonic spirituality. Instead of eternal life, the film's Jesus calls moderns to a modern, liberal ethic (see Walsh, 2003: 121–46). Jesus' followers do not need to be more ethereal than Barabbas and Judas are. They simply need to recognize the futility of violence or, more precisely, the political irrelevance of Jesus' teaching. This perspective belies the film's apparent rejection of violence and of politics. This Jesus simply does not speak to such issues. Thus, the film's spectacular Sermon hardly balances the film's epic battle scenes. Even more tellingly, while Jesus (supposedly) teaches (his liberal ethic) in the Temple, the film offers an epic battle. The film's message may be with Jesus, but its camera follows the battle.

The film's heart is really Lucius, the centurion, who is in charge of the Roman forces whenever they come into contact with the Jesus or Barabbas story. As a result, Lucius becomes a witness—with the audience—of the gospel story and of the biblical epic. He does not, however, believe in God, and he is thoroughly complicit in the Roman Empire's violence and colonization. Gradually, however, he comes to admire Jesus. At the Roman trial, Pilate appoints Lucius as Jesus' advocate, and Lucius strenuously asserts Jesus' innocence and, not incidentally, the apolitical nature of Jesus' teaching. At the cross, then, Lucius, the centurion, can confess that Jesus is the (spiritual) Christ without abandoning his Roman loyalties or his imperial military career. Unlike Judas, Lucius conveniently compartmentalizes Jesus and his teaching.

Thereby, Lucius grants the modern audience an entrée into the Jesus story (see Walsh, 2003: 127–28). In particular, his legal defense of Jesus

---

73. Of the various political Judases in film, the other most De Quincey-like Judas appears in Young's *Jesus* (1999).

4 *The Ascetic Judas* 115

separates Jesus' teaching from the realities of politics and empire. Jesus' ethic is for private individuals. By contrast, De Quincey's Judas and the Judas of *King of Kings* improperly mix religion/the spirit with political and social affairs.[74] Modernity accepts and relishes the spirit when it is a symbol for subjective depths or for personal expression (when, e.g., it is Jesus' striking blue eyes). The spirit troubles modernity when it intrudes into the reasonable, bureaucratic world of politics.[75]

Furthermore, the spirit frightens modernity when it augurs the transcendent. For moderns, transcendent spirits are haunting, uncanny specters.[76] Vis-à-vis this spirit, modernity, like Runeberg's second Judas, is spiritually ascetic. So, too, is the modern quest for the historical Jesus. It rejects spiritual myths or the otherworldly Christ of the church in favor of the human Jesus. Thus, the Jesus of Reimarus, the critic whom Schweitzer locates at the very beginning of the quest, is as spiritually blind as the Johannine Christ's interlocutors or as De Quincey's Judas. Like the De Quincey Judas, Reimarus' Jesus desires an earthly Jewish kingdom. The spiritual Christ is the later creation of the disciples (1985: 65–67, 98–102, 129–34, 240–48).

While most historians have not followed Reimarus' specific reconstruction,[77] two features of subsequent historical research share a fundamental similarity with his spiritual asceticism. First, most historical Jesuses are this-worldly figures. These modern Jesuses, however, are more comfortable with modern social and political arrangements than Reimarus' Jesus is. They are more similar to Lucius and, accordingly, understand religion as a matter of individual ethic or of subjective depth, not a matter of the transcendent or the political. These Jesuses do not threaten or even speak to modern political and social arrangements. While this description is patently true of the liberal Jesus of the Old Quest, it is also true of most of the apocalyptic Jesuses created by historians since Schweitzer. In

---

74. As the vices of Judas are ones that modernity would like to disown, they are understandable vices for moderns. See Chapter 5, Walsh, 2006a: 43–47, Pyper, 2001, and Reinhartz, 2007: 151–77. Reinhartz claims that Judas represents the viewing audience who must decide whether to follow or betray Jesus (2007: 177).

75. Cf. the non-apocalyptic resurrection of *Jesus of Nazareth* and of Acts (or, for that matter, of the New Testament as a whole apart from Revelation).

76. This fear dominates religious horror films like *The Exorcist* (1973) and its progeny. See Chapter 5. Cf. the horrible, consuming divine in the fates of Judas in *Jesus Christ Superstar* (1973) and of Jesus in *The Last Temptation of Christ* (1988).

77. On Jesus and a political kingdom, see Brandon, 1967; Eiseman, 1997; Maccoby, 1992: 27–33, 141–59; and Tabor, 2006. The idea has also attracted recent novelists. The most well known is Dan Brown's *The Da Vinci Code* (2003). See also Baigent, Leigh, and Lincoln, 2004.

the hands of most scholars, apocalyptic becomes everyday mysticism, a primitive form of existentialism, or Buddhism lite. Apocalyptic becomes a worldview that enables individuals to cope individually with modern socio-political realities without transforming them.[78] Put differently, such apocalyptic Jesuses are simply another way of valuing modern subjectivity, not some transcendent reality (Walsh, 2003: 173–85). In fact, one might see the apocalyptic Jesus as scholars' successful domestication of Reimarus' more troublingly political figure.

Second, historical Jesus research routinely arrives at a Jewish Jesus. At first blush, the Jewish Jesus offers less support for modern Christians than the apocalyptic Jesus does (see Schweitzer, 1968: 398–99; and Miles, 2001: 266); however, this appraisal overlooks the post-Holocaust context of the most recent, most ardent Christian assertions about Jesus the Jew. Put simply, while Jesus the Jew does not justify any form of modern *Christ*ianity, the horror of the Holocaust calls for desperate measures. Accordingly, recent Christian apologetics, like Runeberg's speculations, have shifted from metaphysical and epistemological concerns to ethics. These apologists deny the spirit—the problematic, otherworldly claims of traditional Christianity vis-à-vis secular, scientific modernity—to focus on Christianity's relationship to "the other" in this present, material world.

Unlike that of Runeberg's second Judas, however, this scholarly asceticism does not consider the spiritual (transcendent) world it sacrifices the pearl of great price. It makes these "sacrifices" painlessly in order to make a place for itself in materialistic modernity. Moreover, despite apologetic claims, such Christian or academic myth-making does not necessarily rehabilitate Judaism or foster religious dialogue.[79]

For Maccoby, however, such spiritual asceticism or the rejection of Christian theology is a first step toward the restoration of Judas/Judaism. He claims that the early Christian writings betray several stages in the development of what he calls "the Judas myth": (1) a historical Judas, the brother and disciple of Jesus (see the other Judas in Lk. 6:16); (2) the Pauline church's creation of the spiritual Christ myth and the claim that those not accepting this myth, like Judas and the Jerusalem "church," are spiritually blind (see the question of the other Judas in Jn 14:22); and (3)

---

78. For a discussion of Schweitzer that leads to a similar conclusion, see Blanton, 2007: 129–72. If one understands apocalyptic so, little separates the apocalyptic Jesus from its recent rival, the cynic sage Jesus.

79. See Arnal's insightful critique of the (often Christian) mythic work covertly accomplished through the symbol of the Jewish Jesus (2005: 39–72).

4 *The Ascetic Judas* 117

the invention of the betrayal and its attachment to Judas because of his name (1992: 25–29, 146–54).[80]

In this analysis, the fiction of the betrayal serves the interests of spiritual Christianity by covering up those early followers of Jesus who are "more" Jewish and who contend with early Pauline Christianity. For Maccoby, these other followers include the family of Jesus who share his expectations of a restoration of the Davidic Kingdom (remember Reimarus). After Jesus' death, his brothers, including "Prince Judas," head a nationalistic messianic movement in Jerusalem. The movement, which includes Zealots, differs from the Zealots largely because it (and the apocalyptic Jesus) relies more heavily on divine intervention than the Zealots did (1992: 141–59).

In this scenario, Jesus and Judas become difficult to distinguish.[81] They are so many Jewish "princes" working for a restored Jewish kingdom. One is again in a Borgesian world where figures switch places at a bewildering pace. Of course, only mavericks, like Maccoby, carry the spiritual asceticism of modern, historical Jesus and Judas research to such lengths. Runeberg's second Judas, for example, is a more Christian figure. His spiritual asceticism is a sacrifice. He makes this sacrifice not to adapt to modernity, but to become a figure worthy of his Lord. More modern Judases and Jesuses make no such sacrifice when they excise the spirit. In modernity, the spirit distracts one from more valuable, this-worldly matters.

The use of Judas in Theodore Rozak's *Flicker* is illustrative of this modern rejection of an otherworldly spirit. The novel tells the tale of Jonathan Gates' education in film and sex in a grubby, repertory film house, *The Classic*, and as a film professor and critic. In the process, Jonathan discovers the B-movies of a little-known director, Max Castle, one of whose "classic" films was *Judas Jedermann (Judas Everyman)*, which sets the Judas story in a modern setting with a Judas who "rats" on a political comrade. Many film visuals descend staircases in engulfing shadows in order to create a sense of shame, panic, and damnation. Through these visuals the audience experiences how it feels to be Judas. Jonathan's basic experience is revulsion, but the most telling review of the film's effect

---

80. Klassen's reconstruction of the historical Judas is more popular with scholars than Maccoby's. Klassen also finds beneath the calumny of betrayal—at its height in John's world-above gospel—a loyal disciple and a good Jew, struggling to do what is right vis-à-vis his Jewish traditions and Jesus. See Chapter 3. Cf. also Greenberg, 2007.

81. Is it relevant that the book of James, often associated with Jewish Christianity and even with the brother of Jesus, contains so many echoes of the teachings of Jesus without attributing them to Jesus?

comes from Jonathan's unsophisticated lover: "It's enough to put you off sex for the rest of your life" (2005: 116).

While Jonathan thinks little of her remark at the time, he ultimately discovers that the movies are the greatest conspiracy of all time. The flicker of film is an analogue for and a device implementing the theology of the Cathari, who believe the world to be a struggle between the light/spirit and the darkness/flesh. They produce films, with hidden messages (Jonathan finds a device that allows him to see these messages), that demean the material world in favor of the spirit. Like *Judas Jedermann*, they create a sense of revulsion about life in this world. Their bleak and sadistic images sexually repulse their audiences. Although Jonathan discovers this conspiracy, the novel ends bleakly. The Cathari kidnap Jonathan and exile him on a deserted island with Max Castle. Max and Jonathan spend their (last?) days together making film clips out of earlier films to create various apocalyptic scenarios. The world as it is seems lost to the powers of the dark spiritual gods.[82] The novel's one note of hope is that Jonathan begins writing his memoirs on the island and his first sentences sound like the beginning of the novel in which he stars.

Conspiracies, secret plots, and phantoms with no meaningful will of their own are, of course, common modern themes. What *Flicker* does, which Runeberg's second Judas does not, is to show how these themes, when combined with an exaltation of the spirit, leave this world enslaved to dark powers. Many have seen gnosticism or the Cathari as guilty on this point. For Borges, Christianity poses the same threat, and heretics, like Runeberg, simply pursue ideas inherent in Christianity to their (absurdly) logical results. Hence, Runeberg's second Judas does not provide an exact analogue to the rise of modernity and its valuation of this world. Instead, he is, like the Cathari and like spiritual Christianity, one who devalues this world in favor of another. His ethic only seems modern. The implicit praise of sex in *Flicker* is far more modern.

Incidentally, so too, is the premise of *The Da Vinci Code*, which has characters who claim that the spiritual Christ of orthodox Christianity is a massive cover-up of the earthly dynasty of Jesus and his wife, Mary Magdalene. More importantly, *The Da Vinci Code* also claims that the Christian spiritual message covers up, not just this one *Sang Real* (Holy Blood or holy lineage), but the eternal feminine, which exalts sex and this

---

82. Cf. how the idealist Tlön threatens to consume the world in Borges' "Tlön, Uqbar, Orbis Tertius" (1962: 17–35). Once again, Borges' fiction serves as a prophylactic against metaphysical and theological certainties. See the discussion in Chapter 1.

life. Vis-à-vis the patriarchal church and the spiritual Christ, the fiction's premise democratizes and secularizes the sacred. Runeberg's second Judas does not chart such waters. He remains too entrenched in spiritualizing Christian discourse. Runeberg's third Judas, Judas the god, comes closer to this modern hallowing of the individual and his/her life in this world.

Chapter 5

JUDAS THE GOD

Runeberg's Third Judas: Judas the Incarnate God

After some years, Runeberg publishes his second manuscript, *Dem hemlige Fralsaren* (*The Secret Savior*), with the epigraph, "In the world he was, and the world was made by him, and the world knew him not" (Jn 1:10). The quotation concisely summarizes Runeberg's argument against orthodox Christology. Jesus cannot be the incarnate God because he is well known as such. The secret plan assumption makes orthodox Christology laughable. Runeberg further contends that Jesus cannot be the incarnate God because the suffering of a mere afternoon (the crucifixion) is not the perfect sacrifice befitting God.[1] Instead, God must become a man to the point of his own damnation. He must be despised as the least of men. Adroitly, Runeberg refers to Isa. 53:2-3:

> For he grew up before him like a young plant,
>   and like a root out of dry ground;
> he had no form or majesty that we should look at him,
>   nothing in his appearance that we should desire him.
> He was despised and rejected by others;
>   a man of suffering and acquainted with infirmity;
> and as one from whom others hide their faces
>   he was despised, and we held him of no account.

For Runeberg, this passage prophesies Judas precisely. It does not fit the orthodox Christ. Therefore, Runeberg concludes succinctly: God is Judas. For Runeberg, the indifference with which the theologians receive his ideas corroborates his views.[2] His own lack of notoriety is the corollary of

---

1. A footnote says that the crucifixion goes on forever: Judas now receives the bribe; returns the money; and knots the hangman's noose. The parody of the "eternal time" of the Eucharist is obvious. Jeffers, "Dear Judas," also imagines the betrayal repeated throughout eternity, but his scenario reflects an eternal return, rather than the *in illo tempore* of ritual time (1971: 2: 5–45).

2. Cf. the comic scenes in *Monty Python's Life of Brian* (1979) in which Brian's

the secret identity of the savior (as Judas), and he prays to share hell with his God.[3]

Borges' Judas: Gnosticism or Orthodoxy?

The orthodox narrator of "Three Versions of Judas" describes Runeberg as a latter day gnostic, and many of Runeberg's musings do suggest gnosticism. Runeberg's first Judas mirrors the divine Christ; and these twins cleave reality respectively into the human/material and the divine/spiritual. For orthodox theologians, such a metaphysical dualism is an unmistakable sign of gnosticism.[4] On the basis of this dualistic metaphysic, Runeberg's second Judas enacts an ethic of unworthiness, which the orthodox also often associate with gnosticism.[5] The deification of Judas in Runeberg's third Judas is yet another indication of gnosticism because the gnostics often lionize orthodox villains (e.g., Cain). Moreover, the notion that Judas is God suggests a degradation of the deity similar to the gnostic idea that a divine fall led to the creation of the gnostic pantheon and the material world.

The notion that Judas is the incarnate God, however, is hardly gnostic. Instead, the incarnation is a crucial orthodox idea. As a result, while Runeberg flirts with gnosticism, he also remains troublingly orthodox in some ways. In addition to the incarnation, he affirms orthodox notions like the infinite (infallible) Bible, the secret plan, magical oracles, symbolic (or spiritual) truth, and the degradation of Judas. The Christian narrator's assertion (he refers to "the year of our Lord"), then, that Runeberg

---

denials that he is a messiah convince the messiah-making crowd, which the film spoofs, that he is the messiah.

3. The divine Judas still reaches his canonical fate. As with his opening assumption of the infinite book, Runeberg's speculations are uncomfortably close to orthodoxy because Borges is asserting that his speculations are inevitable within orthodoxy. See Borges, 1964: 211.

4. Before the eighteenth century, such dualism was normally called Manichaeism. See R. Smith, 1990: 522. Some current scholars challenge the dualistic definition of gnosticism and define it instead as a pursuit of awareness of the (divine) self. Even that definition is likely too broad, so current scholars speak of gnosticisms. See M. Williams, 1996; Pagels, 2003; and King, 2003. Borges' knowledge of gnosticism antedates these new views. Some trace Borges' knowledge of gnosticism to Mead, 1962.

5. The qualifications, which asserts that gnosticism appears a metaphysical dualism and so forth to the orthodox, are necessary because of recent debates about what gnosticism is and because the previous chapters have associated a neoplatonic metaphysic and an ethic of human unworthiness with orthodoxy itself.

is a gnostic defends orthodoxy against confusing heretics like Runeberg. Runeberg hopelessly mixes orthodoxy and gnosticism (see Chapter 6). It is no wonder, then, that the orthodox theologians of the story ultimately ignore him. Ignoring him protects their worldview.

Borges himself also confuses metaphysical systems even though gnosticism admittedly fascinates him.[6] In "A Defense of Basilides the False," Borges professes an admiration of gnosticism for its "quiet resolution of the problem of evil by means of a hypothetical insertion of a gradual series of divinities between the no less hypothetical God and reality" (1999b: 67). Borges hones in further on the chain of deities and worlds as yet another example of *structure en abîme* or infinity.[7] The Creator becomes a lesser divine being, a demiurge, a deity spawned by some higher deity. This Creator is an analogue to the priest in Borges' "The Circular Ruins," a Creator who is himself a creation (1962: 57–63).[8] In the poem, "Chess," Borges abandons analogies and reduces God to one of a series:

> God moves the player, he in turn the piece.
> But what god beyond God begins the round
> of dust and time and sleep and agonies?" (2000a: 103)

The suggestion of a chain of deities also figures in Borges' "The Approach to Al-Mu'tasim," a story in which Borges' narrator reviews a novel (imagined into existence by Borges) whose Muslim protagonist murders a Hindu in Bombay (or thinks he does) and flees, spending his life on the run among the vile (1962: 37–43). In the presence of one of the vilest, he senses a reflection of a noble soul; thereafter, he searches for this soul "through the subtle reflections which this soul has left in others." He looks for what he calls "Al-Mu'tasim" (1962: 40). The novel ends with the protagonist entering a curtained room from which the voice of Al-Mu'tasim has issued.

The narrator offers various interpretations of this novel. One, which he calls stimulating, is "the conjecture that the Almighty [Al-Mu'tasim] is also in search of Someone, and *that* Someone in search of some superior Someone (or merely indispensable or equal Someone), and thus on to the end—or better, the endlessness—of Time, or on and on in some cyclical

---

6. Bloom describes Borges as imaginatively a gnostic (1986:1). Bloom has admitted his own fascination with gnosticism. See Bloom, 1992.
7. Cf. the discussion of Borges' fantastic fiction in Chapter 1.
8. Cf. Borges, "The Golem" (2000a: 192–97). The films *The Thirteenth Floor* (1999) and *eXistenZ* (1999) are similar world-within-world stories.

5 Judas the God

form" (1962: 41–42). To support this interpretation, the narrator reveals that "Al-Mu'tasim" means "the Seeker of Shelter."

The discovery of the noblest in the vile, which sparks this seeker's search, parallels Runeberg's discovery of the incarnate God in the despised Judas; however, the Muslim goes beyond Runeberg's rather orthodox approach to the divine. The Muslim assumes multiple reflections and, in one of the reviewer's interpretations, multiple gods who are themselves seekers. The chain of deities resembles the gnostic πλήρωμα and Borges' infinity. Not surprisingly, seeker and sought mirror one another, and the novel's fitting subtitle is *A Game with Shifting Mirrors*. A footnote about a Persian poem continues the motif. The poem describes the birds' search for their king, the Simurg, who has left a feather behind. Losing many of their number along the way, thirty birds finally come to the mountain of the Simurg. Not coincidentally, the name "Simurg" means "thirty birds." Accordingly, the thirty birds conclude that they are the Simurg. Once again, the searcher and the sought are one (1962: 43).[9] Matters, to a large degree, are comparable with Runeberg and his Judas, although Runeberg's orthodoxy (or that of the narrator) prevents this self-knowledge.

For Borges himself, as Runeberg's ambiguities indicate, orthodoxy and heresy are mirrors and/or narrative rivals. They require one another for self-definition.[10] Thus, in Borges' "The Theologians," two "orthodox" theologians contend with one another as they fight heresy (1964: 119–26). Early on, John of Pannonia bests his rival Aurelian by writing a brief refutation of the Monotone heresy which teaches that history is a circle. Later, another heretical group, the Histriones, claims that events and people are inverse mirror images of those in heaven (cf. Runeberg). Some of these heretics also teach that there is no repetition. In refuting the Histriones, Aurelian inadvertently uses the words of John of Pannonia to describe their views. As a result, the authorities accuse John of the Histrione heresy and, as he cannot recant without becoming a Monotone, burn him as a heretic. Intriguingly, orthodoxy vanishes. At least, it is not a viable option for John. For him, there is no (non-heretical) space between

---

9. Cf. Borges, "The Simurgh [sic] and the Eagle" (1999b: 294–97).

10. See the discussion of plot rivals in Chapter 4. The canon assumes that heresy is the evil transformation of orthodoxy (e.g., Acts 20:29–30; Jude). Scholars, however, now routinely assume that a variety of Jesus movements preceded the development of orthodoxy, whose eventual development rendered other early versions heretical. In this reconstruction, orthodoxy is the version of early Christianity that eventually gained the power to label its competitors heretical and, thereby, to recreate itself continually. In either view, heresy is orthodoxy's constant shadow.

the two heresies. Some years later, Aurelian also dies in a lightning strike. Thereafter, in heaven, "Aurelian learned that, for the unfathomable divinity, he and John of Pannonia (the orthodox believer and the heretic, the abhorrer and the abhorred, the accuser and the accused) formed one single person" (1964: 126).[11]

After concluding a similar story about life-long artistic rivals, the narrator of "The Duel" observes, "Only God (whose aesthetic preferences are unknown to us) can bestow the final palm" (1999a: 385). The experience of Auerlian might lead one to add, "If there is a final palm." The introduction of God—the Western symbol of infinity—at the end of both "The Theologians" and "The Duel" effectively undermines human judgments about and distinctions between heroes and villains (see Chapter 4) and between orthodoxy and heresy. In Borges, the infinite corrupts everything. For Runeberg, too, the corruption of Christian discourse that his third Judas represents begins with reflections on the infinite (book). Runeberg stops there (in death), but Borges is not Runeberg.

For Borges, the play of possibilities continues. Thus, the degradation of Borges' Runeberg also mirrors the secret, degraded divinity. As he seeks to follow the incarnate Judas, Runeberg reprises the role of his first Judas vis-à-vis this third divine Judas. As a result, Borges' "Three Versions of Judas" returns to its beginning, inscribing a circle like that imagined in "The Approach to Al-Mu'tasim." This circle—or the parallel between Runeberg's first Judas and Runeberg's own obsessive life—illustrates both the corrupting power of infinity and the fraternal rivalry between orthodoxy and gnosticism. Borges uses Runeberg, who is his Judas, to confusingly blend such rivals. For Borges, such confusion, or mystery itself, is more important and interesting than devotion to any system.[12]

---

11. Cf. the conclusion of Borges, "Story of the Warrior and the Captive" (1964: 127–31).

12. As noted previously, Borges' description of his character Dunraven sounds like a self-description (1999a: 260). The notion of mystery is equally important in Borges' "The Sect of the Phoenix" (1962: 163–66), in which a sect differs from the common mass by possessing a secret, trivial rite because of which God grants eternity to humans. The rite's necessary materials include cork, wax, or gum arabic. The sect has no mythology, no priesthood, and no temples. The rite cannot be spoken of respectably. While many critics have claimed that this secret rite is sex, the cork, wax, and gum arabic are puzzling necessities if this is the case. While Borges once told Ronald Christ that the secret was sex, Christ himself is skeptical and has proposed other alternatives. In passing, Christ mentions De Quincey's observation that secret societies often have no secret (or, more accurately, that their secret is some mundane matter that has to be cloaked in secrecy in order to be awe-inspiring). See Christ,

Narrative Rivals and Perspectives Again: The Gospel of Judas

Like Runeberg, some ancient gnostics lionize Judas. At least, according to Irenaeus, a group of gnostics possessed a Gospel of Judas that depicts Judas as the only disciple who understands Jesus and who, therefore, accomplishes "the mystery of the betrayal" (Irenaeus, *Against Heresies*, 1.31.1). For centuries, no copies of such a gospel were extant, but, in 2006, the National Geographic Society published an ancient manuscript bearing the name of the Gospel of Judas with much fanfare.[13] Many of those associated with that text's marketing have claimed it to be the gospel to which Irenaeus refers.

The recently published gospel reports Jesus' secret revelations to Judas. It begins, after the winnowing of the disciples who do not believe correctly, with a true disciple's correct confession (Gospel of Judas 33–36).[14] The scene resembles Jn 6:60-71. In that passage, John elevates Peter and twice dismisses Judas, once as disloyal and once as a devil (6:64, 70-71). By contrast, the Gospel of Judas exalts Judas and vilifies the twelve. The twelve are spiritually blind, and they worship the god of this world. The twelve do not know Jesus even though he appears to them in various forms. When Jesus laughingly mocks their false beliefs and (Eucharistic)

1969: 155–59. De Quincey's observation seems closer to Borges' aesthetic worldview than does the notion that the secret is sex. One might restate De Quincey's observation in a fashion that recalls the discussion of Eco's *Foucault's Pendulum* (1990) in Chapter 3 above: the only secret is that someone claims to have a secret. One believes in that secret (plot) and pursues it to one's peril. In a slightly different but intriguing interpretation, Crossan suggests that the secret in Borges' "The Sect of the Phoenix" is "play," the human fabrication of world and the consciousness of that act (1976: 50–54). Borges' "The Sect of the Phoenix" does include this Latin proverb: "*Orbis terrarum est speculum Ludi*" (1962: 165).

13. The text was publicized and published by the National Geographic Society. For in-house accounts of the text's history and discovery, see Krosney, 2006; Kasser, 2006: 47–76; and Kasser, 2007: 1–33. For an alternate account, see Robinson, 2006. Most of the initial popularity of the gospel had to do with its potential to rewrite early Christian history. See n30 below.

14. The numbers refer to manuscript pages in Codex Tchacos. The discussion here cites the translation included in Kasser and Wurst, 2007: 183–235. This critical edition includes photos of the Coptic manuscript and transcriptions of the Coptic. Kasser, Meyer, and Wurst published an earlier translation (2006), which has been more widely read and used, particularly as it was briefly available on the internet. DeConick offers criticisms of the earlier translation, some of which do not apply to the critical edition (2007: 45–61). For a discussion of her reading of the Gospel of Judas, see below.

rituals,[15] the disciples become angry and blaspheme. Jesus responds by challenging them to stand before him. Only Judas accepts the challenge and then confesses, "I know who you are and where you have come from. You have come from the immortal realm of Barbelo. And I am not worthy to utter the name of the one who sent you" (Gospel of Judas 35). Judas alone recognizes that Jesus represents the ineffable God, not the lesser demiurge who created the world. Recognizing Judas' insight, Jesus separates Judas from the others and predicts Judas' suffering at the hands of the others and his eventual replacement by them (35–36, cf. 44–46). When Judas asks a question, however, Jesus leaves without answering.

When Jesus returns, he tells the disciples that he has been with a holy generation (in the spiritual realm), which they cannot hope to comprehend. He, then, interprets their vision of a temple as their service in the false religion of the god of this world (36–43). When Judas distinguishes himself again by asking about the fruit of this generation, Jesus claims that some spirits will rise after death (43–44). When Judas describes his visions of the twelve stoning him and of a great house, Jesus explains that the house is the spiritual realm and that Judas is the thirteenth δαίμων, the one who will be cursed by the others but who will rule over them (44–47).[16]

Jesus, then, takes Judas aside for private revelations. The instruction, partly from a speaking, luminous cloud, concerns gnostic cosmology, the great invisible Spirit, and the bloody lesser deities who made this world and humans (47–55). Jesus also promises Judas that his star will reign over the thirteenth aeon (55). Laughing at the error of those (the twelve) who worship the demiurge, Jesus tells Judas "… everything that is evil. But you will exceed all of them. For you will sacrifice the man who bears me" (56).[17] After a poem eulogizing Judas, Judas is transfigured. He enters the luminous cloud while those left behind hear a heavenly voice (57). The scene resembles Jesus' transfiguration in the Synoptic Gospels or the moment the heavenly voice marks the beginning of Jesus' glorification in Jn 12:28–30. The betrayal follows immediately and ends the gospel, but in a decidedly anticlimactic fashion.

As in the canonical gospels, Judas' betrayal follows Jesus' imperial oracle (56). Unlike the canonical gospels, however, the Gospel of Judas

---

15. The winnowing of the disciples in John follows the bread from heaven discourse, which many see as a discourse with Eucharistic overtones.

16. Cf. the "woe" pronounced upon Judas at the Last Supper (Mt. 26:24; Mk 14:21; Lk. 22:22).

17. The text has several gaps rendering its precise meaning uncertain. See below.

prepares Judas and its readers for Judas' betrayal through extensive lessons in gnostic cosmology. The instruction provides a metaphysical context for Judas' act. Judas sacrifices the man who bears Jesus, a "man," which is the creation of the demiurge. The sacrifice will release Jesus' spirit into the higher spiritual realm. Confusing elements do, however, certainly exist. For example, it is not altogether clear why Jesus' death—or, more precisely, that of his "man"—is necessary. After all, Jesus already comes and goes from the heavens at will. Nevertheless, the gospel amply prepares Judas for the idea that death is the release of the spirit for those who belong to the heavenly generation (Gospel of Judas 43–44). Jesus' cosmological lectures to Judas are, then, the functional equivalent of the Synoptic passion predictions or the Johannine farewell discourse. While the Johannine discourses educate everyone but Judas, the Gospel of Judas depicts the spiritual education of Judas alone. The others are now the ones left outside in the dark.

So read, the Gospel of Judas is the story of Judas' spiritual enlightenment, and Judas models what it means to follow Jesus. Judas' story—and one presumes the story of the gospel's believers as well—begins with a gnostic confession, moves through enlightenment in gnostic cosmological teachings, eschews (Jewish and) orthodox rituals and leadership, and climaxes with the believer's transfiguration/glorification. The contrast with John is again instructive. John climaxes with Judas' demonization and Jesus' glorification. Here, Judas is the glorified one. If one takes Irenaeus' comment that Judas "accomplished the mystery of the betrayal" as a key to this gospel, then the betrayal is the moment of "the mystery," the ritualistic climax of Judas' enlightenment.

When Judas betrays Jesus, Judas enacts the key soteriological teaching of the gospel, the notion that his master's death is a spiritual release.[18] By assisting his master's departure, Judas himself reaches a stage of mystic enlightenment like that of his master, but Judas does not yet leave the world. He remains behind, like the apostles in the canonical gospels, to teach others by his example. Accordingly, the gospel twice predicts Judas' future: his passion, his replacement, his curse, and his damnation for all time by the spiritually blind apostles. Borges' Runeberg agrees.

---

18. Irenaeus refers to the gnostics that used the Gospel of Judas as Cainites. No other record of such a group exists, and most critics today associate the recently published Gospel of Judas with Sethian Gnosticism. For discussions of this type of gnosticism, see Meyer, 2006: 137–69; and Turner, 2001. Meyer suggests that "Cainite" was a derogatory nickname applied by the orthodox to this group (2006: 137). It is an appropriate nickname for a "brother killer."

Here, gnosticism does to orthodoxy what Christianity does to Judaism in the gospels. Gnosticism claims knowledge of a secret plot, a symbolic/spiritual story, which the other (here orthodoxy) does not know. The Christian canon claims that the Old Testament is the hidden truth of the Hebrew Bible. The Gospel of Judas claims that the real story of Jesus' betrayal and passion is the story of the enlightenment and mystic initiation of Judas. Once again, the story is not unlike John's, which also makes Jesus' passion into a story of the believer's spiritual enlightenment through its elaborate farewell discourse.

This gospel, then, is not the Gospel according to Judas. It is not something that Judas reports. It is the Gospel of Judas, the story of the good news about what happens to Judas (see Kasser, Meyer, and Wurst, 2006: 45n151). The news is not the oracular Judas. That notion is the very heart of the canonical Judas. The news is not that Judas cooperates with Jesus in the betrayal as Jesus' intimate friend and leading disciple. The latter may have been news in its day, but moderns are quite familiar with the idea because of theological reflections on the gospels and because of fictions like those of Borges, Kazantzakis, and Scorsese. The news is that Judas' betrayal of Jesus completes Judas' enlightenment and initiates him into the mysteries. The passion of Jesus is absent.[19] At least, the present text of the gospel ends with the betrayal. As a result, the Gospel of Judas makes Judas, rather than Jesus, the sacred center of the gospel narrative. He, not Jesus, is the mythic model for all who would follow. Like the story of Runeberg's third Judas, the Gospel of Judas rewrites Christianity with different names.

John's Demonic Judas

In this reading, the Gospel of Judas parallels John more closely than it does the Synoptic Gospels. Of course, John was the canonical gospel that was most appealing to the gnostics. Some have even argued recently that the Johannine community defined itself through a debate with the (gnostic?) community of the Gospel of Thomas about whether to emphasize belief (John) or experience (Thomas). Thus, in John alone, Thomas is the disciple who doubts until he "touches," and John extols those who believe without seeing (or touching) (Jn 20:29-31) (Riley, 1995; and

---

19. For some gnostics, the "real" Jesus did not suffer the passion, having already departed. The physical suffering was a matter for the "man" or physical body left behind. In the Gospel of Barnabas, Judas takes Jesus' place on the cross. Something similar happens here as this gospel predicts Judas' suffering, not Jesus'.

Pagels, 2003: 30–75). Do the close parallels between John and the Gospel of Judas also indicate that the communities of these texts also defined themselves vis-à-vis the other? If so, would that help account for John's particularly damning portrait of Judas? Is John deliberately demonizing another community's mythic hero?[20] Conversely, is the Gospel of Judas lionizing the other's devil?

Such scenarios may have only aesthetic appeal; nonetheless, the connection of the two gospels adds context to the fact that John demonizes Judas far more than the other canonical gospels do. Luke 22:3 does report that Satan entered Judas, but John's Judas is a devil from his first introduction (Jn 6:70-71). In fact, John makes this devilish point before even naming Judas. For John, then, the devil precedes Judas just as the Christ (or λόγος) precedes Jesus (cf. Jn 1:1-18). Not incidentally, the Gospel of Judas also refers to Judas as a δαίμων (Gospel of Judas 44). In the Hellenistic world, δαίμων is not necessarily a "demon" or an evil spiritual being. It may simply refer to a spiritual being. Read so, Judas the δαίμων is metaphysically superior to the world and to the other apostles. It classes him with the gnostic's and Runeberg's Christ.[21]

John's διάβολος is another matter. It places Judas securely in Satan's camp. Nonetheless, if one reads John as Borges' precursor, Christ/Jesus and Satan/Judas become mirror images of supernatural possessions. One thinks again of those magical knives in Borges' "The Encounter" (1999a: 364–69). In the Gospel of Judas, these possessions indicate the two's superior status and knowledge. In John, it makes them fraternal rivals. In John, two "demons" possess two humans in order to enact the ancient conflict myth. Thus, John's demonization of Judas threatens to reanimate the creation through conflict myth, normally suppressed in biblical literature (see Chapter 2).

In the Synoptic Gospels, a personified devil engages in conflict with Jesus in the temptation narrative; however, Jesus bests Satan there, and Satan plays only a minimal role thereafter (but see Lk. 22:3). The exorcisms of the Synoptic Gospels display Jesus' divine control over what is a mere remnant of the ancient conflict monster. In the exorcisms, as in Gen. 1, divine fiat dismisses the opposition. John, however, has no personified devil, no temptation narrative, and no exorcisms and, thus, creates a different scenario altogether. While various characters and the narrator do

---

20. DeConick suggests that orthodox theologians began to reflect on Judas' role in Jesus' passion after the writing of the Gospel of Judas (2007: 133–38).

21. See Kasser, Meyer, and Wurst, 2006: 31n74. DeConick argues that δαίμων identifies Judas as an evil figure, not a hero (2007: 48–51, 109–24). See below.

speak of Satan, Satan takes an active role only in Jn 13:27 (cf. 13:2) where he enters Judas to empower the betrayal (see Eslinger, 2000: 48–50). For John, then, Judas truly is the devil (6:70-71) (Kermode, 1979: 85).

The result is a Judas/Satan versus Jesus/Revealer from Above conflict, which potentially creates a Dragon versus God (world below versus world above or evil versus good) motif normally associated with non-biblical creation stories or with the apocalypse. In keeping with general tendencies in biblical literature, however, John thoroughly emasculates this mythology through a constant emphasis upon the passion as God's plan and as Jesus' action. Thus, a long passage ending Jesus' public ministry in John 12 identifies the passion as the divine program before the narrator's notes about Satan and Judas in Jn 13:2, 27. In Jn 12:23, Jesus decides that the time has come for the passion, and, in Jn 12:28, a voice from heaven seconds this decision. Immediately thereafter, Jesus describes his passion as his victory over the world and Satan (12:31–32). As a result, when Satan subsequently possesses Judas to arrange the passion, Satan/Judas simply does the divine bidding and plays out the secret divine plot. John's Judas is doubly determined, first by God/Christ and then by Satan. In John, Satan/Judas has absolutely no chance. After all, the Johannine prologue has already announced that the darkness, the world, or Satan cannot "comprehend"—either understand or overwhelm—the one from above (1:5 KJV).

Satan's confinement to Judas in John trivializes the ancient conflict mythology. The Exodus story demythologizes Pharaoh and the conflict mythology by having YHWH control Pharaoh's action through the device of the hardened heart and by having YHWH defeat Pharaoh by fiat (miraculous mention). The enemy of YHWH becomes a mere human or even something less, a phantom in the secret plan. Something similar happens in John with the confinement of Satan to Judas.[22] However demonically enthused, a mere human resists (and cooperates unknowingly with) the divine plan. Thereby, the conflict mythology becomes absurdly laughable (Eslinger, 2000: 59).[23]

---

22. The conflict would be less trivial if God's opponent in the passion narrative were Pilate or Rome. Revelation plays out this more serious story. Certain gospel stories also contain seeds of the defeat (e.g., Mk 5:1-20) or manipulation (e.g., Lk. 2:1) of Rome. Jesus' kingdom message and his resurrection are more important examples of a triumph over Rome. In the passion narrative, however, the opposition is largely Jewish, and the narrative treats Pilate, the representative of Rome, quite leniently. Many have rightly noted the anti-Semitic potential in the shift of responsibility for Jesus' death from Pilate to the Jewish leaders. See, e.g., Crossan, 1995.

23. He also describes the scenario as evil "on a leash" (Eslinger, 2000: 62). Paffenroth similarly says that the combination of Satan and Judas in John 13 makes evil both

5 Judas the God

By contrast, the Gospel of Judas lionizes Judas. Its glorification of Judas, replete with heavenly voice, rivals John's glorification of Jesus in his passion. Perhaps, one responds to the other. Mythically, it hardly matters. Whether demonic or glorified, Judas represents a mythic community's attempt at self-definition through drawing boundaries between good and evil, insiders and outsiders. At the level of myth work, John is not so far from the Gospel of Judas or from Runeberg's reflections as some might like to assume.

Gnosticism Redivivus: The Sacred, Modern Individual

The discussion to this point assumes that the meaning of the Gospel of Judas is clear and that its Judas is a gnostic hero, the one disciple who understands Jesus and accomplishes "the mystery of the betrayal" at the request of his mentor Jesus.[24] On this interpretation, the gospel squares nicely with the Cainite Gospel of Judas that Irenaeus denounces polemically (*Against Heresies*, 1.31.1). Judas' modern heroic interpreters, of course, treat the gnostic Judas differently than the ancient bishop did. That which the bishop tries to harry out of existence fascinates and attracts them. These modern readers empathize with the heroic Judas and with the gnostic communities he supposedly represents. Their empathetic search for the "human" in Judas is, as will be discussed below, the essential characteristic of modern depictions of Judas.

A minority, however, disputes this heroic interpretation. This minority contends that the heroic interpretation inappropriately allows Irenaeus' brief remarks about a lost gospel to function as a "title" for this recently discovered gospel and that this "title" over-interprets the gospel's enigmatic and fragmented text.[25] They also assert that the heroic interpretation

---

cosmic and trivial (2001b: 34). The conflict is even more laughable in the late Gospel of Barnabas 215–17. Angels thwart Judas' attempt to have Jesus arrested by translating Jesus to heaven. God transfigures Judas into Jesus' double and Judas suffers crucifixion.

24. Despite differences in detail, the following are all advocates of the hero reading of the Judas of the Gospel of Judas: Krosney, 2006; Kasser, Meyer, and Wurst, 2006; Robinson, 2006; Ehrman, 2006b; Meyer, 2007; and Pagels and King, 2007.

25. In a session of the Nag Hammadi and Gnosticism Section at the 2006 Annual Meeting of the Society of Biblical Literature, Craig Evans and John Turner disputed the heroic interpretation of the Gospel of Judas. Evans based his reading in part on a lecture delivered at the University of Ottawa in the fall of 2006 by Louis Painchard, "À Propos de la (Re)découverte de *L'Évangile de Judas*." See also DeConick, who reports more dissent at a 2006 conference on the Gospel of Judas at the Sorbonne (2007: xviii–

serves a politically correct agenda, which reads current concerns about anti-Semitism back into antiquity (see Wright, 2006b: 110–16; and DeConick, 2007: 144–54). For this minority, if one leaves aside these extraneous influences, the Judas in the Gospel of Judas is far from clearly heroic.

According to April DeConick, the heroic interpretation also rests upon a series of questionable translation choices (2007: 45–91). Instead of building upon the admittedly fragmentary and enigmatic "you will exceed all of them" (Gospel of Judas 56) as heroic interpreters do, DeConick highlights the fact that Jesus refers to Judas as the thirteenth δαίμων (Gospel of Judas 44) and locates Jesus' revelations to Judas solidly in the context of the cosmological teachings of Sethian Gnosticism (2007: 22–42; cf. Turner, 2001; and Meyer, 2006: 137–69).

While she acknowledges that δαίμων can mean "spirit" in early Greek literature, she points out that it routinely means a demonic spirit in early Christian literature and that it refers specifically to the rebellious Archons, including the demiurge Ialdabaoth, in Sethian Gnosticism. She claims further that "thirteen" is associated with Ialdabaoth, who rules over twelve Archons. As the thirteenth δαίμων, then, Judas acts demonically on behalf of this demiurge, not on behalf of the true gnostic deity. Judas makes the correct confession, like the demons in Mark's Gospel, simply because he has supernatural knowledge. Judas is not a true gnostic or one who belongs to the heavenly realm of the Aeons (2007: 48–51, 95–116).

For DeConick, the demon Judas receives special revelations from Jesus so that Judas himself may grieve (Gospel of Judas 35) and in order that the gnostics may mock apostolic Christianity. After all, the Jesus of this gospel repeatedly laughs (mockingly) at Judas and the disciples. Jesus' revelations inform Judas that he does not belong to the holy generation of the Aeons. Instead, Judas will, with Ialdabaoth, rule over the twelve (apostolic Christianity), whose various beliefs and rituals serve that demiurge (46). While Judas objects to this fate, Jesus' subsequent revelations simply fix Judas even more firmly "in his place." Similarly, various references to Judas' star (45, 56, 57) refer to his (astrological) fate.[26] If anything, then, this gospel determines Judas even more completely than the canon does.

In this reading, the enigmatic passage in Gospel of Judas 56 about Judas exceeding the others takes on a quite different meaning. For DeConick, it

---

xix). The dissent led to DeConick's own book. Papers from the Sorbonne conference are now available in Scopello, 2008.

26. She suggests that Judas may be locked into his fate because he has not undergone gnostic baptism (2007: 121–24). For DeConick, Judas' pathetic, unsuccessful objection to his fate in the Gospel of Judas 46 is the narrative crux of the gospel (2007: 142).

means Judas exceeds the twelve in evil. He does the worst thing possible. He is the ill-starred demon who sacrifices Jesus to Ialdabaoth. He does not set Jesus' spirit free from his body or work in cahoots with him (2007: 54–61, 125–33). When Judas enters the cloud (57), he is not transfigured among the gnostic Aeons. The cloud belongs to the realm of Ialdabaoth because stars surround it and the Aeons dwell above the stars. Judas has merged with Ialdabaoth in order to betray Jesus unto death (58) (2007: 116–20). Judas does to Jesus what the demiurge Ialdabaoth has done to all the spirits trapped in a finite, evil world.

Nonetheless, Judas and Ialdabaoth ultimately rule over the twelve because the twelve's understanding of the atonement and their ritual practices (particularly, the Eucharist) serve Ialdabaoth (33–34, 38–44). For DeConick, as for the heroic interpreters, the Gospel of Judas parodies apostolic Christianity. Unlike the heroic interpreters, however, DeConick finds within the Gospel of Judas either "Good Old Judas" or an even more demonic, determined Judas than that of the canon.[27]

Now that DeConick has offered a full-length exposition of a demonic Judas in the Gospel of Judas, which contests the more popular heroic interpretation, the modern debate provides an analogue of the debate hypothesized above between John and the (heroically read) Gospel of Judas. More intriguingly, some of those who castigate the heroic interpreters have claimed that these interpreters (like ancient gospel writers) are engaged in their own (politically correct) mythic projects. While DeConick does not pursue this point, she observes by looking at a few film portrayals of Judas that modern consciousness needs a good Judas and wonders if this motivates heroic interpretations like that of the National Geographic Society translation (2007: 148–54).[28]

For N. T. Wright, the heroic interpretation of Judas revives gnosticism.[29] Judas' heroic defenders are so many Runebergs retelling the story of Christianity with different names. According to Wright, these advocates of Judas replace the canonical, episcopal story of Christian origins, which he advocates, with a myth that suits their own modern identities. First, in place of the divine Christ who dies for the sins of the world and is

---

27. The phrase comes from the title of part two of DeConick's book.

28. She also opines that the good Judas may represent collective guilt about the Holocaust.

29. Pagels (2003) openly champions the experiential religion of the Gospel of Thomas against that of either John or Irenaeus. Similarly, DeConick extols the Gospel of Judas for calling modern readers to trust their inner spirit, rather than external authority (2007: 144).

resurrected, they posit a human Jesus who teaches a subversive wisdom. Second, instead of an early, emergent apostolic Christianity, they postulate a great diversity of early Jesus movements and christianities gradually brought into line by power-hungry bishops and by Constantine's desire to have a monolithic, imperial religion. Third, instead of a message of social reform and world transformation, they imagine the essence of religion to be the knowledge of the divinity within the elite (2006b: 120–23).[30]

Wright first characterizes this myth as "a soft version of Buddhism," which is "in tune with the hopes of liberal American academics from the 1960s onwards, especially those who had grown up in somewhat strict versions of the Christian faith" and have since rejected it (2006b: 122). He subsequently describes this religion as a selective, modernized version of gnosticism (2006b: 122–34). As Wright acknowledges, many critics have previously argued that popular American religion is gnostic.[31] After all, given the separation of church and state in the United States, American popular religion is inevitably sectarian. When one couples that sectarianism with the intense emphasis on expressive individualism in recent decades, the sect often becomes a sect of one.[32] Thus, recent religion in

---

30. Cf. Ehrman's assessment of the "revolutionary" status of the Gospel of Judas: (1) truth comes from secret revelations to Judas, not the twelve, who are spiritually blind, not the pillars of the faith; (2) Jesus is not the son of the Creator, but represents a higher mysterious God; and (3) salvation comes when the elite follow Jesus' teaching about escaping this world, not through Jesus' death (2006: 119–20). Wright critiques here the scholars involved in the Gospel of Judas discussion, like Ehrman and Pagels, but he similarly impugns those involved in historical Jesus research, like Crossan, Mack, and many of those associated with the Jesus Seminar, in 2006a. Other critics have attacked these same scholars for creating (modern) Jesuses that are implicitly "anti-Semitic." For the ideological/mythological work going on in such critiques, see Arnal, 2005. He argues that those making such charges are, among other things, rejecting German criticism of the gospels as fragmented, edited texts in favor of (implicit) claims about the truth of the gospels' narratives, essentializing both Judaism and Christianity, construing Judaism so that it makes a convenient "other" for Christianity, and asserting a supernatural, creedal Christianity (2005: 29–30, 41–43, 56–68). Incidentally, Arnal includes Wright among the critics of the so-called, non-Jewish Jesus (2005, 46–47). Arnal's description would make an intriguing starting point for describing the mythic work that Wright displays in his attack on the heroic Judas interpreters.

31. See Bloom, 1992; Lee, 1987; and Walsh, 2003: 162–65, 173–85. R. Smith briefly charts various uses of gnosticism in the mythic development of modern self-identities (1990). O'Regan objects to the equation of gnosticism with modernity and restricts the label "gnostic" to certain theological critiques of biblical narrative (2001).

32. On expressive individualism, see Bellah, Marsden, Sullivan, Swindler, and

the United States is an intensely private, interior matter. It is not surprising, then, that American popular religion has affinities with gnosticism.

Both ancient and modern gnosticism offer the individual escape from the evils of the world.[33] However, as Wright notes, while some varieties of ancient gnosticism ascetically denied the world, modern gnosticism is a religion of self-expression normally involving a pursuit of (material) happiness in the world (2006b: 57, 71, 91, 125, 129–30).[34] Modern gnostics do not see the material world as evil or their (spiritual) self as tragically trapped in that world. As a result, the "selves" of ancient gnosticisms and of popular American gnosticism are not quite the same. They inhabit different metaphysics. Harold Bloom describes the modern, divine American self succinctly:

> Freedom, in the context of the American Religion, means being alone with God or with Jesus, the American God or the American Christ. In social reality, this translates as solitude, at least in the inmost sense. The soul stands apart, and something deeper than the soul, the Real Me or self or spark, thus is made free to be utterly alone with a God who is also quite separate and solitary, that is, a free God or God of freedom. What makes it possible for the self and God to commune so freely is that the self already is of God; unlike body and even soul, the American self is no part of creation, or of evolution through the ages. (1992: 15; cf. Lee, 1987: 140–60)

The key words are "already is of God." The tone is joyous, not the angst of a spiritual being trapped in an evil material world. The relatively relaxed, modern gnostic *already* knows the bliss of the divine self. They do not need to learn this through religious discipline. They do not await salvation from the material world. All that awaits the modern gnostic is the fuller self-expression of the wonder that is the unique individual or the total triumph of the individual's truest, deepest, most private self (see Walsh, 2003: 173–85). By contrast, ancient gnostics expected to find within their material body a divine "self" that differed so dramatically from the present

---

Tiption, 1985: 33–35. Lee claims that the journey into the self is "very near" the heart of gnosticism (1987: 140).

33. For a discussion of the importance of escape to modern self-identity, see Cohen and Taylor, 1992. Cf. also Lee, 1987: 115–39.

34. Bloom claims that American gnosticism differs from ancient varieties by its emphases on democracy and materialism (1992: 21–27, 260–65). Wright, however, thinks modern gnosticism is elitist (2006b: 125). Perhaps, the elitism he detects is academic, not religious; and Bloom's analysis is more accurate. Incidentally, Pagels also argues that (ancient and modern) experiential religion is democratic, not elitist (2003: 46). But see Lee, 1987: 161–75.

individual that such a salvation would seem like absorption into a transcendent divine being and the resulting loss of the precious, independent self to a modern individual.[35]

Despite their differing anthropologies and ethics, ancient and modern gnostics do share a degree of social radicalism. Both position the individual polemically vis-à-vis the social world and reject "worldly" institutions. Such anti-institutionalism is endemic to popular American religion, and both popular and academic American rhetoric often supports rebels and cynicism.[36] As Wright observes, the heroic interpretation of the Judas of the Gospel of Judas belongs to this culture and, in fact, reenacts the typical story of American liberation (2006b: 133). But the rebel is not simply American. The notion of the lone individual who stands against larger, usually institutional, corruption or, at least, oppression is a trope common to the novel as well as to Hollywood. In fact, some see the assertion of the self vis-à-vis social constraints as the essential feature of modern individualism (cf. Cohen and Taylor, 1992).[37] It is also, as Kermode notes, endemic to modern criticism of literary texts, which following modern cultural training invariably looks for character (1979: 76–77).

Given this modern location, heroic readers of the Gospel of Judas "naturally" (cf. Barthes, 1972) celebrate and empathize with the Judas who stands against the twelve and, thus, the corrupt or oppressive (apostolic) institution. Such a Judas offers them the bare bones of a modern character, a simulacrum of an individual, that most sacred of all modern things. Traditional texts and readers function differently (see Chapter 2 above). The ancient person is embedded in larger wholes. Traditional readings, therefore, are mesmerized with plot. Thus, traditional readers are far more likely to find the lonely Judas the dupe of some larger plot than they are to find him a hero. For traditionalists, Judas is oracle and/or possessed.

---

35. Borges' notion of infinity also disrupts modern individualism. See Chapter 1. According to Rollo May, modern individuals fear absorption and ostracism above all else (1991). For May, individualism is the flimsy mythic construct that attempts to bridge and thereby ameliorate these twin, opposed fears.

36. It also supports skepticism vis-à-vis an institution demanding belief. This element of modern gnosticism is what disturbs Wright most deeply. He observes that the furor over the Gospel of Judas is about what people do not want to believe (2006b: 26). Cf. Robinson, 2006: 87; and Pyper, 2001. Prothero claims similarly that the American fascination with Jesus has partly to do with many Americans' desires to reject the institutional church while simultaneously embracing spirituality or ethic or some other value that they lodge in Jesus (2003: 9–16).

37. For a discussion in the context of the recent debate about the Gospel of Judas, see Walsh, 2006b.

5 Judas the God

In an attempt to damn what he calls the "new myth" of Christian origins by association, Wright compares its "conspiracy theories" to that of Dan Brown's *The Da Vinci Code* (2006b: 13; 2006a). For Wright, Brown's novel and many of Judas' academic supporters wrongly allege that the canon obscures secret truths, which modern critics are now in a position to reveal. Wright's comparison is apt,[38] but it obscures the fact that secret plots enthrall the gospels and the canon more than they do modern conspiracy buffs (see Chapter 2 above; and Walsh, 2007). Thus, Dan Brown and the heroic Judas' supporters are right to observe the mechanism of the secret plot in the canon even if they may be wrong about that plot's specific contours. They are also, however, quite modern when they attempt to extract a heroic character—or Judas specifically—from the snares of these secret plots. The gospels, by contrast, never consider this salvific possibility. The gospels and the canon seek to embed everyone in their secret divine plots. Moderns may talk about secret plots as incessantly, but they do so in order to indulge fantasies of the disclosures of these plots (conspiracies) and of heroic, individualistic escapes.

The heroic Judas appeals, then, because he enacts something like modern rebellion and alienation.[39] While the canonical gospels alienate Judas, they wrongly—for moderns—depict the rebel as villain, not hero. Further, they do not develop Judas as a character sufficiently for modern mythologies (see Walsh, 2006b). In addition to their obsession with secret plots, the canonical gospels concentrate too relentlessly on Jesus. In fact, even the gospel Jesus lacks modern character appeal. He, too, is mere cog in the divine machine. Further, the gospel Jesus is all externals—he is what he says and does. He has no subjectivity for moderns to emulate (see Walsh, 2003: 21–43). He is also the aristocratic Christ. He is absolute virtue, standing well above the (democratic) fallible mass (cf. Happel, 1993). He is to be imitated, but mere mortals necessarily fail at that task. The canonical, aristocratic Christ is, quite simply, not a very good modern mythic hero.

---

38. The comparison, however, merely notes that the heroic interpreters, the novel, and the subsequent film all belong to modern culture and share several features of its worldview: e.g., (1) anti-institutionalism; (2) celebration of the rebel hero; and (3) a this-worldly, materialistic, hedonistic ethic (which the novel and film express in terms of a celebration of the eternal feminine). See Walsh, 2007.

39. That which Judas rebels against is less important than the mere fact that he rebels. Critics often see the products of modern media as anti-religious because their heroes rebel against religious institutions. These heroes are, however, more anti-institution than they are anti-religious. They typically value privatized, subjective religion.

Here lies the genius of the academy's historical Jesuses. They are excellent modern mythic heroes:

> Their Jesuses are not aristocratic (or divine) Christs, but the mediocre heroes typical of the novel, persons inevitably out of place/time, persons at odds with their society. The plot of the typical historical Jesus novel concerns such an individual's tension vis-à-vis society and its resolution, not the delivery of a heroic/divine message or salvation. Accordingly, the historical Jesus is on one hand a revolutionary, an apocalyptic doomsayer, or a cynic sage—that is, a partial dropout vis-à-vis a particular culture—or on the other hand a universal ethicist rising above the fray of a particular society. This novelized Jesus idealizes, as it realizes, the alienated, modern individual. (Walsh, 2005b: 163–64)

The modern Judas—particularly, the hero of the Gospel of Judas—is a similar modern mythic hero. Like so many of the historical Jesuses, he is a rebel or a misfit out of place in the society of his own time.[40] Most importantly, both the historical Jesus and the heroic Judas resist absorption into the (transcendent) divine. Instead, they deify the modern (rebellious) individual. Incidentally, that the Gospel of Judas ends with the betrayal may be essential to its modern popularity. If the gospel continued, it might include Jesus' or Judas' ascent to the divine. Such absorption would terrify modern individuals.

God as Uncanny Horror

The heroic Judas satisfies modern desires for a simulacrum of the modern individual. The canonical Judas does not. In the canon, terrible, villainous forces deny Judas even the semblance of character. Oracles and supernatural beings overwhelm Judas and prevent his subjective individuation. He is a mere phantom. For moderns, such determinism is a malevolent oppression, a demonic possession, rather than divine providence. The determined Judas is a victim of a malign monotheism (Mark, John), an evil empire (Luke), or a Torah squabble (Matthew). For moderns, then,

---

40. Many scholars have critiqued the rebel/misfit Jesus as anti-Semitic. See n30. In the analysis here, modern mythology—not anti-Semitism—is the main explanation for the rebel Jesus. The hero of virtually every novel and film is alienated in a sense, but one of the best examples of modern alienation is Thomas Pynchon's "preterite," "the many God passes over when he chooses a few for salvation" (1995: 554–57). The pages exegete and extend Borges' "Three Versions of Judas" as Pynchon imagines an alternative U.S. history. The preterite becomes thereby an example of the victim-Judas written large. See below.

the fate of the canonical Judas is a horror story (cf. the portrayal of Judas in *The Passion of the Christ*).

Modern resistance to this horror creates a Judas-as-victim reading of the gospels, which is a first step toward a modern Judas. Such readings, as Kermode has astutely noted, aspire to leave plot, tradition, and determinism behind for character (cf. Walsh, 2006b). From this modern perspective, the canonical Judas becomes one who stands apart. He is the one left outside the divine plan. Or, even more tellingly, he is the one who escapes the boundaries of the gospel plot altogether (in Mark, Luke, and John). Such readings, however, eschew canonical confines and read wildly.[41] They search the canon desperately for a better story, a story of the rebel who resists the group or institution. They do so in order to salve modern fears about absorption (or supernatural possessions).

Such fears are innately religious. Many have said that modernity rejects religion and/or the spiritual. That is not quite the case. Modernity rejects—perhaps only in its fantasies—institutional religion.[42] Modernity celebrates, as noted above, privatized, subjective religion. This romanticized psychology abandons traditional transcendence, the dualist metaphysic of the spiritual world above in favor of the indwelling divine self (spirit). The spirit within, which, for moderns, does not differ from the true individual self, is the modern sacred. By contrast, the idea of an absorbing supernatural spirit is modern horror. At the edges of rational modernity, lingers the terrifying horror of a monstrous external divine/spirit that threatens to absorb the desperately defended divine individual. As the enduring popularity of religious horror like *The Exorcist* (1973) illustrates, such a deity remains a significant feature of the repressed, modern uncanny.[43] The cinema of religious horror also indicates that, for

---

41. Borges' Runeberg never reads so wildly. He is as obsessed with oracles and secret plots as the canon. Borges himself is no advocate of individualism. He eschews individualism for a play with infinity that disdains modern fears of absorption. See n35 and Chapter 1.

42. See n39. In a sense, modernity creates religion. For a discussion in terms of modern biblical studies, see Blanton, 2007. For a broader discussion of the relatively late appearance of the word/concept "religion," see W. Smith, 1963. Cf. as well Borges' notion that authors (and readers) create their precursors (1964: 199–201).

43. The sense of cosmic alienation in Lovecraft's horror is another good example of the fears inherent to the modern uncanny. See Beal, 2002: 1–10, 173–92; and the discussion of the uncanny in Freud, Todorov, and Borges in Chapter 1. Stephen King's fiction nicely illustrates Freud's notion of the uncanny as superstitions repressed by reason as King's novels often depict childhood fears become adult reality. See, e.g., *Salem's Lot*; *The Shining*, *Cujo*, or *It*.

moderns, such possessing deities are far more satanic than benevolent. The divine modern individual despairs in the face of the possibility of mysterious forces beyond rational control (like the magical mentions and secret plots of the canon).[44]

The canonical Judas, the Judas of *The Passion of the Christ* (2004), and other victims of religious horror fascinate moderns because they represent these modern fears (see Chapter 4). They symbolize that which moderns do not wish to be, the individual swallowed by larger powers.[45] This Judas represents the problems of determinism, fate, infinity, the possibility of freedom's illusion, and the unfathomable realities of external evil. This Judas represents more than the (pre-religious or irreligious) horror of cosmic alienation. He represents the Lovecraftian horror of a victim hunted down by some satanic deity. Giotto's depiction of Judas' meeting with the priests in the Arena Chapel in Padua depicts this horror wonderfully. Behind Judas, egging him on and obviously controlling him, is a dark, ghoulish Satan.[46] Vis-à-vis such a malign deity, conscious (modern) alienation is far more preferable. In fact, vis-à-vis fears of absorption, alienation becomes a sacred place/identity. Not surprisingly, then, many moderns look for inklings of the victim-Judas in the canon and welcome the merest hint of a heroic Judas. That quest negotiates and massages deep modern fears.

---

44. One might also see Thomas Pynchon's *The Crying of Lot 49* as a commentary on this fear. Throughout the novel, Oedipa Mass senses the imminence of a revelation that does not quite occur (cf. Borges' notion of aesthetic near revelations). That aura drives her story which ends without resolution (cf. "The Approach to Al-Mu'tasim" [Borges, 1962: 37–43]). Near the end, the narrator muses about the uncomfortable options open to Oedipa: something mysterious may be about to be revealed; Oedipa may be crazy; etc. (1999: 140–51). Cf. the discussion in Chapter 1. *The Matrix* is a more popular manifestation of similar fears. There, Neo becomes the One only after the Oracle tells him that he is not. The modern myth of individualism requires that Neo choose this identity, rather than having it foisted upon him. Subsequent episodes in *The Matrix* trilogy deal with Neo's freedom less optimistically.

45. Critics often observe that the victims of horror provide lessons about vices that the audience should avoid. In older horror films, e.g., sexually active females were often the first and goriest victims. Interestingly, unbelievers (often scientists) often come to similar fates (if they do not learn to believe in the horror's reality).

46. Photographs of *The Payment of Judas* are readily available on the internet. See, e.g., http://www.wga.hu/index1.html (accessed 7–26–09) and the reproduction on the cover of this book. According to Schiller, depictions of Judas receiving the money are rare and the presence of Satan in the scene rarer still (1972: 2:24). Satan's presence at Judas' death is more common in art. See Schiller, 1972: 2:77.

The play with determinism in the characters of Jesus, Judas, and Satan in Roger Young's TV *Jesus* (1999) illumines these very fears. Young's Judas is a version of the De Quincey Judas. Disenchanted with Jesus' failure to lead a revolution, he betrays Jesus to force Jesus to begin the revolt. By contrast, Young's Jesus repeatedly resists the temptation to force other people to conform to his will. Unlike Judas, Jesus respects the free will of individuals. In fact, Young's Jesus lives and dies in order that individuals may freely choose God (and love). Young's Jesus makes this stance clear in his struggle with Satan at Gethsemane. There, Jesus prophetically sees the violence that will be done in his name. Satan uses these troubling visions to tempt Jesus to forego his self-sacrificial plans to evoke human love. Satan tempts Jesus to impose the ethic he desires (as king or a god) upon his subjects. Jesus rejects this temptation by asserting that people are good enough to choose for themselves. When he dies thereafter, then, Jesus does so on behalf of that most sacred of modern values—individual freedom. A benign deity, he refuses to possess or determine his followers.

Implicit in this struggle is the possible end of or even the illusoriness of human freedom. Mighty forces work against it. Nonetheless, the movie resolves these deep mythic anxieties quite rationally. God/Jesus stands for good, that is, for individual freedom. God/Jesus will not absorb, determine, or possess the individual. Satan stands for evil, that is, the attempt to overwhelm human freedom. Satan would possess the individual.

Judas falls prey to that evil. Ironically, despite its massaging of modern mythic concerns, the movie's Judas is quite canonical. He is still the insider who becomes outsider. He still represents the evil to be purged. In fact, the movie's Judas is even more reprehensible than that of the canon. The canonical dupe becomes the modern would-be seducer. Like John's Judas, this Judas becomes Satan as he tries to consume others' individual freedom.

Judas' Motivation: The Modern Subjective Individual[47]

Modern individuals are not only alienated; they are also subjective individuals. Judas, then, is not a modern character unless he has an understandable motivation. Here, the canonical gospels are worthless. They simply say that Judas is oracular or, in its inverted form, that he is satanic.

---

47. On the motivation of film Judases, see Walsh, 2006a; Reinhartz, 2007: 151–77; and the discussion in Chapter 4. On Judas in film, see also Paffenroth, 2001a. The discussion here relies heavily on the information about Jesus films in Staley and Walsh, 2007.

Matthew's note about the request for money and John's note that Judas is a thief are just that, mere slanderous notes providing no credible motivation.

Film, the modern medium par excellence, "naturally" (cf. Barthes, 1972) provides Judas with understandable modern motivations. Perhaps, the most common motivation is political, the creation of some version of the De Quincy Judas who tries to coerce Jesus into establishing a Jewish kingdom (see the discussions in Chapters 3–4). The clearest example in the Jesus film tradition is in Nicholas Ray's *King of Kings* (1961) although the Judas of Roger Young's *Jesus* (1999) has this, as well as other motivations, as do the Judases of Raffaele Mertes' television *Judas* (2001) and Charles Robert Carner's television *Judas* (2004).

The Judas in Martin Scorsese's The *Last Temptation of Christ* (1988) also aspires to a Jewish political kingdom, but he never attempts to force Jesus' hand on this point despite his frequent threats to do so. Specifically, he does not murder Jesus, as he has promised, when Jesus departs from the plan of revolt against Rome. Instead, Jesus seduces Judas into betraying him in order to bring about the spiritual kingdom that Jesus desires. Like the De Quincey Judas, Scorsese's Judas never understands this spiritual kingdom (except perhaps as a phantom in Jesus' final fantasy).

The Judas in Zeffirelli's *Jesus of Nazareth* (1977) also wants political freedom, but believes that negotiations can create it. He and another of Jesus' disciples have left the Zealot movement behind for Jesus' peaceful mission. During Jesus' Jerusalem days, however, Judas presses for political solutions to the problems of his people. He thinks that negotiations with Zerah, an aide to the Sanhedrin, will bring about a political summit between Jesus and the Sanhedrin that will lead to the public acknowledgment of Jesus as king. Once again, like the De Quincey Judas, this Judas misunderstands the spiritual nature of Jesus' kingdom. In the language of this movie, Judas, a man of the "head," never understands the "heart," which is the focus of Jesus' mission. Consequently, Judas realizes he has betrayed Jesus only after the fact. He believes that Jesus' address to him at the Supper indicates Jesus' support for Judas' scheme. When Jesus is arrested, a shocked Judas hurries to the Sanhedrin meeting. When Zerah tells Judas that the meeting is a trial for blasphemy, rather than a political summit, refuses him entry, and tosses him some money, Judas breaks. His political hopes dashed, he realizes that he has "killed" Jesus. Accordingly, this Judas commits suicide almost immediately, without returning the money.

Jewison's Judas in *Jesus Christ Superstar* (1973) is yet another political figure. This Judas believes that Jesus is about to catalyze a disastrous revolution because Jesus wrongly believes he is the messiah/celebrity that people are saying he is. For Judas, these claims are a (false) myth. When Judas cannot separate the myth from the man, he betrays Jesus to prevent the myth's destruction of the people by the Romans. While he acts politically, this Judas resembles the Johannine Caiaphas (Jn 11:50) far more than he does the Zealots.

The popularity of a political motivation for film Judases is perhaps most evident in the humorous spoof of Jesus films, *Monty Python's Life of Brian* (1979). Its Jewish revolutionary movements are ineffectual and sectarian. They spend far more time listing Roman offenses and fighting amongst themselves than revolting against the Romans. Moreover, most of Brian's comic misadventures occur because of his infelicitous involvement with these revolutionaries. Among these revolutionaries is Judith with whom Brian has a brief tryst before the crowds acclaim him as messiah and the Romans arrest him as a revolutionary. Predictably, his arrest on such a charge endears Brian to Judith. He becomes her ideal, revolutionary man as he becomes a martyr for her cause. Unlike the canonical and most De Quincey Judases, however, Judith works to liberate Brian after his arrest. She tries vainly to stir the liberation movement to save Brian and, then, successfully incites the crowd to demand Brian's release at his trial. Pilate acquiesces with their demands, but the crucifixion party comically frees the wrong man. Such is Brian's hard luck life. At the cross, Judith misguidedly thanks Brian for his noble death for her cause. Then, however, she deserts him even before he expires.

These political motivations for Judas are popular in modernity for a number of reasons. First, the move from theological (God/Satan) to political motivations is a sensible updating of the story. Politics is more understandable and more important than theology for most modern audiences. In fact, many critics see nationalism as a modern form of (quasi-)religion. Further, the move from theology to politics deftly sublimates the horror of theological determinism and/or absorption. Second, the conception of Judas as a politician—particularly as a freedom fighter—makes ideal fodder for the conventions of action and epic film. It also supports American myths about individual self-identity as free individuals or, even, as rebels (see above). Third, and most importantly, most of these political portrayals of Judas define religion "correctly" for moderns by insisting that Judas misunderstands the spiritual nature of Jesus' kingdom by trying to politicize his message.

Modern religion is necessarily a private, subjective matter. It is, then, a particular kind of spirituality, perhaps best described as some modern form of gnosticism (see above). Modernity cannot brook a religion—other than something like nationalism—that interferes with politics or society. The political Judas, who tries to relate Jesus' message directly to the world, is, then, pathetically wrong. Perhaps, then, the ultimate appeal of the political Judas is this spiritual naiveté. This depiction of Judas allows films to articulate acceptable (subjective spirituality) and unacceptable (those meddling with political or social realities) religious identities.

Not all films, however, rely upon political motivations for Judas. Some rely upon more traditional motivations, like greed or divine determinism. Greed, which often motivates medieval Judases, is relatively rare in film. It is most significant in Sydney Olcott's *From the Manger to the Cross* (1912), in Cecil B. DeMille's *The King of Kings* (1927), and in Paoli Pasolini's *The Gospel according to St. Matthew* (1965). The scene with the greedy Judas haggling for money with the priests is one of the more memorable visuals in Olcott's film. At the supper, Olcott's Judas also greedily snatches the identifying and damning bread from Jesus and runs off with it into the night.[48] In fact, the shadows become a completely black screen, a visualization of the Johannine night. Olcott's Judas and that of DeMille as well owe a great deal to the depiction of Judas in medieval art, in Giotto's Arena Chapel, and in the passion play tradition. Associations in that tradition of the greedy Judas with cultural perceptions about greedy Jews eventually proved too troublingly anti-Semitic for most filmmakers to utilize this motivation.

Thus, the greedy Judas already troubles the capitalist DeMille. Accordingly, he makes his ambitious Judas desire exotic, aristocratic—not good middle-class—wealth. The depiction worked so well in the capitalist U.S. that it eventually became a stereotypical portrayal of vile characters. For such films, economic self-sufficiency is not bad, and the desire for such is not bad. It is the pursuit of wealth beyond middle-class self-sufficiency that is hubris. Thus, DeMille's Judas is not merely greedy. He hungers for power, which provides a touch of the De Quincey Judas, as well. From the very beginning, this Judas expects Jesus to become a king who will line Judas' pockets. Perhaps, the most important scene, however, comes during Jesus' triumphal entry. In the Temple, Satan tempts Jesus to become king. Tellingly, Judas holds a crown for Jesus. Jesus, however, rejects these two tempters simply by holding a lamb. Incidentally, it is Judas' misguided, public attempt to crown Jesus that provides Caiaphas with leverage against

---

48. Many artistic representations of the Supper depict Judas' outing. He reaches into the dish or takes bread from Jesus as Jesus speaks the oracle about betrayal. See Schiller, 1972: 2:31–35.

Judas. To escape Caiaphas' subsequent death threats, Judas agrees to betray Jesus for the traditional thirty pieces.

Thereafter, the greedy Judas vanishes from American Jesus films either because the greedy Judas raises uncomfortable questions for capitalist Americans or because he smacks of anti-Semitism. The greedy Judas, however, appears in the Marxist Pasolini's *The Gospel according to St. Matthew* (1965). Although ostensibly filming Matthew alone, Pasolini inserts the Johannine account of Judas' complaint about the anointing waste before segueing to Judas' bargain with the priests. Greedy traitor, Judas smiles horribly as he does so and seals his fate.

Denys Arcand's *Jesus of Montreal* (1989) is a Canadian film that critiques greedy participation in a consuming society. The film, which hosts repeated versions of a passion play within a framing Christ-figure story, has no real Judas figure in its passion play proper. "Judases" play a role, however, in the frame story. The film opens with a theatrical presentation of part of Dostoevsky's *The Brothers Karamazov*. After the play ends, critics laud the protagonist, who adopts a John the Baptist persona by pointing to a "real" actor in their midst, Daniel Coulombe. Daniel is back in town from points unknown in order to stage and star in a passion play. As he plays the role of Jesus, that persona bleeds into his "real" life, and he becomes a Christ-figure. As the film nears its end, Daniel is fatally injured when he is knocked from his cross in a brawl between the security guards who have been told to close down Daniel's play and the spectators who wish it to continue. Unable to find help in a hospital, he, attended by two of his female actresses/disciples, collapses in the subway. He does so in the midst of an apocalyptic rant about the abomination of desolation after he sees the Dostoevsky's actor's head on an advertising billboard. Here, then, is the narrative standard. Those who "sell out," as this actor has by accepting the bribes of consumer society, betray themselves. They lose their personal integrity for filthy lucre. Instead of a Judas, then, this film offers "Judases," who betray themselves, not Jesus.[49]

Some films even flirt with the idea of Judas' divine determinism. Almost all Jesus films include the magical Supper oracle. Some associate Judas with Satan as tempter of Jesus, like DeMille and Young. Others, even more

---

49. The priest Leclerc is another of these "Judases" because he betrays his aesthetic dreams and his knowledge of the truth about Jesus for the comfort of his place in the institutional church. Most of Daniel's disciples also betray their integrity by making a deal with a sleazy lawyer figure to open a theater in Daniel's name after his death. In fact, one might easily see institutions and their true believers as the symbolic Judas of this film. The film esteems individual artistic integrity. See Walsh, 2003: 45–68.

troublingly, imagine Judas' possession by Satan (cf. Sykes and Krisch's *The Jesus Film* [1979], Saville's *The Gospel of John* [2003], and Mel Gibson's *The Passion of the Christ* [2004]). Such depictions frighten modernity because they resurrect the uncanny horror of divine determinism;[50] therefore, films often transform divine determinism into human dupery.

Thus, in Nicholas Ray's *King of Kings* (1961), Barabbas misleads Judas. Convincing Judas that he will wait and see what Jesus will do in Jerusalem, Barabbas plots a revolt to coincide with Jesus' entry into Jerusalem. In a real sense, Barabbas' dupery leads to Judas' betrayal of Jesus because Barabbas' revolt is unsuccessful and Judas subsequently betrays Jesus in order to save his friend Barabbas. In Zeffirelli's *Jesus of Nazareth* (1977), Zerah tricks Judas into "betraying" Jesus. As noted above, Judas believes that he is arranging a clandestine political summit between Jesus and the Sanhedrin that will result in the acclamation of Jesus as king. Such modifications of determinism are typically modern. They make Judas the victim, not of divine forces, but of larger cultural forces that Judas wrongly thinks he can manipulate.[51] The story of such victims is so popular in modern mythology that the institutional victim motif plays some role in the characterization of other film Judases as well (cf. the Judases of *The King of Kings*, *The Gospel according to St. Matthew*, and *Monty Python's Life of Brian*).

The Judas in Norman Jewison's *Jesus Christ Superstar* (1973) is modern in a different way. Whether or not that Judas is actually a divine dupe, he sees himself as such. The canon is full of oracles, but it relates nothing of their emotional impact upon Judas. By contrast, Jewison's film visualizes Judas' angst in the face of divine determinism. Only here in the Jesus film tradition does Judas actually converse with Jesus about the oracle that creates him. Like some modern Job, Judas rails against the divine decrees that create him. In fact, Jesus has to chase Judas from the picnic Supper to force his betrayal.[52] Before Jesus' Roman trial ends, Judas hangs himself, accusing God of manipulation and murder to the bitter end.

God, however, never appears in the film unless one finds him in Jesus' demands or in the montage of crucifixion paintings that accompany Jesus' Gethsemane prayer. As a result, this Judas' divine determination

---

50. Of course, they try to salve this fear by an ethic that asserts that only the evil are demonically possessed. Cf. n45.

51. Here, Judas fails as modern hero. A film hero would successfully manipulate these institutional forces. Cf. the Judas in Rayner's *The Knifeman* (1969).

52. This Judas has already made his deal with Caiaphas, but Jesus' physical hounding of Judas is striking.

is far less certain than that of the Judas of the canon. Shifting from the canon's providential perspective to Judas' perspective shifts the divine from tradition to Judas' subjectivity. Consequently, the only evidence for Judas' divine determination is his own testimony (or one's memory of the tradition). The divine has become, for Judas, a horror within.[53] No one else can know these subjective, alienated depths. This Judas is a wonderful simulacrum for the modern, divine individual's fears.

Our Judases, Ourselves[54]

In summary, film depictions depart from the canonical Judas by creating motivations for him that rely on modern notions of character and that render Judas a simulacrum of a modern, subjective individual. When filmmakers do not avail themselves of this opportunity, modern critics may question their sensitivity, if not their ethics (cf. the effect of the Judases in *From the Manger to the Cross* [1912], *The Jesus Film* [1979], *The Gospel of John* [2003], and *The Passion of the Christ* [2004]). In addition to subjectivity, modernized Judases also provide a figure, who is alienated from the tradition. Such aliens help articulate modern Christian identities.[55] If the canonical Judases make Judas the excluded, non-personal other (the object) that identifies the insider's true (religious) human identity by way of contrast, recognizably modern Judases help reinforce the modern understanding of people as both subjective and alienated individuals.

The Judas of all these Jesus films, however, fails. He is no hero nor does he successfully individuate. In a success-oriented society, failure is the ultimate cause of ostracism, which is, other than absorption, the great fear of moderns.[56] When modern Judases fail, moderns join traditionalists in

---

53. The position of the film's Jesus is quite similar, particularly in the Gethsemane scene. He also rails against the God who holds every card and demands his death. Here, too, one has only his word for the divine demand.

54. This phrase adapts the title of Nina Auerbach, *Our Vampires, Ourselves* (1995). For discussion, see Pippin, 2002: 24–41. Cf. Beal, who titles his final chapter, "Our Monsters, Ourselves" (2002: 173–92) Incidentally, Dracula is Judas in *Dracula 2000*, and that accounts for Dracula's aversion to silver and to crosses. Cf. *The Librarian: The Curse of the Judas Chalice* (2008).

55. In J. Smith's description, religion is always an exegesis of a tradition which does not quite match reality or the present. The incongruity is what makes religion useful, and he often cites Borges' "On Exactitude in Science" (1999a: 325) to illustrate this point. He does, however, see the awareness of this incongruity as the peculiarly academic sense of religion. See J. Smith, 1978: 289–309.

56. As noted in n35, Rollo May sees ostracism and absorption as the twin fears of

eschewing Judas. After all, they must avoid such fates. Succinctly, Judas still represents that which moderns cannot be. Moderns cannot misunderstand Jesus' spiritual message and try to impose his "kingdom" on the political/social world. They cannot greedily pursue wealth and ambition beyond prescribed middle-class values. They cannot "sell out" to consumer society and abandon the deity within, their personal integrity. They cannot afford to be a dupe of others or institutions. Above all else, they must avoid the uncanny horror of the determining divine because that would disrupt the very contours of sacred individualism.[57] More positively, moderns must be triumphant and true individuals (see Walsh, 2003: 173–85).[58] Few, if any, conceive Judas as such a figure.

---

modern individualism. He also opines that moderns, particularly Americans, have few mythic resources for dealing with failure and with death (1991).

57. In one sense, the cooperative Judas, like that in Scorsese's *The Last Temptation of Christ* (1988), is the most horrible Judas possible. He cooperates with his dupery. See Chapter 3 above.

58. Judas remains a significant failure even in two recent television movies, which, like Jewison's *Jesus Christ Superstar* (1973), are passion plays from Judas' perspective. In Raffaele Mertes' *Judas* (2001), Judas desperately desires Jewish independence and declares Jesus king at the triumphal entry. Thereafter, Judas is a man on the run from the Romans. Matters worsen, when Judas' fiancée, Sarah, tricks him into providing thirty pieces of silver for an assassination attempt masterminded by her brother. After Jesus cleanses the Temple, Pilate demands that the Jewish leaders (including merchants) turn Jesus over to him. When Sarah's brother's assassination plot fails, Pilate arrests leading families, including Judas'. When Sarah confesses her deceit, Judas suddenly becomes cynical. When Jesus stoops to wash his feet, Judas rejects him as a slave, a shadow of his former messianic self, and accuses Jesus of betraying them all. After the Supper oracle, Judas betrays Jesus, hoping to obtain thereby his family's release and to bring in the kingdom. Judas maintains this hope until Jesus dies, even though Peter and Sarah beg him to ask for forgiveness. When Jesus dies, Judas realizes that he has killed Jesus and lapses into a despair that leads to his suicide.

Mertes' Judas reprises that of De Quincey, but tracks the mistakes, dupery, deceit, heroism, and pride that bring Judas to his demise. In short, this Judas is a full, complicated, subjective individual. He combines both good and evil. As in many traditional interpretations of Judas, however, his pride and despair make it impossible for him to accept forgiveness, even though Peter and Sarah repeatedly offer him forgiveness. In a novel touch, Peter tries to comfort Judas after Jesus' death and chases him futilely as Judas races to his death. When he finds Judas hanging, Peter sobs and asks vainly why Judas did it. The moment visualizes Christian claims about forgiveness and the traditional idea that Judas' suicide, not his betrayal, is his ultimate failing (see Chapter 3).

From a modern perspective, Judas' suicide is his ultimate sin because it dispatches the sacred individual. As a result, this Judas is as much a modern failure as he is a Christian one, however sympathetically the movie tries to portray him. Notably, the

Typically, film Judases fall ultimately to internal weaknesses. Ignorance, pride, fear, and despair—not deities—dispatch them. Perhaps, the Judas in George Stevens' *The Greatest Story Ever Told* (1965) is most revelatory. As discussed previously, the visuals of Stevens' film associate Judas with the satanic Dark Hermit. What was not noted previously, however, was that the script for the film identifies the Dark Hermit as the dark voice within the individual.[59] If so, Stevens' Judas, a simulacrum of the modern and his/her fears, succumbs to his own dark voices. Divine determinism becomes psychological mystery.

Given their failures, these modern Judases remain the excluded other, the humans that moderns do not want to be, although moderns may have some nagging suspicion that they may be precisely that Judas-person. As that is never more than a suspicion, moderns may have sympathy, but they never have empathy for these Judases.[60] Like the canonical Judas, these

---

movie constantly alienates Judas. Jesus is always in white; Judas in dark clothing. Judas is rich and from Jerusalem. The rest of the troupe is rural. He is often visually alone or seen departing from the group. No one else is.

Charles Robert Carner's television *Judas* (2004) portrays an equally conflicted Judas. A prologue shows the crucifixion of Judas' father and a host of others for insurrection. Thus, Judas has a personal reason to desire freedom from Rome. When he sees Jesus cleanse the Temple, Judas believes Jesus is the long desired messiah. When Judas' mother dies, however, Judas bargains with Caiaphas to betray his messiah. Surprisingly, Judas' motives for the betrayal are not as clear as one might expect for a modern story. More confusingly, after the betrayal, Judas tries vainly to secure Jesus' release. When this fails, Judas commits suicide. The movie ends, even more hopefully than Mertes' does, with the apostles deposing Judas' body and praying Jewish prayers for the dead. As the movie ends, Jesus' voice joins the apostles' prayer and, finally, continues alone as the screen fades to black.

Intriguingly, the filmmakers describe their goal as twofold. First, they want people to sympathize or even to identify with Judas. Second, they want their audience to recognize the horror of Judas' "sin." Proceeding from an avowedly Christian stance, the filmmakers also want to use Judas to provide a point of entry into the Jesus story for what they consider to be "our conflicted" age. Consequently, they have provided yet another modern Judas, an alienated, subjective figure who is not quite what moderns wish to be. Poor, unfortunate Judas is here, as elsewhere in modernity, doubly alienated. He fits neither the tradition nor modernity.

59. The temptation narrative in the wilderness may visualize this interior voice in Jesus because Jesus meets the Dark Hermit only after he goes into a dark cave (the soul?). Moreover, the soundtrack allows the audience, thereafter, to hear the voices of the prophets in Jesus' head as well as that of the Dark Hermit.

60. One exception is the empathetic, heroic reading of the Gospel of Judas discussed above. One might also read the Judas in Callaghan, *A Time for Judas* (1984), heroically, but his character is more than a little ambiguous. This Judas heroically

modern Judases still function primarily as a mythic boundary marker, as a warning sign. If the traditional, canonical Judas is determined (by oracle), scapegoat, and demonic, the modern Judas is victim, alien, and failure.

When the modern individual replaces God, character does not replace myth. Character bespeaks myth, as Kermode has rightly observed. Determined, demonic Judases bespeak canonical myth. Victimized, fallen Judases bespeak modern myth. In both cases, Judas remains trapped in the amber of some mythology or ideology in whose service he remains a mere object. In an important sense, then, it hardly matters whether Judas is demon or divine hero. Such roles are, as Borges' fiction illustrates, readily reversible. Only a particular story's fictional perspective (or a culture's dominant myth) is capable of clearly distinguishing such roles. Of course, that perspective is also the place where both demons and deities are born.[61] Both reveal more about their makers than any other entity. "Our Judases," then, are truly "ourselves." They represent human desires and fears.

---

accepts his role for the purpose of the story, but he betrays Jesus (a second time) by revealing this secret to Philo, who ultimately betrays Judas by burying his story in a jar, rather than destroying it. The Judas in Rayner's *The Knifeman* (1969) acts heroically to save Jesus (who mistakenly thinks that he died and was resurrected) and Ruth (Judas' lover) from a Zealot plot, but he ultimately falls to forces larger than himself (establishment and Zealot plots and Christian mythmaking). Dupe seems to outweigh hero here.

61. Borges plays with such mythopoesis and mythoclasm (or demythologizing) in "Theme of the Hero and Traitor" (1962: 123–27). A certain Ryan discovers that his famous, heroic ancestor Kilpatrick, whose autobiography he is writing, was a traitor to the Irish revolution. The populace's lionization of him, however, dictated that his fellow revolutionaries dispatch the traitor as a hero. A certain Nolan, charged with creating this scenario and pressed for time, plagiarizes Shakespeare. Ryan discovers this plot in his researches because of the literary parallels between Kilpatrick's death and the assassination of Julius Caesar. Ultimately, Ryan elects to leave the cover-up in place. Once again, the connection of myth and secret plots is clear. Cf. the need for secrecy in Callaghan's *A Time for Judas* (1984).

Chapter 6

ADDING EVIL TO THE SON

Corrosive Infinity

Like other Borgesian endings, the narrator's parting observation—that Runeberg adds "the complexities of calamity and evil" to the Son (Borges, 1962: 157)—calls attention to "Three Versions of Judas'" fictional status. As the Son is orthodoxy's symbol of the good, the addition of evil startles and demands conscious interpretation.[1] The comment's basis may lie in orthodoxy's assertion that gnosticism is a metaphysical dualism valuing the spirit and demeaning matter (see Chapter 5 above). Runeberg's Judases all assume this metaphysical ethic. Runeberg's first and second Judases, for example, clearly value the spiritual Christ over the human Judas. Runeberg's focus on the human Judas, however, adds material evil to the

---

1. In a very real sense, Runeberg's reflections and his Judases are quite orthodox. Runeberg begins with obsession with the infinite book and its magical mentions (oracle) and moves through symbolism/spirituality to degradation/evil. That is the route of the true believer. See Chapter 3 above. It is also the route of the canonical Judas. That Judas begins with, and is essentially, oracle. See Chapter 2 above. Beyond that, in the canon, there is only Judas' disappearance, just destruction, or demonization. From oracle to evil, then, is the story of Runeberg, his Judas, and the canonical Judas. If one is willing to read so heretically, one may discern the same pattern in the canonical Jesus as well. His story also moves from oracle (from John the Baptist and Jesus' own predictions) to a Roman cross (a shameful death in imperial, if not in Christian, discourse). See Walsh, 2008b. Borges himself tells such a Jesus story, if one sees Baltasar Espinosa as a Jesus figure. See, e.g., 1999a: 397–401.

Incidentally, the Spanish phrase that ends "Three Versions of Judas" is *"del mal y del infortunio."* *"Mal"* means "evil," "harm," "injury," "hurt," "mischief," etc. *"Infortunio"* means "misfortune," "ill luck," "calamity," or "fatality." If one chooses to emphasize the last meaning of *"infortunio,"* one has a Borgesian trajectory from the infinite to fate or chance (as in "The Babylonian Lottery," 1962: 65–72). Secure identities—the stability of the orthodox Jesus and Judas—vanish in the corrosions of infinity. See Chapter 1 above; and Borges 1964: 202. If one reads from infinity to fate/chance, then Runeberg and his Judases become more Borgesian and less canonical.

spiritual Christ. Runeberg's incarnate Judas hopelessly adds evil to good by mixing spirit and matter, Jesus and Judas. In short, Runeberg's Judases bring together matters that gnosticism's metaphysical dualism separates.

The incarnation itself, however, is an idea that belongs to orthodoxy, rather than gnosticism. In gnosticism, the divine descends "into" the material world as the divine falls or degenerates into the multiple beings of the πλήρωμα. Ultimately, the demiurge, one of the lesser divine beings, creates the material world. That creation traps lesser spiritual beings within it. Creation itself, then, is an evil or a metaphysical fate to be overcome. Gnostic salvation occurs when one comes into possession of the knowledge that allows one to surmount this metaphysical damnation. Gnostic salvation, then, reverses the divine descent. It is not a further descent into the degraded material world. Further, while the saving gnosis often comes through the descent of a heavenly revealer, that figure appears like a phantom in the world of the demiurge.

Despite the orthodox narrator's allegations about his gnosticism, Runeberg clearly does not think in these terms. For Runeberg, the ultimate divine descent is the incarnation (of one spirit), and the notion of the *incarnate* Judas is more at home in orthodoxy than in gnosticism. While Runeberg's incarnation is degradation, not the crucial salvific moment that it is in orthodoxy (but see Phil. 2:5-11), the turn to the incarnation makes Runeberg seem more orthodox than gnostic.[2]

In short, Runeberg's Judases are equally alien to and at home in both orthodoxy and gnosticism. More accurately, Runeberg's Judases reflect both systems enigmatically, disturb both discourses, and confuse the boundaries between the two.[3] It is little wonder, then, that the orthodox narrator sees Runeberg as adding evil to the Son. It is not metaphysical dualism, which despite orthodox claims is as present in orthodoxy as it is in gnosticism, that adds evil. It is the confusion of the clear borders between the good (orthodoxy, Jesus) and the evil (gnosticism, Judas).

2. The perspective on Borges' fiction here (see Chapter 1) does not see degradation as salvation. More precisely, it does not see Runeberg's obsession as salvation. If one thinks of degradation as equal to mortality, then Borges' immortals would disagree. See Borges, 1964: 105–18. They find death a desideratum because it separates humans from the inhuman territory of immortality (or the infinite). Perhaps, one should be more precise then. Borges' fictions take a stand against obsession with human constructs. They do not take a stand against mortality. Death is a human's certain fate. Here, too, certain, stable identities vanish.

3. Orthodox theologians complain that gnosticism separates creation and salvation, matters held together by orthodox theology. Despite his reputed gnosticism, Runeberg also unites them, but in a strikingly unorthodox fashion.

In Borges' fictions, such confusions are the consequence of the infinite. The infinite corrodes all identities (1964: 202). Nothing holds. God, the individual, and the author (Shakespeare) are everyone and, thus, no one. Traitor and hero are one. Jesus and Judas are reversible roles. The vilest augurs unspeakable virtue. Such confusions resemble the effects of the ambiguous sacred, the source of both life and death, both good and evil. Religion tames this chaos (or the infinite) with the orders of myth and ritual. Its narratives and theologies separate good and evil, orthodoxy and heresy. It is not surprising, then, that the orthodox narrator claims that Runeberg adds evil to the (good) Son. Runeberg's confusion of orthodoxy and heresy destroys orthodoxy's mythic order (see below). It reintroduces the chaos of the sacred/infinite.

Of course, Runeberg is hardly confused. He is as certain of theological truth—which for him is the incarnate Judas—as any orthodox or gnostic true believer. Perhaps, then, the narrator's observation that Runeberg adds evil to the Son refers neither to metaphysical dualisms nor to the corrosions of the infinite but to Runeberg's degrading obsessions. In Borges' aesthetic worldview, metaphysical systems—those of the orthodox, the gnostic, and Runeberg—are branches of fantasy. None of these theologies represent reality, however logical or realistic their conventions; they all add to reality (yet another marker, by the way, of the infinite). Accordingly, true believers, who cling obsessively to their orthodoxies, come to bad ends. In Borges, if there is an ethic, a path to the good, it lies in turning away from such true beliefs. Perhaps, then, Runeberg adds evil to the Son simply through his certainty that he knows the Son's true identity.

In a piece that James Irby refers to as a parable, "*Paradiso*, XXXI, 108," Borges muses nostalgically on the lost face of Jesus, opining that the face is "the key to all parables." He claims that one might come across that face in the mundane round without knowing it. His penultimate remarks, however, leave such nostalgia behind: "Perhaps some feature of that crucified countenance lurks in every mirror; perhaps the face died, was obliterated, so that God could be all of us" (1964: 238–39). While one can read these lines as reflective of modern gnosticism, as yet another paean to the divinity of the individual, this reading seems unlikely given Borges' agnosticism and his disenchantment with modern individualism. It seems more likely that the lines gesture once again at the infinite and its corrosiveness. Like the infinite series of seeking divinities in "The Approach to Al-Mu'tasim," the God who is "all of us" belies the notion of one incarnate one, whether it is Jesus or Judas or Rurik (Borges, 1962: 156).

In the face of the infinite, obsession with one identity is evil or, better, degrading and destructive. Instead of Runeberg's mania, Borges espouses an ethic of living non-obsessively in the face of the enigmatic infinite, of forsaking divine myths for terrestrial ones and of embracing lucidity and fairness. Like Camus, Borges occasionally, deliberately opposes this ethic to Christian teachings.[4] While Borges admires the gospel as literature, his sympathies do not lie with Jesus Christ. Thus, in various pieces, Borges revises Jesus' teaching, equates his cross with those of others, and, most importantly, rejoices that Jesus' face is lost.[5] Jesus fixes the infinite too definitively for Borges.[6] Like Sophocles, Borges' interests lie instead with humans, like Runeberg, who confront the infinite.[7]

Of course, Borges also deviates from the gospel because it has already been told (so well). Vis-à-vis this classic, Borges always tells a different story. If he tells a Jesus story, he renames Jesus as Baltasar Espinosa. If he tells a Judas story, he relates a story in which believers venerate Judas or he renames Judas as John Vincent Moon, Jacob Fischbein, or Nils Runeberg. The result is heresy, a deliberate choice to deviate from the canonical story.[8] The result disrupts and demythologizes Christian orthodoxy.[9] "Three Versions of Judas" is particularly corrosive of the Christian myth because it conjoins an orthodox narrator and an allegedly gnostic theologian, whose lifework the narrator recounts. While knowing that Runeberg adds evil to the Son, the narrator apparently does not notice how disruptively close to orthodoxy Runeberg and his Judases stand. Borges does. Of course, Borges' fiction is fantastic, not mythic.

Outing Evil in Myth

In comparative studies, myth is a cultural story that provides communal self-definition in terms of some powerful, desirable other (a god,

---

4. See Borges, "A Prayer" (1999a: 33); and "Fragments From an Apocryphal Gospel" (2000a: 292–95). Cf. Camus, 1991: 117–18. On the problems of deriving an ethic from Borges, see Chapter 1.

5. For the first in this series, see the references in n4 above. For the second, see Borges, "Christ on the Cross" (2000a: 470–71). The third is discussed in the text above.

6. One can imagine a story in which Jesus is a Borgesian obsessive like Runeberg. See n1.

7. Thus, Borges calls Job the one sublime book in the Bible (1990).

8. The root meaning of heresy is choice. Sturrock asserts, "Heresy, with Borges, is identical with authorship in general, both in its motives and its products: it reorganizes the old fiction which it hates into new ones" (1977: 173).

9. See the demythologizing play in Borges' "Theme of the Hero and Traitor" (1962: 123–27).

the sacred, or simply an ideal).[10] The powers and institutions of a culture inculcate and enforce the communal myth and cultural structure (see Barthes, 1972; Foucault, 1979). Those marginalized by such dominant myths have perceptively pointed out that while mythic self-definition strives to draw believers (invariably imagined as the elite) closer to the sacred or the ideal, it also seeks to separate them from the monstrous other, or more broadly speaking, from evil (a role in which those marginalized often find themselves placed by the dominant).[11] More generally, as Claude Lévi-Strauss has concluded, myth is work done between being and non-being (1981: 694). Myth, then, is adversarial self-creation vis-à-vis the doubled other, sketching out a living space between the desired and the demonized. Such work establishes boundaries which include and exclude, creating and defending the world in which mythic believers live (Walsh, 2001: 10–12, 51).[12]

Jackson Pollack's *Guardians of the Secret* visualizes this mythic work. At the center of the painting is a light-colored rectangular box, ambiguously separated from its surroundings. Various mythological, monstrous figures surround the box on all sides, either guarding or threatening the box (Walsh, 2001: 165).[13] In the interpretation here, the box represents the mythic enclosure and its insiders while the monstrous figures symbolize all that true believers know of anything beyond their mythic system. The secret may be the (communal) box, the monsters, or both. As the community creates both the box and the monsters,[14] the claims of those like

---

10. More popularly, myth is a sacred story or a story of the gods. The statement above restates the popular in academic language. The classic statement of communal self-definition by means of the ideal/religion is Durkheim, 1975: 424–25. See also Walsh, 2001: 13–53.

11. Important works on the creation of the other include De Beauvoir, 1974; and Said, 1978. In myth studies, see Detienne, 1986; and Lincoln, 1999. In biblical studies, see Walsh, 2001; Arnal, 2005; Blanton, 2007; and Aichele, Miscall, and Walsh, 2009. The paragraph defining myth above slightly revises material from the last source.

12. So seen, myth is the community's common sense and the hermeneutic through which the community defines life and meaning. Myth, i.e., is both map and mapping. It establishes and defends the communal status quo and, thereby, supports the interests of the dominant in the community by repeating itself *ad nauseam* throughout society and by portraying itself as the real, the true, or the natural. See Barthes, 1972; and, with respect to biblical studies, Crossan, 1975.

13. Photographs are available on the internet. See, e.g., http://sfmoma.museum/artwork/259 (accessed 7-26-09).

14. The film, *The Village* (2004), illustrates this feature of myth as well. The village elders tell the story—and act the part—of monsters in the surrounding woods in order to protect the village from the outside world. Here, quite vividly, the mythic

De Quincey, Borges, and Eco that the only secret is that someone claims to possess and reveal it are obviously quite pertinent.

Christian discourse is such a mythic—secret (or enigma) creating—box. It establishes itself in the spaces between the desired and the demonic, God and Satan, Christ and Judas. Judas is a—if not the—essential Christian boundary marker.[15] Created by the discourse, he serves as the monster on the border that protects and threatens the boundary at the same time. He symbolizes the Christian experience of evil.[16] Thus, he is possessed by Satan for Luke and is a devil for John. But, Judas also represents the Christian attempt to conceptualize (to create a theodicy) and to out evil (through ritual). With Judas, Christian discourse creates its secrets—its box and its monsters—or its mythic meaning. Judas is, then, a—if not the—Christian secret. It is no wonder that theologians and artists in Christian cultures have found him enigmatic. Ireneaus' gnostics were right to speak of him in terms of "mystery."

As illustrated in preceding chapters, the oracular Judas lays a sacred, providential meaning over chaos and inexplicable evil. The cooperative Judas continues that basic mythic work as it sacrifices the true believer, which the cooperative Judas symbolizes, to the mythic system. The scapegoat and demonic Judas exorcise evil and create a safe, mythic space for insiders.

While the heroic Judas provides a simulacrum of the alienated, subjective modern individual, that figure, despite relentless quests for him, is quite rare.[17] Most often, modern interpretations continue to depict Judas as a failure. Accordingly, the modern Judas still functions quite like the canonical Judas. He exorcises the modern fears of absorption and ostracism. Casting out Judas the failure establishes and defends modern

---

community creates its own monsters. Cf. the discussion of rivals' creation of one another in Chapters 4–5 above.

15. Maccoby (1992) and Arnal (2005) argue in different ways that Judaism often functions in this fashion for Christian thinkers as well.

16. From this perspective, then, the narrator of "Three Versions of Jesus" rightly opines that Runeberg adds evil to the Son when he concludes that Judas—the Christian marker of evil—is the incarnate one.

17. In mythic terms, it matters little whether Judas is demonic or divine. See Chapter 5; and the discussion of myths that demonize the other (e.g., those of tradition and the Enlightenment) and those that desire the other (e.g., those of Romanticism) in Walsh, 2001: 13–53. Whether demonic or divine, Judas is a product of mythic discourse and reveals nothing about the other or the outside. He is a mythic insider's fiction. In Borges, the reversibility of fictional roles and the infinite's corrupting influence also mean that it matters little whether Judas is demonic or divine.

identities by imagining the modern ideal self, in relief, as triumphant and true. The Menard-like repetition of the canonical Judas in modernity by neo-traditionalists works differently. That attempt to repeat the canonical Judas in modernity establishes and defends a sectarian identity/mythic enclosure in the midst of and against the threatening modern world.

The mythic creation and exorcism of Judas (or his deification for that matter) dispels insecurities about the truth and goodness of true believers and their myth. Thus, if Judases reflect a fascination with evil, they do not explore evil. They exclude it and look voyeuristically at it from afar, from inside the safe, sacred enclosure. As a device of mythic discourse, Judas defines true believers as *not* damned outsiders, *not* victims, *not* failures, and so forth.[18] Judas' ostracism defines true believers positively as saved, triumphant, true, and so forth. In such myths, Judas is never known in any meaningful way. Judas warns true believers not to venture into certain precincts. He is myth's boundary, shadow, or monstrous outside. He is mysterious and enigmatic. The insider discourse formed by such boundaries cannot speak meaningfully of the boundary or of the outside. Myth always speaks within enclosures.[19] As a result, Judas is a Christian or, more accurately, a product of Christian mythic discourse (see Maccoby, 1992; J. Robertson, 1927; and Tarachow, 1960). Baum puts it aptly: Judas is the gargoyle on the Christian cathedral (1916: 623).[20]

Borges' "Three Versions of Judas" differs dramatically by adding evil to the Son. In the Christian myth, Judas represents all that is evil and demonic while the Son represents all that is virtuous and sacred. The Christian myth exorcises Judas and connects the true believer with the Son. Joining Judas and Jesus, then, completely confuses this mythic work. Joining insider and outsider, good and evil, highlights the artificiality of mythic boundaries by calling attention to them. Such actions degrade Runeberg and his Judas because they reject myth's deifying intentions.[21]

---

18. On this type of mythic use of Judas in Jesus films, see Walsh, 2006a. Lawrence Besserman provides a nice overview of the theological issues with which artists and theologians struggle in their interpretations of Judas (1992: 418–20). Paffenroth deals with many of the same theological issues throughout his volume (2001b).

19. Or it speaks of the divine creation of the mythic world *in illo tempore*, a time different from but providing the sacred basis of the present order and a time continuing in that religious order's rituals.

20. Anderson similarly says that Christians need Judas to draw off the demonic (1991: 32). Kennelly's Judas says that his story will feed the children "who need a monster to hate and fear" (1991: 47).

21. Once again, it is not at all clear that Borges thinks one can escape degradation. See n2. Of course, Borges engages in heresy, not mythology.

Myth safely separates good and evil, Jesus and Judas, life and death, and other binaries. Borges' "Three Versions of Judas" and his other fictions restore the rivalry resolved by such myths:

> Two ideas, two aspects of reality, two attributes or "beings" vie for the attention of the consciousness; one must be victorious over the other; so Scharlach kills Lönnrot, the Negro kills Martín Fierro, Bandeira kills Otálora, and so on. The fate of the subordinate idea is a cause for lament, in Borges' view, and although the victory of one is necessary, it is nevertheless deplorable because the victor is only a perspective, a partial image of reality. (Wheelock, 1969: 64–65)[22]

By focusing on Judas, the monster excluded by Christian discourse, Borges' "Three Versions of Judas" gestures at the incompleteness of and *the evil within* the Christian myth.

Nonetheless, Borges does not explore external evil, the other, the outside, truth, reality, or the infinite any more than the Christian myth does. In fact, Borges' Runeberg imagines the character or career of Judas in a fashion strikingly like that of the Judas of the canon. The Judases of both the canonical gospel and of Runeberg begin with oracle (or the infinite) and proceed directly to dismissal, destruction, and degradation (or evil). As a result, "Three Versions of Judas" does not provide an antimyth contesting or replacing the Christian myth. "Three Versions of Judas" is much more uncomfortably close to home than an antimyth.[23] It dwells on the border of the Christian myth. It is Christological fantasy or parable.[24] It provides stories alongside the canon, exposing Christian mythwork, challenging the Christian myth's values, and fictionalizing the whole mythic process. Thereby, Borges' "Three Versions of Judas" asserts that "our Judases/our evil, ourselves."

While the tone of "Three Versions of Judas" is serious, its effect resembles that of *Monty Python's The Life of Brian* (1979). In that parody of Jesus epics, everything is slightly off kilter because the film focuses on

---

22. Aizenberg discusses this same element in Borges in terms of his repeated retelling and revision of the Cain and Abel story (1984: 108–48). Here, it is worth remembering that Irenaeus refers to the gnostics who have a Gospel of Judas as Cainites.

23. One may think of "Three Versions of Judas" as the uncanny or as exposing the uncanny (*unheimlich*) within the homely (*heimlich*) world of the canon. Freud begins his discussion of the uncanny with lengthy reflections on the etymological relationships between *heimlich* and *unheimlich*. See Freud, 2003; and the discussion in Chapter 1.

24. Borges refers to "Three Versions of Judas" as Christological fantasy in 1962: 106. On myth, antimyth, and parable, see Crossan, 1975. On Borges' fantastic fiction, see Chapter 1.

Brian, not Jesus. Thus, the audience of *The Life of Brian* is outside the glowing manger of the nativity, at the back of the Sermon on the Mount where they cannot understand Jesus' teaching, in the presence of a former leper disgruntled with the miracle that put him out of his (begging) job, and at Golgotha on what appears to be the wrong day. The result leaves one laughing out loud. Borges causes less laughter. One hardly laughs at Runeberg's degradation. One may, however, smile when reading Borges. If so, it is a wry smile at one's own displacement, at the self-awareness that one has taken a Zahir too seriously. Borges' fantasy/parable displaces the metaphysical and ethical certainties of Christian myth both by presenting other stories and by calling attention to itself as fiction. Fictions, of course, are matters of near belief, not true belief (see Aichele, 1985).

Fictional Lessons

Borges' fantastic fictions offer an ethic for living graciously in the face of enigmatic reality (the infinite) and in the presence of various, competing myths (e.g., of Judas) that claim to illumine that reality.[25] At bottom, this ethic is a joyful, playful acceptance of the human condition. Borges' description of his own Dunraven best expresses both Borges' playful awe in the face of the infinite and his suspicion of systems: "Dunraven, who had read a great many detective novels, thought that the solution of a mystery [a system] was always a good deal less interesting than the mystery itself [the infinite]; the mystery had a touch of the supernatural and even the divine about it, while the solution was a sleight of hand" (1999a: 260).[26]

Despite this agnosticism, Borges' fictions never deny the human need for myths. The life of Funes the Memorious, immersed in reality without syntax, is sub-human. To live, humans need perspective, order, and meaning. Myths provide such necessities. Nonetheless, Borges never endeavors to supply a new, better myth.[27] His fictions always abut some other story (or even the concept of story itself). By telling multiple fictions, stories alongside other (dominant) stories, Borges prevents one's unconscious, obsessive alignment with any one story and/or myth.

---

25. For Borges' parables alongside or rewritings of the gospel, see nn4–6 above.

26. Cf. Camus' invitation to think of Sisyphus as happy in the face of the absurd (1991: 123).

27. One might read his description of his artistic style as an eschewal of new myth making: "The composition of vast books [myth] is a laborious and impoverishing extravagance.... A better course of procedure is to pretend that these books already exist, and then to offer a résumé, a commentary" (1962: 15).

His fictions constantly remind one that myth is not reality. Myth is a human construct or, better, a human attempt to map reality in order to navigate life. As Jonathan Z. Smith has frequently asserted, it is precisely its difference from reality that makes a myth or map useful and interesting (1978: 289–309). In making this point, Smith frequently cites Borges' "On Exactitude in Science." That story imagines cartographers who make an increasingly precise map of their empire until they create "a Map of the Empire whose size was that of the Empire, and which coincided point for point with it" (1999a: 325). This map is as useless a navigational tool as Funes' unmediated, un-abstracted experience of reality. Not surprisingly, the map spells the end of geography in the empire. Ironically, then, myths are useless unless they are imprecise and incomplete. Fortunately, they are inherently so. Unfortunately, true belief ignores this fact.

Accordingly, Borges' fictions also show the dangers of this obsessive, true belief or of mistaking myth for reality. True belief makes everything and everyone subservient to the mythic system. It is the path to Runeberg's death and Judas' suicide. True belief manufactures and silences—in fact, it renders unknowable—the other. It scapegoats and demonizes Judas. Finally, true belief deifies the true believer at the other's expense. Borges' "Three Versions of Judas" provides a story alongside the canonical Judas that makes these problems inescapable. It begins by pointing out gaps and inconsistencies in the canonical Judas; it proceeds by telling other, more interesting stories about Judas, which provide, not incidentally, a parody of both the canonical Judas and the (modern) lionization of Judas; and it concludes by adding evil to the Son.

That last, enigmatic line in "Three Versions of Judas" reminds one that myths afford better versions of the self and the community by externalizing evil. That (particular) evil becomes, thereby, unknowable, unthinkable, and unspeakable within the mythic community. However, the community easily forgets that it has fabricated this evil and that, therefore, corruption also still lies within it and within the nature of the mythic process itself.[28] The end of "Three Versions of Judas" makes this mythic complicity with evil inescapable. With respect to Judas, it illustrates that "our Judases, ourselves."

The first chapter of this book claims that Borges' fictions provide a prophylactic against metaphysical certainty. As a human, one cannot

---

28. The argument here does not deny the horrors of the human experience of evil and the desperate need to deal with it intellectually (in theodicy) and practically (in ritual, etc.). This study simply calls attention to myth's inevitable complicity with that which it deems evil. True belief and its mythic clarities easily obscure this point.

6 *Adding Evil to the Son* 161

know the infinite. Moreover, within a myth, one cannot know the myth's outsider or other (that is, an insider in another myth). Vis-à-vis such matters, Borges helpfully insists that humans always dwell in uncertainty. Thus, in the story of "Pedro Salvadores," Borges' narrator muses on the character of the story's highly questionable protagonist. Pedro hides in a cellar from a dictator for nine years, leaving his wife to face the horrors of the situation alone. Although the dictator falls and Pedro emerges from the cellar, he and his family are reduced to poverty. The narrator ends the sad, perhaps cowardly story with a line that speaks, with the mere change of a name, of both the canonical and modern understandings of Judas: "We see the fate of Pedro Salvadores [Judas], like all things, as a symbol of something that we are just on the verge of understanding…." (1999a: 337).[29] Borges' story about Pedro brings to the fore the aesthetic near revelations, near beliefs, and uncertainty at which Borges' fictions always gesture (see Borges, 1964: 188).

While one might wish to rush to condemn, excuse, or eulogize Judas in light of some mythic certainty, Borges' fictions insist on uncertainty.[30] It makes little difference whether one demonizes or deifies Judas, whether one asserts the canonical or the modern heroic Judas.[31] Either mythic certainty is equally pernicious.[32] Vis-à-vis such obsessions, the playfulness of fictions—the plural is crucial—and near belief may be the only way to avoid the gallows.[33]

---

29. See Chapter 1. Cf. Kennelly, who imagines Judas responding to a poet, Kennelly himself, by saying, "I'm tickled to death/By people who think they know/Shallows and depths of somebody else" (1991: 359).

30. Borges describes the attempt to create uncertainty as an enduring feature of his fictional style (1999a: 331).

31. Perhaps, one should sing with Bob Dylan, "But I can't think for you/You'll have to decide/Whether Judas Iscariot/Had God on his side." The lyrics are part of his anti-war "With God on Our Side." Like Borges' fiction, the song critiques the deadly effects of mythic certainty. The lyrics are available at http://www.bobdylan.com/#/songs/god-our-side (accessed 7-26-09).

32. For a devastating critique of the murderous effects of ideology (or mythic certainty), see Camus, 1956. Camus says, e.g., "Ideology today is concerned only with the denial of other human beings, who alone bear the responsibility of deceit. It is then that we kill. Each day at dawn, assassins in judges' obes [sic] slip into some cell: murder is the problem today" (1956: 5).

33. On near belief, see Chapter 1. For an argument that one can live with such fictions, see Walsh, 2001: 133–74. Nietzsche's version of such "near belief" is a call to temporary habits (or the courage to change one's convictions).

Near belief calls one to live more graciously than mythic certainty does.[34] On one hand, it calls one to recognize that evil belongs to one's own myth and myth-making process. Specifically, it compels one to acknowledge that one's Judas is one's mythic creation, the symbol of one's own fears and desires. On the other hand, it implies, as some postmodern thinkers might say, that Judas also represents nothing less than the demand of the (unknowable) other. After Nietzsche, such a demand may be the important rumor left of transcendence.

34. Theologians occasionally offer a similar ethic. With respect to Judas, see, e.g., Anderson, 1991; Klassen, 1996; and Paffenroth, 2001b: 139–44. The distinction between these theologians and the agnostic Borges is the question of whether or not a healthy union with the infinite is possible. Like Camus', Borges' ethic is closer to revolt at this point than submission. See n7 and Chapter 3.

Bibliography

Aichele, George. 1985. *The Limits of Story*. Philadelphia: Fortress.
—1997. *Sign, Text, Scripture: Semiotics and the Bible*. Sheffield: Sheffield Academic Press.
—2001. *The Control of Biblical Meaning: Canon as Semiotic Mechanism*. Harrisburg: Trinity Press International.
—2006. *The Phantom Messiah: Postmodern Fantasy and the Gospel of Mark*. New York and London: T&T Clark.
Aichele, George, (ed.). 2000. *Culture, Entertainment and the Bible*. Sheffield: Sheffield Academic Press.
Aichele, George and Richard Walsh, (eds.). 2002. *Screening Scripture: Intertextual Connections Between Scripture and Film*. Harrisburg: Trinity Press International.
—2005. *Those Outside: Noncanonical Readings of Canonical Gospels*. New York: T&T Clark.
Aichele, George, Peter Miscall, and Richard Walsh. 2009. "An Elephant in the Room: Historical Critical and Postmodern Interpretations of the Bible." *Journal of Biblical Literature* 128.2 (Summer): 399–419.
Aizenberg, Edna. 1984. *The Aleph Weaver: Biblical, Kabbalistic and Judaic Elements in Borges*. Potomac, MD: Scripta Humanistica.
Aizenberg, Edna, (ed.). 1990. *Borges and His Successors: The Borgesian Impact on Literature and the Arts*. Columbia and London: University of Missouri Press.
Alazraki, Jaime. 1986. "Kabbalistic Traits in Borges' Narration." In Bloom, 1986: 79–91.
Alter, Robert. 1981. *The Art of Biblical Narrative*. New York: Basic Books.
Anderson, Ray S. 1991. *The Gospel according to Judas*. Colorado Springs: Helmers & Howard.
Aristotle. *Poetics*. 1999. Ed. and trans. Stephen J. Halliwell; Loeb Classical Library, 199; Cambridge: Harvard University Press.
Arnal, William. 2005. *The Symbolic Jesus: Historical Scholarship, Judaism and the Construction of Identity*. London: Equinox.
Auerbach, Nina. 1995. *Our Vampires, Ourselves*. Chicago: University of Chicago Press.
Auerbach, Erich. 1968. *Mimesis: The Representation of Reality in Western Literature*. Trans. Willard R. Trask; Princeton: Princeton University Press.
Augustine. 1984. *The City of God*. Trans. Henry Bettenson; New York: Penguin.
Baigent, Michael, Richard Leigh, and Henry Lincoln. 2004. *Holy Blood, Holy Grail*. New York: Delta.
Barrenechea, Ana María. 1965. *Borges: The Labyrinth Maker*. Ed. and trans. Robert Lima; New York: New York University Press.
Barth, Eugene Howard, (ed.). 1972. *Festschrift to Honor F. Wilbur Gingrich*. Leiden: E. J. Brill.
Barthes, Roland. 1972. *Mythologies*. Trans. Annette Lavers; New York: Hill and Wang.
Baum, Paull Franklin. 1916. "The Mediaeval Legend of Judas Iscariot." *Publications of the Modern Language Association* 31.3: 481–623.

—1922. "Judas's Red Hair," *Journal of English and Germanic Philology* 21.1: 520–29.
Beal, Timothy K. *Religion and Its Monsters*. 2002. New York/London: Routledge.
Bellah, Robert N., Richard Marsden, William M. Sullivan, Ann Swindler, and Stephen M. Tiption. 1985. *Habits of the Heart: Individualism and Commitment in American Life*. Berkeley: University of California Press.
Besserman, Lawrence. 1992. "Judas Iscariot." In Jeffrey, 1992: 418–20.
Blanton, Ward. 2007. *Displacing Christian Origins: Philosophy, Secularity, and the New Testament*. Chicago: University of Chicago Press.
Bloom, Harold. 1992. *American Religion: The Emergence of the Post-Christian Nation*. New York: Simon & Schuster.
Bloom, Harold, (ed.). 1986. *Jorge Luis Borges*. Modern Critical Views; New York: Chelsea House.
Borges, Jorge Luis. 1962. *Ficciones*. Ed. and with an introduction by Anthony Kerrigan; New York: Grove Press.
—1964. *Labyrinths: Selected Stories and Other Writings*. Ed. Donald A. Yates and James E. Irby; New York: New Directions Books.
Borges, Jorge Luis. 1990. "The Book of Job." Trans. Edna Aizenberg; in Aizenberg, 1990: 267–75.
—1999a. *Collected Fictions*. Trans. Andrew Hurley; New York: Penguin Books.
—1999b. *Selected Non-Fictions*. Ed. Eliot Weinberger; trans. Esther Allen, Suzanne Jill Levine, and Eliot Weinberger; New York: Penguin Books.
—2000a. *Selected Poems*. Ed. Alexander Coleman; New York: Penguin Books.
—2000b. *This Craft of Verse*. Ed. Calin-Andrei Mihailescu; Cambridge: Harvard University Press.
—2005. *The Book of Imaginary Beings*. With Margarita Guerrero; trans. Andrew Hurley; New York, Viking Penguin.
Boyarin, Daniel. 1999. *Dying for God: Martyrdom and the Making of Christianity and Judaism*. Stanford: Stanford University Press.
Brandon, S. G. F. 1967. *Jesus and the Zealots: A Study of the Political Factor in Primitive Christianity*. New York: Scribner.
Brelich, Mario. 1988. *The Work of Betrayal*. Trans. Raymond Rosenthal; Marlboro, VT: Marlboro Press.
Brown, Raymond. 1994. *The Death of the Messiah*. 2 vols; New York: Doubleday.
Brown, Dan. 2003. *The Da Vinci Code*. New York: Doubleday.
Bultmann, Rudolf. 1955. *Theology of the New Testament*. 2 vols; trans. Kendrick Grobel; New York: Charles Scribner's Sons.
Burkert, Walter. 1983. *Homo Necans: The Anthropology of Ancient Greek Sacrificial Ritual and Myth*. Berkeley: University of California Press.
Callaghan, Morley. 1984. *A Time for Judas*. Toronto: Avon.
Campbell, Joseph. 1969. *The Masks of God*. New York: Penguin Books.
Camus, Albert. 1956. *The Rebel*. Rev. edn; trans. Anthony Bower; New York: Vintage Books.
—1991. *Myth of Sisyphus and Other Essays*. Trans. Justin O'Brien; New York: Vintage International.
Castelli, Elizabeth A. 1991. *Imitating Paul: A Discourse of Power*. Louisville: Westminster John Knox.
Christ, Ronald J. 1969. *The Narrow Act: Borges' Act of Allusion*. New York: New York University Press.
Christianson, Eric S., Peter Francis, and William R. Telford, (eds.). 2005. *Cinéma Divinité: Religion, Theology and the Bible in Film*. London: SCM.

Bibliography

Cohen, Stanley and Laurie Taylor. 1992. *Escape Attempts: The Theory and Practice of Resistance to Everyday Life*. 2nd edn; London: Routledge.

Conzelmann, Hans. 1961. *The Theology of St. Luke*. Trans. Geoffrey Buswell; Philadelphia: Fortress.

Crossan, John Dominic. 1975. *The Dark Interval: Toward a Theology of Story*. Niles: Argus Communications.

—1976. *Raid on the Articulate: Comic Eschatology in Jesus and Borges*. New York: Harper & Row.

—1991. *The Historical Jesus: The Life of a Mediterranean Peasant*. San Francisco: HarperSanFrancisco.

—1995. *Who Killed Jesus? Exposing the Roots of Anti-Semitism in the Gospel Story of the Death of Jesus*. New York: HarperSanFrancisco.

Crossley, James G. 2006. *Why Christianity Happened: A Sociohistorical Account of Christian Origins (26–50 CE)*. Louisville/London: Westminster John Knox.

Dalman, Gustaf. 1973. *Jesus Christ in the Talmud, Midrash, Zohar and the Liturgy of the Synagogue*. New York: Arno Press.

Daube, David. 1994. "Judas." *California Law Review* 82: 95–108.

De Beauvoir, Simone. 1974. *The Second Sex*. Trans. H. M. Parsely; New York: Vintage.

DeConick, April D. 2007. *The Thirteenth Apostle: What the Gospel of Judas Really Says*. London: Continuum.

De Man, Paul. 1986. "A Modern Master." In Bloom, 1986: 21–27.

De Quincey, Thomas. 1897 (original, 1857). "Judas Iscariot." In Mason, 1897: 8:177–206.

Derrida, Jacques. 1981. *Dissemination*. Trans. Barbara Johnson; Chicago: University of Chicago Press.

—1987a. *Glas*. Trans. J. P. Leavey, Jr. and Richard Rand; Lincoln: University of Nebraska Press.

—1987b. *The Truth in Painting*. Trans. Geoff Bennington and Ian McLeod; Chicago: University of Chicago Press.

Detienne, Marcel. 1986. *The Creation of Mythology*. Trans. Margret Cook; Chicago: Chicago University Press.

Dieckmann, B. 1991. *Judas als Südenbock. Eine verhängnisvolle Geschichte von Angst und Vergeltung*. Munich: Kösel.

Droge, Arthur J. and James D. Tabor. 1992. *A Noble Death: Suicide and Martyrdom among Christians and Jews in Antiquity*. New York: HarperSanFrancisco.

Durkheim, Emile. 1975. *The Elementary Forms of Religious Life*. Trans. Karen E. Fields; New York: The Free Press.

Eco, Umberto. 1990. *Foucault's Pendulum*. Trans. William Weaver; New York: Ballantine Books.

Ehrman, Bart. 2006a. "Christianity Turned on Its Head: The Alternative Vision of the Gospel of Judas." In Kasser, Meyer, and Wurst, 2006: 77–120.

—2006b. *The Lost Gospel of Judas Iscariot: A New Look at Betrayer and Betrayed*. Oxford: Oxford University Press.

Eiseman, Robert. 1997. *James the Brother of Jesus: The Key to Unlocking the Secrets of Early Christianity and the Dead Sea Scrolls*. Viking Penguin.

Eliade, Mircea. 1959. *The Sacred and the Profane: The Nature of Religion*. Trans. Willard R. Trask; New York: Harcourt Brace & World.

Emerson, Ralph Waldo. 1998. *Self-Reliance and Other Essays*. New York: Dover.

Enslin, Morton S. 1972. "How the Story Grew: Judas in Fact and Fiction." In Barth, 1972: 123–41.

Epiphanus. 1990. *The Panarion.* Trans. P. R. Amidon; New York and Oxford: Oxford University Press.
Eslinger, Lyle. 2000. "Judas Game: The Biology of Combat in the Gospel of John." *JSNT* 77.1 (March): 45–73.
Exum, J. Cheryl, (ed.). 2006. *The Bible in Film—The Bible and Film.* Leiden: Brill.
Foucault, Michel. 1979. *Discipline and Punishment: The Birth of the Prison.* Trans. Alan Sheridan; New York: Vintage.
Fox, Richard Wightman. 2004. *Jesus in America: Personal Savior, Cultural Hero, National Obsession.* New York: HarperSanFrancisco.
Freud, Sigmund. 1950. *Totem and Taboo.* Trans. James Strachey; New York: W. W. Norton.
—1989. *The Future of an Illusion.* Ed. and trans. James Strachey; New York: W. W. Norton.
—2003. *The Uncanny.* Trans. David McLintock; New York: Penguin Classics.
Frye, Northrop. 1982. *The Great Code.* New York: Harcourt Brace Jovanovich.
Genette, Gérard. 1980. *Narrative Discourse: An Essay in Method.* Trans. Jane E. Lewin; Ithaca: Cornell University Press.
Girard, René. 1965. *Deceit, Desire, and the Novel: Self and Other in Literary Structure.* Trans. Yvonne Freccero; Baltimore: Johns Hopkins University Press.
—1972. *Violence and the Sacred.* Trans. Patrick Gregory; Baltimore: Johns Hopkins University Press.
—1986. *The Scapegoat.* Trans. Yvonne Freccero; Baltimore: Johns Hopkins University Press.
—1987a. *Job: the Victim of His People.* Trans. Yvonne Freccero; Stanford: Stanford University Press.
—1987b. *Things Hidden since the Foundation of the World.* Trans. Stephen Bann and Michael Metteer; Stanford: Stanford University Press.
Goldstein, Morris. 1950. *Jesus in the Jewish Tradition.* New York: Macmillan.
Graves, Robert. 1946. *King Jesus.* New York: Creative Age.
Greenberg, Gary. 2007. *The Judas Brief: Who Really Killed Jesus?* New York and London: Continuum.
Greimas, A. J. 1984. *Structural Semantics: An Attempt at a Method.* Trans. Ronald Schleifer, Daniele McDowell, and Alan Velie; Lincoln: University of Nebraska Press.
Gundry, Robert Horton. 1967. *The Use of the Old Testament in St. Matthew's Gospel.* Leiden: E. J. Brill.
Halas, R. B. 1946. *Judas Iscariot: A Scriptural and Theological Study of His Person, His Deeds, and His Eternal Lot.* Washington, D.C.: Catholic University Press.
Hand, Wayland D. 1942. *A Dictionary of Words and Idioms Associated with Judas Iscariot.* Berkeley: University of California Press.
Happel, Stephen. 1993. "The Postmodernity of Judas: Religious Narrative and the Deconstruction of Time." In Jasper, 1993: 91–119.
Hengel, Martin. 1977. *Crucifixion: In the Ancient World and the Folly of the Cross.* Trans. John Bowden; Philadelphia: Fortress.
Hobbes, Thomas. 1958. *Leviathan.* Indianapolis: Liberal Arts.
Hughes, Kirk T. 1991. "Framing Judas." *Semeia* 54: 223–38.
Hunt, T. (ed.). 1971. *The Collected Poetry of Robinson Jeffers.* Stanford: Stanford University Press.
Irwin, W. R. 1976. *The Game of the Impossible: A Rhetoric of Fantasy.* Urbana: University of Chicago Press.
Jasper, David, (ed.). 1993. *Postmodernism, Literature, and the Future of Theology.* New York: St. Martin's Press.

Jeffers, Robinson. 1971. "Dear Judas." In T. Hunt, 1971: 2: 5–45.
Jeffrey, David Lyle, (ed.). 1992. *A Dictionary of Biblical Tradition in English Literature.* Grand Rapids: Eerdmans.
Jeremias, Joachim. 1971. *New Testament Theology: The Proclamation of Jesus.* Trans. John Bowden; New York: Scribner's.
Jeremias, Joachim. 1977. *The Eucharistic Words of Jesus.* Trans. Norman Perrin; Philadelphia: Fortress.
Jursch, Hanna. 1952. "Judas Ischarioth in der Kunst." *Wissenschaftliche Zeitschrift der Friedrich Schiller Universität* 1: 101–105.
Käsemann, Ernst. 1982. *Essays on New Testament Themes.* Trans. W. J. Montague; Philadelphia: Fortress.
Kasser, Rodolphe. 2006. "The Story of Codex Tchacos and the Gospel of Judas." In Kasser, Meyer, and Wurst, 2006: 47–76.
—2007. "Introduction." In Kasser and Wurst, 2007: 1–33.
Kasser, Rodolphe, Marvin Meyer, and Gregor Wurst, (eds.). 2006. *The Gospel of Judas.* Washington, D.C.: National Geographic.
Kasser, Rodolphe and Gregor Wurst. 2007. *The Gospel of Judas Together with the Letter of Peter to Philip, James and a Book of Allogenes from Codex Tchacos: Critical Edition.* Washington, D.C.: National Geographic.
Kennelly, Brendan. 1991. *The Book of Judas.* Newcastle upon Tyne: Bloodaxe Books.
Kermode, Frank. 1979. *The Genesis of Secrecy: On the Interpretation of Narrative.* Cambridge: Harvard University Press.
King, Karen L. 2003. *What is Gnosticism?* Cambridge: Harvard University Press.
Klassen, William. 1996. *Judas: Betrayer or Friend of Jesus?* Minneapolis: Fortress.
Klauck, Hans-Josef. 1987. *Judas: Ein Jünger des Herrn.* Freiburg: Herder.
Klausner, Joseph. 1944. *Jesus of Nazareth: His Life, Times, and Teaching.* Trans. Herbert Danby; New York: Macmillan.
Krosney, Herbert. 2006. *The Lost Gospel: The Quest for the Gospel of Judas Iscariot.* Washington, D.C.: National Geographic.
Kuryluk, Ewa. 1987. *Salome and Judas in the Cave of Sex: The Grotesque: Origins, Iconography, Techniques.* Evanston, IL: Northwestern University Press.
Lagerkvist, Pär. 1968. *Barabbas.* Trans. Alan Blair; New York: Bantam.
Lee, Philip J. 1987. *Against the Protestant Gnostics.* New York: Oxford University Press.
Lévi-Strauss, Claude. 1981. *The Naked Man: Introduction to a Science of Mythology, IV.* Trans. John and Doreen Weightman; New York: Harper & Row.
Lincoln, Bruce. 1999. *Theorizing Myth: Narrative, Ideology, and Scholarship.* Chicago: University of Chicago Press.
Lindstrom, Naomi. 1990. *Jorge Luis Borges: A Study of the Short Fiction.* Twayne's Studies in Short Fiction, 16; Boston: Twayne Publishers.
Lovecraft, H. P. 2005. *At the Mountains of Madness.* With an introduction by China Miéville; New York: Modern Library.
Maccoby, Hyam. 1982. *The Sacred Executioner.* London: Thames & Hudson.
—1992. *Judas Iscariot and the Myth of Jewish Evil.* New York: Free Press.
Mack, Burton L. 1988. *A Myth of Innocence: Mark and Christian Origins.* Philadelphia: Fortress.
Martel, Yann. 2001. *Life of Pi.* Orlando: Harvest Book.
Mason, David, (ed.). 1897. *The Collected Writings of Thomas De Quincey.* London: A. & C. Black.
May, Rollo. 1991. *The Cry for Myth.* New York: Delta.

McMurray, George R. 1980. *Jorge Luis Borges*. Modern Literature Monographs; New York: Frederick Ungar Publishing.
Mead, George. 1962. *Fragments of A Faith Forgotten*. New Hyde Park, NY: University Books.
Meier, John. 2001. *A Marginal Jew*. 3 vols.; New York: Random House.
Mellinkoff, Ruth. 1982. "Judas's Red Hair and the Jews." *Journal of Jewish Art* 9: 31–46.
Meyer, Marvin. 2006. "Judas and the Gnostic Connection." In Kasser, Meyer, and Wurst, 2006: 137–69.
—2007. *Judas: The Definitive Collection of Gospels and Legends about the Infamous Apostle of Judas*. New York: HarperCollins.
Meyer, Marvin W. and Charles Hughes, (eds.). 2001. *Jesus Then and Now: Images of Jesus in History and Christology*. Harrisburg: Trinity Press International.
Miéville, China. 2007. *Un Lun Dun*. New York: Ballantine Books.
Miles, Jack. 1996. *God: A Biography*. New York: Vintage.
—2001. *Christ: A Crisis in the Life of God*. New York: Alfred A. Knopf.
Moore, Christopher. 2002. *Lamb: The Gospel According to Biff, Christ's Childhood Pal*. New York: Harper Perennial.
Moore, Stephen D. 1989. *Literary Criticism and the Gospels: The Theoretical Challenge*. New Haven: Yale University Press.
—1996. *God's Gym: Divine Male Bodies of the Bible*. New York: Routledge.
Morrow, James. 1994. *Towing Jehovah*. San Diego: Harcourt Brace.
—1996. *Blameless in Abaddon*. San Diego: Harcourt Brace.
—1999. *The Eternal Footman*. San Diego: Harcourt Brace.
Neusner, Jacob. 1993. *A Rabbi Talks to Jesus: An Intermillenial, Interfaith Exchange*. New York: Doubleday.
Nickelsburg, George W. E. 1980. "The Genre and Function of the Markan Passion Narrative." *Harvard Theological Review* 73: 153–84.
Nietzsche, Friedrich. 1873. "On Truth and Lies in a Nonmoral Sense." Trans. Daniel Breazeale; in Pearson and Large, 2006: 114–23.
—1954. *The Antichrist*. In Walter A. Kaufmann, (ed. and trans.); *The Portable Nietzsche*, 1954: 565–656; New York: Viking.
—1966. *Beyond Good and Evil: Prelude to a Philosophy of the Future*. Trans. Walter Kaufmann; New York: Vintage.
—1974. *The Gay Science*. Trans. and with a commentary by Walter Kaufmann; New York: Vintage Books.
—1996. *Human, All Too Human: A Book for Free Spirits*. Trans. R. J. Hollingdale; Cambridge: Cambridge University Press.
Nortje, L. 1994. "Matthew's Motive for the Composition of the Story of Judas's Suicide in Matthew 27:3–10." *Neotestamentica* 28.1: 41–51.
O'Regan, C. 2001. *Gnostic Return in Modernity*. Albany: SUNY.
Otto, Rudolf. 1958. *The Idea of the Holy: An Inquiry into the Non-Rational Factor in the Idea of the Divine and its Relation to the Rational*. Trans. John W. Harvey; New York: Oxford University Press.
Paffenroth, Kim. 1992. "The Stories of the Fate of Judas and Differing Attitudes towards Sources." *Proceedings: Eastern Great Lakes and Midwest Biblical Societies* 12: 67–81.
—2001a. "Film Depictions of Judas." *Journal of Religion and Film* 5.2. Available at htpp://avalon.unomaha.edu/jrf/judas.htm (accessed 7-26-09).
—2001b. *Judas: Images of the Lost Disciple*. Louisville: Westminster John Knox.
Pagels, Elaine. 2003. *Beyond Belief: The Secret Gospel of Thomas*. New York: Random.

Pagels, Elaine H. and Karen L. King. 2007. *Reading Judas: The Gospel of Judas and the Shaping of Christianity*. New York: Viking.
Pearson, Keith Ansell and Duncan Large. 2006. *The Nietzsche Reader*. London: Blackwell.
Pelikan, Jarslov. 1985. *Jesus Through the Centuries: His Place in the History of Culture*. New Haven: Yale University Press.
Pippin, Tina. 1999. *Apocalyptic Bodies: The Biblical End of the World in Text and Image*. New York: Routledge.
—2002. "Of Gods and Demons: Blood Sacrifice and Eternal Life in *Dracula* and the Apocalypse of John." In Aichele and Walsh, 2002: 24–41.
Pojman, Louis P. 1994. *Philosophy: The Pursuit of Wisdom*. Belmont, CA: Wadsworth.
Popkes, W. 1976. *Christus Traditus: Eine Untersuchung zum Begriff der Hingabe im NT*. ATANT, 49; Zurich: Zwingli Verlag.
Propp, Vladimir. 1968. *Morphology of Folktale*. 2nd edn; trans. Laurence Scott; Austin: University of Texas Press.
Prothero, Stephen. 2003. *American Jesus: How the Son of God Became a National Icon*. New York: Farrar, Straus and Giroux.
Pynchon, Thomas. 1995. *Gravity's Rainbow*. New York: Penguin.
—1999. *The Crying of Lot 49*. HarperPerennial.
Pyper, Hugh S. 2001. "Modern Gospels of Judas: Canon and Betrayal." *Literature & Theology* 15.2 (June): 111–22.
Rabkin, Eric. 1976. *The Fantastic in Literature*. Princeton: Princeton University Press.
Rayner, William. 1969. *The Knifeman*. New York: William Morrow & Co.
Reimarus, H. S. 1985. *Fragments*. Ed. with an introduction by Charles Talbert; trans. Ralph S. Fraser; Chico, CA: Scholars.
Reinhartz, Adele. 2007. *Jesus of Hollywood*. Oxford: Oxford University Press.
Riley, Greg. 1995. *Resurrection Reconsidered: Thomas and John in Controversy*. Minneapolis: Augsburg Fortress.
Robertson, David. 1973. "The Book of Job: A Literary Study." *Soundings* 56: 446–69.
Robertson, J. M. 1927. *Jesus and Judas: A Textual and Historical Investigation*. London: Watts.
Robinson, James M. 2006. *The Secrets of Judas: The Story of the Misunderstood Disciple and His Lost Gospel*. New York: HarperSanFrancisco.
Robinson, James M., (ed.). 1990. *The Nag Hammadi Library in English*. 3rd rev. edn; New York: HarperSanFrancisco.
Rodríguez-Luis, Julio. 1991. *The Contemporary Praxis of the Fantastic: Borges and Cortázar*. Latin American Studies, 1; New York: Garland.
Roszak, Theodore. 2005. *Flicker*. Chicago: Chicago Review Press.
Saari, A. M. H. 2006. *The Many Deaths of Judas Iscariot: A Meditation on Suicide*. London and New York: Routledge.
Said, Edward W. 1978. *Orientalism*. New York: Random House.
Sarlo, Beatriz. 1993. *Jorge Luis Borges: A Writer on the Edge*. Ed. John King; London: Verso.
Schaberg, Jane. 2004. *The Resurrection of Mary Magdalene: Legends, Apocrypha, and the Christian Testament*. New York/London: Continuum.
Schiller, Gertrud. 1972. *Iconography of Christian Art, Vol. II: The Passion of Jesus Christ*. Trans. Janet Seligman; Greenwich, CT: New York Graphic Society.
Schonfield, Hugh. 1967. *The Passover Plot*. New York: Bantam.
Schwartz, G. 1988. *Jesus und Judas: Aramistische Untersuchungen zur Jesus-Judas-Überlieferung der Evangelien under der Apostelgeschichte*. BWANT 123; Stuttgart: Kohlhammer.

Schweitzer, Albert. 1968. *The Quest of the Historical Jesus: A Critical Study of Its Progress from Reimarus to Wrede.* Trans. W. Montgomery; New York: Macmillan.

Scopello, Madeleine, (ed.). 2008. *The Gospel of Judas in Context.* Nag Hammadi Studies 62; Leiden: Brill.

Senior, Donald. 1974. "A Case Study in Matthean Creativity (Matthew 27:3–10)." *Biblical Review* 19: 23–36.

—1982. *The Passion according to Matthew: A Redactional Study.* Leuven: Leuven University Press.

Shepherd, David, (ed.). 2008. *Images of the Word: Hollywood's Bible and Beyond.* Semeia Studies; Society of Biblical Literature.

Smith, Jonathan Z. 1978. *Map is Not Territory: Studies in the History of Religion.* Leiden: E. J. Brill.

Smith, Richard. 1990. "The Modern Relevance of Gnosticism." In Robinson, 1990: 532–49.

Smith, Wilfred Cantwell. 1963. *The Meaning and End of Religion.* New York: Macmillan.

Sperling, S. David. 2001. "Jewish Perspectives on Jesus." In Meyer and Hughes, 2001: 251–59.

Stabb, Martin S. 1991. *Borges Revisited.* Twayne's World Author Series, 819; Boston: Twayne.

Staley, Jeffrey L. and Richard Walsh. 2007. *Jesus, the Gospels, and Cinematic Imagination: A Handbook to Jesus on DVD.* Louisville: Westminster John Knox.

Stendahl, Krister. 1968. *The School of St. Matthew and Its Use of the Old Testament.* Philadelphia: Fortress.

Stern, Richard C., Clayton Jefford, and Guerric DeBona, O.S.B. 1999. *Savior on the Silver Screen.* Mahwah, NJ: Paulist.

Sturrock, John. 1977. *Paper Tigers: The Ideal Fictions of Jorge Luis Borges.* Oxford: Clarendon Press.

Tabor, James D. 2006. *The Jesus Dynasty: The Hidden History of Jesus, His Royal Family, and the Birth of Christianity.* New York: Simon & Schuster.

Tarachow, Sidney. 1960. "Judas the Beloved Executioner." *Psychoanalytic Quarterly* 29: 528–54.

Tatum, W. Barnes. 2004. *Jesus at the Movies: A Guide to the First Hundred Years.* Rev. and expanded edition; Santa Rosa: Polebridge.

Telford, William R. 2005. "The Two Faces of Betrayal: The Characterization of Peter and Judas in the Biblical Epic or Christ Film." In Christianson, Francis, and Telford, 2005: 214–35.

Tilley, Terrence W. 1991. *The Evils of Theodicy.* Washington, D.C.: Georgetown University Press.

Todorov, Tzvetan. 1973. *The Fantastic: A Structural Approach to a Literary Genre.* Tran. Richard Howard; Cleveland: The Press of Case Western Reserve University.

Topping, Coral. 1970. *Jewish Flower Child: An Historical Novel.* Toronto: McClelland & Stewart.

Turner, John D. 2001. *Sethian Gnosticism and the Platonic Tradition.* Québec: University of Laval Press.

Unnik, Willem C. van. 1974. "The Death of Judas in Saint Matthew's Gospel." *Anglican Theological Review Supplementary Series* 3:44–57.

Voragine, Jacobus de. 1941. *The Golden Legend.* 2 vols; trans. Granger Ryan and Helmut Ripperger; London: Longmans, Green.

Walsh, Richard. 2000. "Recent Fictional Portrayals of God, or: Disney, Shirley MacLaine, and Hamlet." In Aichele, 2000: 44–65.

—2001. *Mapping Myths of Biblical Interpretation*. Playing the Texts 4; Sheffield: Sheffield Academic Press.

—2003. *Reading the Gospels in the Dark: Portrayals of Jesus in Film*. Harrisburg: Trinity Press International.

—2005a. *Finding St. Paul in Film*. New York: T&T Clark.

—2005b. "Three Versions of ~~Judas~~ Jesus." In Aichele and Walsh, 2005: 155–81.

—2006a. "The Gospel According to Judas: Myth and Parable." In Exum: 2006, 37–53.

—2006b. "Gospel Judases: Interpreters at Play in Mythic Fields," *Postscripts: The Journal of Sacred Texts and Contemporary Worlds* 2.1: 29–46.

—2007 (but published in 2010). "Passover Plots: From Modern Fictions to Mark and Back Again." *Postscripts: The Journal of Sacred Texts and Contemporary Worlds* 3.2-3: 201–22.

—2008a. "Barabbas Rewrites the Cross: Parody or Parable?" In Shepherd, 2008: 113–29.

—2008b. "*The Passion* as Horror Show: St. Mel of the Cross." *The Journal of Religion and Popular Culture* 20 (Fall). http://www.usask.ca/relst/jrpc/articles20.html (accessed 7-26-09).

Weeden, Theodore J. 1971. *Mark: Traditions in Conflict*. Philadelphia: Fortress.

Wheelock, Carter. 1969. *The Mythmaker: A Study of Motif and Symbol in the Short Stories of Jorge Luis Borges*. Austin: University of Texas Press.

Whelan, Caroline F. 1993. "Suicide in the Ancient World: A Reexamination of Matt 27:3–10." *Laval Théologique et Philosophique* 49.3: 505–522.

Williams, James G. 1971. "'You Have Not Spoken Truth of Me,' Mystery and Irony in Job." *Zeitschrift für die alttestamentliche Wissenschaft* 83: 231–55.

Williams, Michael. 1996. *Rethinking Gnosticism: An Argument for Dismantling a Dubious Category*. Princeton: Princeton University Press.

Winter, Paul. 1974. *On the Trial of Jesus*. 2nd edn; Berlin and New York: Walter de Gruyter.

Wright, N. T. 2006a. *Decoding Da Vinci*. Cambridge, England: Grove.

—2006b. *Judas and the Gospel of Jesus: Have We Missed the Truth About Christianity?* Grand Rapids: Baker.

Zwiep, Arie W. 2004. *Judas and the Choice of Matthias: A Study on Context and Concern of Acts 1:15–26*. Tübingen: Mohr Siebeck.

Index of Borges' Writings

Aleph, The 13, 18–19, 47
Approach to Al-Mu'tasim, The 5, 16, 18, 122–24, 140, 153
Argentine Writer and Tradition, The 6
August 25, 1983 9, 29
Avatars of the Tortoise 12, 13, 24, 151, 153
Babylonian Lottery, The 32, 49, 75, 151
Biathanatos 2, 32, 51–52
Book of Imaginary Beings, The 12
Book of Job, The 34, 48
Book of Sand, The 19, 48–49
Borges and I 9
Chess 122
Christ on the Cross 33, 154
Circular Ruins, The 11–12, 122
Covered Mirrors 9
Death and the Compass 18, 19, 82, 92
Defense of Basilides the False, A 122
Defense of the Kabbalah, A 47–48
Duel, The 89, 92, 124
Encounter, The 30–32, 50, 92, 99, 129
Everything and Nothing 8
Examination of the Work of Herbert Quain, A. 5
Fearful Sphere of Pascal, The 48
Form of the Sword, The 65–66, 92, 99
Fragments From an Apocryphal Gospel 30, 79, 80, 154
Funes, the Memorious 6–8, 19, 47, 80, 159
God's Script, The 7, 10, 14, 18, 19
Golem, The 122
Gospel According to Mark 32–33, 47, 151
Hakim, the Masked Dyer of Merv 9
History of Angels, A 49
House of Asterion, The 9
Ibn-Ḥakim al-Bokhari, Murdered in His Labyrinth 17, 18, 124, 159
Immortal, The 7, 9, 10, 14, 18, 19, 152
Inferno, I, 32 8

Investigation of the Word, An 8
John Wilkins' Analytic Language 8
Kafka and His Precursors 20, 139
Library of Babel 9, 48–49, 74–75
Mirror of Enigmas, The 109–10, 121
Narrative Art and Magic 29–30, 32, 33, 47
New Refutation of Time, A 7, 11, 13
Note on (Toward) Bernard Shaw, A 8
On Exactitude in Science 11, 40, 147, 160
On the Cult of Books 48
Other, The 9
Other Death, The 19
Paradiso, XXXI, 108 153
Partial Magic in the Quixote 11, 48
Pedro Salvadores 161
Pierre Menard, Author of Don Quixote 4–6, 20–21
Prayer, A 30, 79–80, 154
Postulation of Reality, The 7
Secret Miracle, The 9
Sect of the Phoenix, The 81, 124,125
Sect of the Thirty, The 30–32, 42, 54, 59, 61, 66, 74, 89, 112–13
Simurgh and the Eagle, The 123
South, The 11
Story of the Warrior and the Captive 124
Theme of the Traitor and the Hero 92, 150, 154
Theologians, The 92, 123–24
This Craft of Verse 49
Tlön, Uqbar, Orbius Tertius 9, 10–11, 12–13, 33, 118
Total Library, The 48
Two Kings and the Two Labyrinths, The 9, 18
Unworthy 85–87, 92
Wall and the Books, The 16, 161
Yellow Rose, The 8
Zahir, The 13, 18, 19, 47

Index of Authors

Aeschylus 43
Aichele, G. 14, 15, 16, 17, 109, 159
Aichele, G., P. Miscall, and R. Walsh 66, 155
Aizenberg, E. 34, 47, 158
Alter, R. 43
Anderson, R. 1, 85, 157, 162
Aristotle 27
Arnal, W. 66, 70, 116, 134, 155, 156
Auerbach, E. 47
Auerbach, N. 147
Augustine 54–55

Barrenechea, A. 2, 7, 12, 13
Barthes, R. 39, 136, 142, 155
Baum, P. 86, 106, 157
Beal, T. 139, 147
Bellah, R. 134
Besserman, L. 157
Blanton, W. 66, 116, 139, 155
Bloom, H. 122, 134, 135
Boyarin, D. 54
Brandon, S. 115
Brelich, M. 25, 40, 79, 112
Brown, D. 34, 80, 115, 118–19, 137
Brown, R. 20, 40, 45, 69, 99
Bultmann, R. 27, 67
Burkert, W. 94, 98

Callaghan, M. 29, 31, 57, 63, 66, 149, 150
Campbell, J. 13
Camus, A. 17, 54, 73–74, 80, 84, 154, 159, 161, 162
Caravaggio 26, 96, 101
Castelli, E. 92
Christ, R. 124, 125
Cohen, S. and L. Taylor 80, 135, 136
Conzelmann, H. 71
Crossan, J. 5, 13, 14, 16, 20, 35, 40, 125, 130, 134, 155, 158

Crossley, J. 66, 67

Dalman, G. 91
Daube, D. 26, 40, 59, 103
De Beauvoir, S. 155
DeConick 54, 125, 129, 131–33
De Man, P. 48
De Quincey, T. 2, 20, 67, 68–69, 72, 77, 85, 113–15, 124, 125, 142–44, 148, 156
Derrida, J. 95, 97, 101
Detienne, M. 155
Dieckmann, B. 93, 98
Droge, A. and Tabor, J. 3, 26, 55
Durkheim, E. 155
Dylan, B. 161

Eco, U. 16, 48, 80–82, 125, 156
Ehrman, B. 131, 134
Eiseman, R. 115
Eliade, M. 95
Emerson, R. 68
Enslin, M. 25, 44
Epiphanus 51
Eslinger, L. 37, 130

Foucault, M. 34, 155
Fox, R. 68
Freud, S. 15, 29, 73, 75, 93, 94, 139, 158
Frye, N. 47

Genette, G. 2
Giotto 26, 31, 103, 109, 140, 144
Girard, R. 93–99
Goldstein, M. 90, 91
Graves, R. 63
Greenberg, G. 20, 35, 36, 41, 61, 117
Greimas, A. 27
Gundry, R. 45

Halas, R. 69
Hand, W. 2
Happel, S. 6, 112, 137
Hobbes, T. 94, 98
Hughes, K. 36, 100–101

Irenaeus 51, 125, 127, 131, 133, 158
Irwin, W. 14, 29
Jeffers, R. 62, 66, 76, 77, 120
Jeremias, J. 28, 36
Jursch, H. 86

Käsemann, E. 67
Kasser, R. 125
Kasser, R. and G. Wurst 125
Kasser, R., M. Meyer, and G. Wurst 125, 128, 129, 131
Kennelly, B. 69, 76, 77, 79, 157, 161
Kermode, F. viii, 6, 20, 25, 27–29, 38, 40, 43, 45, 46, 59, 61, 62, 63, 130, 136, 150
King, K. 121
King, S. 139
Klassen, W. vii, 1, 2. 3, 20, 25, 26, 55, 57, 59, 60–61, 63, 68, 69, 71, 91, 117, 162
Klauck, H. 2, 63, 69, 85
Klausner, J. 91
Krosney, H. 125, 131
Kuryluk, E. 86

Lagerkvist, P. 76
Lee, P. 134, 135
Lévi-Strauss, C. 155
Lincoln, B. 155
Lindstrom, N. 9
Lovecraft, H. 17, 73, 139, 140

Maccoby, H. 40, 56, 69, 86, 91, 92, 96, 98–99, 102, 115–17, 156, 157
Mack, B. 67, 134
Martel, Y. 39
May, R. 95, 136, 147
McMurray, G. 17
Mead, G. 121
Meier, J. 40, 68
Mellinkoff, R. 86
Meyer, M. 127, 131, 132
Miéville, C. 82–83

Miles, J. 52–55, 116
Milton, H. 52
Moore, C. 62, 83
Moore, S. 34, 70
Morrow, J. 53

Neusner, J. 71, 109
Nickelsburg, G. 35
Nietzsche, F. 8, 13, 20, 53, 54, 74, 88, 99, 109, 161, 162
Nortje, L. 71

O'Regan, C. 134
Origen 42, 50
Otto, R. 17, 73

Paffenroth, K. vii–viii, 2, 20, 26, 29, 31, 40, 42, 45, 46, 50, 51, 55, 60, 69, 70, 76, 79, 102, 106, 130, 141, 157, 162
Pagels, E. 24, 121, 129, 133, 134, 135
Pagels, E. and K. King 131
Pelikan, J. 68
Pippin, T. 34, 147
Pollack, J. 155
Popkes, W. 60
Propp, V. 27
Prothero, S. 68, 136
Pynchon, T. 15–16, 138, 140
Pyper, H. 51, 65, 115, 136

Rabkin, E. 16
Rayner, W. 44, 57, 61, 62, 77, 81, 146, 150
Reimarus, H. 67, 115–16
Reinhartz, A. 115, 141
Riley, G. 128
Robertson, D. 79
Robertson, J. 25, 31, 40, 93, 157
Robinson, J. 1, 125, 131, 136
Rodríguez-Luis, J. 4, 14–16
Rozak, T. 117–18

Said, E. 155
Saari, A. 1, 3, 20, 55, 102
Sarlo, B. 2, 5, 6, 10, 26
Schaberg, J. 24
Schiller, G. 86, 100, 103, 140, 144
Schonfield, H. 62
Schwartz, G. 60
Schweitzer, A. 61, 62, 67, 68, 115–16

Index of Authors

Scopello, M. 132
Senior, D. 60
Smith, J. 39–40, 68, 147, 160
Smith, R. 121, 134
Smith, W. 139
Sperling, S. 91
Sophocles 42, 43, 50, 106, 154
Stabb, M. 10
Staley, J. and R. Walsh 56, 60, 87, 108, 141
Stendahl, K. 45
Stern, R., C. Jefford, and G. DeBona 56
Strauss, D. 67
Sturrock, J. 4, 6, 8, 10, 15, 30, 92, 154

Tabor, J. 115
Tarachow, S. 92, 93, 96, 98, 157
Tatum, W. 104
Telford, W. 37, 107
Tilley, T. 35
Todorov, T. 15, 17, 139

Topping, C. 76
Turner, J. 127, 131, 132

Unnik, W. 71

Voragine, J. 43, 106–07

Walsh, R. 1, 6, 24, 32, 34, 40, 53, 54, 56, 60, 67, 68, 70, 76, 80, 82, 87, 88, 92, 100, 104, 107, 108, 113, 114, 115, 116, 134, 135, 136, 137, 138, 139, 141, 145, 148, 151, 155, 156, 157, 161
Weeden, T. 24
Wheelan, C. 3, 26, 55
Wheelock, C. 8, 13, 18, 158
Williams, J. 79
Williams, M. 121
Wright, N. 132, 133–37

Zwiep, A. 26, 55, 102, 103

Index of Scriptures

Old Testament

Genesis
1 — 37, 129
3:14–19 — 53
37:26–28 — 44, 45

Exodus
21:32 — 44

Leviticus
16 — 97
16:7–10 — 93

Deuteronomy
13:1–5 — 90–91
13:9 — 91

2 Samuel
12:11–12 — 46
16:20–17:23 — 46
16:21 — 46

Job, book of — 34–35, 47, 52, 61, 76, 79, 83–84, 92, 154
3 — 42

Psalms
22 — 41
41 — 40–43
41:1–3 — 41
41:4–8 — 41
41:4–10 — 41
41:9 — 23, 28, 40–43, 46
41:10–12 — 41
69:25 — 105
109:8 — 105
109:20 — 105

Isaiah
53:2–3 — 3, 120
53:3–5, 7 — 57

Jeremiah
18 — 45
18–19 — 46
18–20 — 45–47
18:1–3 — 45
18:1–11 — 46
18:18 — 46
19 — 45–46
20 — 45–46
32 — 45–47
32:6–15 — 45

Zechariah
11 — 44
11:4 — 45
11:4–17 — 44–45
11:9–12 — 45
11:12 — 45
11:13 — 45
11:15–17 — 45
13:6 — 44
13:7 — 44

New Testament

Matthew
5:11 — 62
7:21–27 — 71
10:4 — 1, 22, 24–25, 60
10:7–8 — 85
13:55 — 92
20:13 — 64
21:18–22 — 107
22:12 — 64
23 — 46, 64
25:31–46 — 71
26:3–5 — 22, 45–46, 107
26:6–13 — 22
26:14 — 45
26:14–16 — 22, 45–46, 64, 71, 88, 101
26:15 — 25, 31, 43, 45
26:17–19 — 101
26:20–25 — 23, 25, 100
26:20–35 — 101
26:21 — 63
26:21–23 — 101
26:22 — 63
26:23 — 40
26:23–24 — 63
26:24 — 101, 126
26:25 — 63, 64, 71
26:26–29 — 100
26:31 — 44
26:36–46 — 101
26:46 — 23
26:47–56 — 23, 101
26:48 — 31–32, 64
26:49 — 64, 71
26:50 — 43, 64, 71

Index of Scriptures

26:64	64	14:21	41, 42, 60, 101, 126	22:48	72
27:3–5	45			23:28–31	72, 92, 103
27:3–10	23, 26–27, 45–47, 59–60, 102–103, 106–108	14:22–25	100	23:34	105
		14:27	44		
		14:27–31	42	*John*	
		14:32–42	41, 70, 101	1:1–18	72, 129
		14:42	23	1:5	73, 130
27:4	27	14:43–50	101	1:10	3, 120
27:5	46	14:43–52	23	2:4	51
27:6–10	45–47	14:45	31–32	6:60–71	125
27:9–10	45–46	15:34	41, 61, 71	6:64	72, 125
27:11	64	16:7	24	6:64–65	102
27:16–17	92	16:8	24	6:64–71	1, 22, 24–25, 88
27:19	27	16:9–20	24		
27:23	27			6:65	72
27:24	27	*Luke*		6:70	63
27:25	44, 46, 92	2:1	130	6:70–71	72, 102, 125, 129–130
		4:1–13	71		
Mark		4:13	71–72		
3:19	1, 22, 24–25, 60	4:16–30	71, 91	7:30	51
		6:16	1, 22, 24–25, 60, 72, 115	8	92
4:10–12	71			8:20	51
5:1–20	130			8:31–47	88–89
6:3	92	7:36–50	22	10:15	51
8:31	41, 42	11:4	72	10:18	51
8:34–35	54	19:41–44	72, 92, 103	11:45–53	22
8:35	113	22:1–2	22	11:50	91, 143
9:30–32	41. 42	22:1–6	71	12	130
10:32–34	41	22:3	28, 40, 71, 72, 101, 129	12:1–8	22, 41
10:32–44	42			12:6	25, 73, 88
13	92			12:23	51, 130
13:12	42, 43, 71, 70–71	22:3–6	22, 25, 88, 101	12:27	51
13:20				12:28	130
13:32–27	70	22:14–38	101	12:28–30	126
14:1–2	22, 25, 41	22:17–20	99–100	12:31–32	130
14:1–21	40–43	22:21	40, 101	13	88, 130
14:3–9	22	22:21–22	72	13:1	51
14:4–9	41	22:21–23	100	13:2	22, 25, 40, 72, 101, 130
14:10–11	22, 25, 41, 88, 101	22:21–27	23, 25		
		22:22	101, 126		
14:12–16	101	22:28	72	13:10–11	22, 73
14:17–21	23, 25, 41, 100	22:31	72	13:11	24
		22:31–34	72	13:18	40, 73
14:17–31	101	22:39–46	101	13:18–19	22, 24
14:18	41	22:40	72	13:21–30	23, 25
14:18–19	40	22:46	72	13:27	28, 40, 72, 101, 102, 130
14:18–20	60, 101	22:47–48	102		
14:18–21	42	22:47–53	23		
14:20	41	22:47–54	101	13:27–30	60

John (cont.)		1:16–26	1, 23, 24,	*1 Corinthians*	
13:30	25–26, 73, 99		26, 36, 102–108	1:31	3, 85
14–17	88	1:18	72, 103	11:23	25, 28–29, 36, 47, 61
14:22	116	1:18–19	81, 103	11:27–32	100
17:1	51	1:20	72, 105	13:12	109–10
17:12	73	1:20–26	105		
18:1–11	23	1:26	106	*Philippians*	
18:3	26, 36	5	103	1:21–24	54
18:3–6	36	7:1–8:4	72	2:5–11	152
18:5	73	12:23	72, 103	2:6–8	51
19:30	51	13:46	72, 106		
20:29–31	128	18:6	72, 106	*Jude*	
		20:29–30	123		123
Acts		28:23–28	72, 106		
1:16	105				
		Romans			
		8:32	61		

OTHER ANCIENT REFERENCES

Gospel of Barnabas		35–36	126	55	126
	92, 128, 131	36–43	126	56	126–27, 132–33
		38–44	133		
		43–44	126–27	57	126, 132–33
Gospel of Judas		44	129, 132		
	51, 55, 66, 125–37	44–46	126	58	133
		44–47	126		
33–34	133	45	132	*Gospel of Thomas*	
33–36	125–26	46	132		92, 128–29, 133
35	126, 132	47–55	126		

Index of Films

American Beauty 39

Barabbas 75–76, 92
Being There 77
Braveheart 39

D.O.A. 39

eXistenZ 122
Exorcist, The 115, 139

From the Manger to the Cross 104, 144, 147

Godspell 61–63, 74, 77
Gospel according to St. Matthew, The 64, 107, 144–45, 146
Gospel of John, The 146, 147
Good, the Bad, and the Ugly, The 99
Greatest Story Ever Told, The 86–88, 100, 107, 149

I Heart Huckabees 89

Jakob the Liar 38–39
Jesus (1999) 56, 77, 113, 114, 141, 142, 145
Jesus Christ Superstar 58, 62, 76–79, 93, 102, 103, 113, 115, 142–43, 146–47, 148

Jesus Film, The 146, 147
Jesus of Montreal 145
Jesus of Nazareth 36, 37, 61, 103, 107–09, 112, 113, 115, 142, 146
Judas (2001) 142, 148–49
Judas (2004) 27, 69, 103, 142, 149

King of Kings 2, 72, 105, 113–15, 142, 146
King of Kings, The 1, 72, 100, 103, 104, 113, 144–45, 146

La ricotta 59, 60
Last Temptation of Christ, The 56–59, 61, 62, 63, 74, 77, 79, 102, 110–12, 113, 115, 128, 142, 148
Life is Beautiful 38
Life of Brian 77, 120, 121, 143, 146, 158–59

Matrix, The 84, 140

Passion of the Christ, The 103–05, 139, 140, 146, 147
Shane 87
Stranger than Fiction 66

Thirteenth Floor, The 122

Village, The 155

CPSIA information can be obtained at www.ICGtesting.com
Printed in the USA
BVOW011743040612

291743BV00003B/9/P

9 781845 537029